The Great Worship
Awakening

The Great Worship Awakening

Singing a New Song in the Postmodern Church

Robb Redman

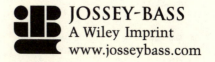

JOSSEY-BASS
A Wiley Imprint
www.josseybass.com

Published by Jossey-Bass
A Wiley Imprint
989 Market Street, San Francisco, CA 94103-1741   www.jossseybass.com

Jossey-Bass books and products are available through most bookstores. To contact Jossey-Bass directly, call our Customer Care Department within the U.S. at 800-956-7739, outside the U.S. at 317-572-3986 or fax 317-572-4002.

Jossey-Bass also publishes its books in a variety of electronic formats. Some content that appears in print may not be available in electronic books.

Unless otherwise noted, the scripture quotations are from the HOLY BIBLE: New International Version, copyright © 1973, 1978, 1984. Used by permission of Zondervan Bible Publishers.

Library of Congress Cataloging-in-Publication Data

Redman, Robb.
The great worship awakening: singing a new song in the postmodern
    church / Robb Redman.—1st ed.
        p. cm.
Includes bibliographical references and index.
ISBN 0-7879-5126-9 (alk. paper)
1. Public worship.   I. Title.
BV15 .R435   2002
264—dc21

                                              2002008115

FIRST EDITION
HB Printing 10 9 8 7 6 5 4 3 2 1

Contents

Acknowledgments

Thanks are due to many people who helped me with this book. Andy Dearman and Christine Blair at Austin Presbyterian Theological Seminary, Greg Ogden at Fuller Theological Seminary, Gayle Beebe and Cathy Schaller-Gregg at Azusa Pacific University, and Greg Bourgond at Bethel Theological Seminary invited me to teach courses on worship that became the anvil on which much of this material was forged. Phil Butin, Paul Detterman, Chuck Fromm, Michael Hamilton, Michael Hawn, David Miller, Sally Morgenthaler, Hughes Old, Randy Rowland, Lester Ruth, Sheldon Sorge, and John Witvliet read portions of the book in earlier stages and made many helpful suggestions. The late Sarah Polster, Sheryl Fullerton, Chandrika Madhavan, and Andrea Flint at Jossey-Bass offered excellent editorial guidance and demonstrated great patience with an overly optimistic writer.

A special word of thanks goes to the students who have worked with me on these issues in course PM706 Contemporary Worship at Fuller Theological Seminary from 1992 to 1999. The two weeks I spent with you was my annual trip to the refreshing well of wisdom and experience. You will recognize your insights and contributions throughout this book, though I am not always able to give you the credit you're due.

To my wife, Pam,
an unceasing source of encouragement
and support from the beginning

Introduction

In the summer and fall of 1995, *Worship Leader* magazine Executive Editor Chuck Fromm convened Worship Leader Roundtables in ten cities across the country. Each Roundtable session included thirty-five music directors and worship leaders. Working in small groups, these worship leaders compiled a list of key trends affecting worship in their churches:

- Seeker services

- Contextualization of worship to North American culture

- Changing forms of communication

- Increasing use of multimedia technology

- Decentralization of authority

- Promise Keepers and other large gatherings

- Youth orientation of culture and innovative churches

- The rise of the Contemporary Christian Music (CCM) industry

These impressions from the frontlines of ministry square with what I've learned from my students at Fuller Theological Seminary and from worship leaders attending the Worship Leader Workshop during the season I directed that program for Maranatha! Music. Nearly everyone I've talked to about worship since 1990 senses we are in a pivotal time. Leaders from nearly every denomination believe God is refreshing the Church through worship. The sweeping changes taking place in worship over the last thirty years are signs of a renewal or awakening among God's people. Even the most superficial benchmarks suggest something significant is happening with worship. Sales of worship CDs and videos are skyrocketing. Books and seminars on worship attract more and more people. As a result, there is a widespread hunger among pastors, church musicians, and lay leaders to understand and respond to these trends, to dig deeper into the phenomenon of the current worship awakening and learn what it may hold for them and their church. Yet church leaders continue to feel they are working from a deficit. In countless conversations over the past decade, I've listened to pastors tell me their seminary classes did not prepare them for what is happening in worship. I heard musicians fret about keeping up with the expectations of the pastor and congregation. I listened to lay leaders plead for guidance and resources to help them make good decisions for their church.

This book covers four major developments, or trends, that make up the worship awakening: the seeker service movement, the "praise and worship" movement, the Christian worship music industry, and the Liturgical Renewal movement. It deals with some important social and cultural factors that have shaped the worship awakening and accelerated the pace of change: ethnic and cultural diversity, generational dynamics, the emerging postmodern worldview, emphasis on personal experience, popular culture, and new communication media and information technology. How church leaders understand these aspects of the worship awakening determines how they respond to it, yet many know little of the worship awakening apart from a visit to a leading megachurch conference or an article in a magazine. My goal is to move beyond simple description of these trends and influences to analyze them and suggest helpful ways of responding that encourage renewal of worship in an established church.

This book is about change in worship. In my experience, nothing in the life of a church generates tension, anxiety, and conflict like change in worship. The first murder in the Bible (Genesis 4:8) was over worship, and the conflict continues to the present. Among established churches, there are strong feelings about the importance of a congregation's worship heritage that often collide with concern over the large decline in membership and attendance in the past thirty years. New, large, and often nondenominational suburban megachurches—sporting food courts, seven-day-a-week programming, and contemporary worship music—appeal to many children of the aging adherents of mainline churches. Writing in the *Atlantic Monthly,* Charles Trueheart observes that "the next church" will look quite different from those of the 1950s, the heyday of Protestantism in North America.[1] Nearly everyone agrees that something should be done to make worship more appealing. But what is being done? What should be done?

Change in worship should not be so painful to us Protestants. Our roots in the Reformation remind us that change—even painful and radical change—is sometimes necessary if we are to be faithful to the scriptures and keep in step with the Spirit of God. Although change is constant, the circumstances of change differ from generation to generation. In our time, the pace of change is troubling to many. Craig Miller writes that "it's not just that things are changing. The problem is that change in the past took time, it had a pace of its own. Today change is accelerating at an ever increasing speed that either forces us to try to stay with it or puts us on the sidelines to wait to see what is going to happen."[2] It seems we never get a chance to catch our breath or appreciate what we've achieved.

Pastor and church consultant Doug Murren observes that "it is better to lead change than to follow it." It is better to understand change than to ignore it, and it is better to know why things are changing than to adopt innovation uncritically.

Protestant church leaders often worry—with some justification—about the suitability of certain worship innovations. At conferences, seminars, and workshops, as well as in books and periodicals, there is often an edge to the case for worship innovation. Each method, style, and resource is peddled as *the way* to rejuvenate worship and attract new attenders. Despite disclaimers to the contrary, innovative churches often have a vested interest in marketing a worship innovation. As a result, church leaders wonder if a magic formula of a worship strategy will work for their congregation. A packaged program developed by a consortium of publishers and ministry innovators may not take into account geographical, demographic, and denominational distinction. As one veteran San Antonio pastor once said, "Texas is a long way from California, and I don't just mean geographically."

So, rather than a offer a blueprint for a new kind of service or make a case for adding new elements to an existing service, I hope this book is more like a travel guide that points out the issues to encounter along the journey. There's no getting out of the hard work of figuring out the significance of these things for yourself; no one can do it for you. To accomplish this, we explore various streams of the worship awakening. It is safe to say that there has been more innovation and change in Protestant worship in the past twenty-five years than in the seventy-five before that. These chapters focus on analyzing the streams rather than describing them, since there are resources available that describe these trends well.[3] Unlike many critics of worship innovation, I believe the worship awakening offers important examples and lessons for the established church. But unlike many champions of worship innovation, I believe they need to be critically evaluated and carefully adapted to the individual congregation.

Innovative churches are trying to be faithful to God's leading in worship; they're trying to respond to the massive changes occurring in our society and culture. It is tempting to disregard the chapters on social and cultural factors as academic theory and generalization.

There is another way to think about them. Ultimately, this theory and generalization is about people and how they think and feel, how they receive and process information, and how they look at the world. These chapters are about the people who come to your church—or those you want to come to your church—and how they think and look at the world.

I have tried to minimize technical references to make the book accessible to a wide audience. The endnotes present references for works cited, and occasional explanation of a technical term or concept. One way for pastors and lay leaders to maximize the benefit of reading this book is to read it as a group, in three meetings, one for each part. A study guide and questions for discussion are available at my Website (www.worshipministry.com).

San Antonio, Texas   Robb Redman
July 2002

Part I

New Ways to Worship

1

The Seeker Service

Evangelism and Worship

Since the mid-1980s, seeker services have generated considerable discussion and debate among pastors and church leaders. Many churches have started services that set aside an established liturgy and church music, eagerly embracing new popular musical styles, the arts, and multimedia communication technology to create what Kimon Sargeant calls "modern liturgies for skeptical seekers."[1]

The seeker service approach builds on a basic assumption: unchurched people have dropped out of church or have stayed away because of traditional liturgy and music. Seeker churches create instead an alternative environment in which to hear the gospel by using styles of music and communication that the seekers already know. By setting aside traditional styles of liturgy and music, pastors and service planners hope to appeal to seekers through creative communication media—drama and the visual arts, but above all music and nontraditional preaching.

There is, of course, more than one way to design a service to attract seekers. A seeker-targeted or seeker-focused service aims at the unchurched or unbelieving attendee; it avoids as much traditional liturgy and music as possible and adopts a high level of cultural relevance in music and communication. Willow Creek Community Church in suburban Chicago is widely regarded as the birthplace of the seeker service movement. The buildings do not look like typical church structures, the atmosphere inside is informal and casual, and the attitude is often intentionally irreverent. "Slice of life" drama sketches, video clips from movies, TV programs and music videos, and message-oriented Christian music (or even secular music) are woven together into a tight thematic package. Different approaches to preaching, often using multimedia visual aids, focus on felt needs of the target audience, rather than on biblical text.

In many cases, a pastor or service planner is reluctant to call a seeker-focused event a worship service because it focuses on the seeker rather than God, and because it doesn't contain many of the elements of worship (such as congregational singing, prayer, and celebration of baptism and communion). A seeker-targeted or seeker-focused service is apologetic in tone and strives to make a clear presentation of the gospel.

Seeker-sensitive services try to incorporate elements of the seeker-focused approach, such as creative communication and appreciation of the seeker's state of mind, within the context of a traditional worship service. Such a service often makes extensive use of contemporary worship music, as well as contemporary Christian music, the visual arts, drama, interviews, and video; it avoids traditional preaching style. Prayers are brief and use contemporary language and a conversational tone. The sacraments may be observed in a simple and contemporary manner, though in many places they are observed at a midweek service for believers.

Both of these approaches attempt to minimize what many believe are the less attractive aspects of traditional worship, namely, uninspiring and uninteresting music, a formalized and ritualistic style of leadership, and too much religious jargon as well as a way of speaking that might confuse or even alienate the newcomer. Pastors and other leaders do not wear robes; they often do not even wear a suit. Attendees are expected to come dressed informally as well. Moreover, the seeker service embraces an emotional approach, making an appeal to the heart as well as to the head, primarily through personal testimony, drama, and music. Clear and practical themes predominate from beginning to end of each service, usually focusing a biblical perspective on personal and family issues. Marriage and family issues feature prominently in these mostly suburban churches. Songs that emphasize the lifelong commitment of Christian marriage reinforce a practical sermon on faithfulness in marriage; there may be an arresting title like "How to Affair-Proof Your Marriage," along with testimony from a couple who worked through infidelity, and a time of prayer for couples who want to experience God's blessing for their marriage in a new way.

To understand the seeker service approach as part of the worship awakening, we need to go beneath the surface to examine its historical roots, its theological foundation, and its connection with contemporary popular culture.

The Roots of the Seeker Church Movement

Today's seeker service may seem like an invention of the 1980s, but it comes from a long family history. Its pedigree includes revivalists and evangelists who sought to combine worship and evangelism, going back at least to colonial America. Among them were important figures in American religious history: John Wesley, George Whitefield, Charles Finney, D. L. Moody, Aimee Semple McPherson, and Billy Graham. Advocates and critics of seeker service acknowledge the movement's roots in American revivalist worship of the eighteenth and nineteenth centuries, but few understand this history or the impact on today's seeker service. The history and influence are more complex and diverse than many admit.

Camp Meetings and Revivalist Worship

As far back as the eighteenth century, evangelists and revivalists such as Whitefield and Wesley knew how to draw crowds of unchurched people.[2] The beginning of the nineteenth century was a period of religious revival throughout much of the new country, particularly in the hills and valleys of the Appalachian Mountains and out on the frontier of the Ohio and Tennessee river valleys. In this wild and untamed setting, the camp meeting emerged as the vehicle for revival and evangelism. These three- and four-day meetings were often modeled on the Presbyterian "communion season," which had been observed in Scotland for more than 150 years.[3] Like the communion season, the camp meeting featured evangelistic preaching from several ministers, often from several denominations and occasionally of other races. On Sunday, usually the final day of the meeting, the pastor served communion and baptized new converts. Increasingly, the services prior to the communion service on Sunday morning became more evangelistic in focus, using new features like popular musical styles, a "mourner's bench" for those "under conviction" of their sins, and a sawdust trail that led the convert to the front for prayer. Many exhibited physical manifestations of repentance and surrender to God: violent shaking, fainting, trances, and "speaking in tongues," which some interpreted as a sign of true conversion.

Methodist quarterly meetings also shaped revivalist worship in early America. These two-day weekend events included several preaching services, prayer meetings, the "love feast" and the Lord's Supper, as well as business meetings and fellowship among the Methodists of a particular area. As Lester Ruth writes, "originally designed as a business meeting to conduct certain affairs of a circuit, these meetings developed—particularly in America—into great worship festivals."[4] As many as ten thousand would turn out for these gatherings between 1780 and 1810. The Methodists coined the term *seeker* to mean a nonsociety member who attended the meeting along with regular Methodists. Although they did not use the term *seeker service*, the early Methodists eventually developed a special evangelistic service for nonsociety members. As Methodists understood it, seekers were those who had some sense of their sinfulness and need for grace.[5] By the early nineteenth century, camp meetings had replaced the quarterly meetings in importance among Methodists, but camp meetings adopted many features of the quarterly meetings, including the distinction between public and private service, and worship for believers and seekers. Not surprisingly, Methodists at the time eagerly endorsed and participated in the camp meetings.[6]

Charles G. Finney, a lawyer of the middle nineteenth century who turned evangelist, took the dynamics of the camp meeting to the urban churches of the Eastern seaboard. Worship historian James White calls Finney "the most influential liturgical reformer in American history"; he sees Finney's contribution as "the domestication of frontier practices . . . which soon spread to all parts of the United States and much of Canada."[7] Finney's approach to worship was purely pragmatic; worship is a means to evangelistic ends. He called his approach to worship the "new methods": songs with a simple and familiar melody and lyrics; a dramatic and engaging style of preaching; and the famous "anxious bench," usually the front row of pews, reserved for those who felt God was calling them to repent of their sins and receive Christ.

Finney justified his new methods by claiming that scripture gives no specific guidance on any particular liturgical style. In his *Lectures on Revivals of Religion* (1835), he wrote that "God has established no particular measures to be used. . . . We are left in the dark as to the measures which were pursued by the apostles and primitive preachers."[8] The pastor should not worry about biblical or historical precedent but should ask, "Will it help lead unbelievers to Christ?" This pragmatic approach differed greatly from the denominational traditions, which claimed biblical support for their distinctive worship styles.

As Finney developed it, revival worship is characterized by emphasis on preaching. Other elements, such as prayer, reading scripture, and congregational singing and choral music (often known as "preliminaries"), are secondary elements and should be related thematically to the sermon to prepare the audience for the message. Unlike established Protestant traditions, which featured either expository preaching through individual books of the Bible or lectionary preaching that was based on selection of scripture assigned throughout the church year, revival preaching is primarily topical, focused on the "plan of salvation" and how one can accept Jesus Christ as Savior and Lord.

The significance of Finney's approach to worship is hard to over-state. Three important aspects deserve our attention here. First, his pragmatic approach emphasized freedom and innovation over tra-dition. Denominational traditions, particularly in the conservative churches in the larger Eastern cities, held many of the innovations of the camp meeting in check. By pointing out that scripture did not require specific styles and forms in worship, Finney managed to relativize all liturgical tradition and break down opposition to innovation.[9]

Second, Finney developed a new way to relate worship to its sur-rounding culture. His new measures created an "indigenous" form of worship suited to the emerging American outlook and culture, largely by embracing popular styles and downplaying the importance of clerical authority. Nathan Hatch observes that "Finney called for a Copernican revolution to make religious life audience-centered. He despised the formal study of divinity because it produced dull and ineffective communication."[10] Having shed many of the European trappings of worship, Finney's services were thoroughly American and egalitarian; they freely indulged the "era of good feelings" that abounded during Andrew Jackson's administration.

Third, Finney reversed the relationship between worship and evangelism. Previously, theologians and pastors believed evange-lism was a secondary by-product of worship, even in a camp meet-ing. Saving souls was a high priority to those early camp meeting and quarterly meeting leaders, but worship was a higher priority. For Finney it was the opposite; evangelism was primary, while worship was a secondary concern. Everything that was said and done, sung and prayed in his evangelistic meeting must happen in a way that maximized the opportunity for conversion.

Revival worship spread quickly among all Protestant churches, touching off controversy in one denomination after another. Among Presbyterians, for example, advocates of revival worship were known as the New School; its more conservative detractors were called the Old School. New School Presbyterians were less committed to their denominational institutions than were the Old School advocates and were more open to any attempt to simplify difficult Puritan theology. The New School sought to loosen up Reformed worship with new music and evangelistic preaching. The Old School responded vigorously to block this innovation, but the two groups were unable to accommodate each other and they split the denomination in 1837.

Methodists and Baptists, on the other hand, adopted revival worship, mostly because they did not share the Presbyterians' theological suspicion of Finney. Emerging denominations such as the Disciples of Christ, the Christian Church, and the Seventh-Day Adventists eagerly embraced Finney's approach to worship, followed later by the holiness churches in the second half of the nineteenth century and the Pentecostals early in the twentieth century. Together, this collection of groups formed the evangelical movement that continues to this day, held together in large part by a common commitment to revivalist worship.

Sister Aimee and Robert Schuller

Aimee Semple McPherson, the pioneer radio evangelist and founder of the Angelus Temple in Los Angeles, is a creative and controversial example of revivalist worship in the early twentieth century.[11] Following the death of her first husband in China, McPherson began touring the United States as an evangelist, quickly gaining attention for her healing ministry and her openness to new forms of music for worship—in particular, black worship music. After World War I, she settled in Los Angeles and founded Angelus Temple as the platform for her ministry. Her innovative services attracted considerable press coverage, as well as the scorn of other church leaders in southern California.

Sister Aimee's Sunday evening service was the prototype for today's seeker service, combining several elements she felt would attract the unchurched. The first was a suitable space. Angelus

Temple was an architectural marvel, in its day one of the largest church buildings ever constructed. The quality of the visual and acoustic features in the twenty-five-hundred-seat sanctuary was well ahead of its time. Designed more like a theater than a church, Angelus Temple boasted an orchestra pit, one of the first sound systems to be used in a church, and no seats with an obstructed view of the stage. The second element of Angelus Temple's worship was the music. Sister Aimee loved music, and the temple was known for its musical excellence, boasting "the best jazz in Los Angeles." The outstanding choir led some classical hymns, though the church was particularly well known for singing gospel songs with gusto.

The final element was McPherson's "illustrated sermons." Taking her cues from neighboring Hollywood, she used drama, scenery, costumes and makeup, and a variety of props and extras (including live animals). Among the more memorable events was her sermon on Jesus the Good Shepherd, in which she preached dressed as Little Bo Peep. She would preach on the wages of sin astride a police motorcycle, dressed as a traffic cop. She was simply too much for her critics, who complained bitterly about her popular services and messages. Sister Aimee was, however, a passionate evangelist with a flair for showmanship. She understood and used emerging popular culture and broadcast technology as a means to communicate the gospel. As a result, her church was popular with the Hollywood crowd; even Charlie Chaplin attended services (incognito) and loitered in the back alley waiting to discuss trade secrets with her afterward. Although she gained her fame as a faith healer, McPherson was an evangelist at heart. "Angelus Temple," she often said, "is a home for people who don't have a home."

Racked by scandal and plagued by financial irregularities, the Angelus Temple faded from the limelight by the end of the 1930s. After McPherson's death in 1944, the temple and the denomination she founded, the International Church of the Foursquare Gospel, had no one who could match her creativity and evangelistic energy; the temple and denomination both settled into a phase of retrenchment and consolidation away from the media spotlight.

But less than twenty years later, the media and pop-culture–savvy approach to revivalist worship she developed would find an unlikely advocate in Robert Schuller, a young pastor in a small Dutch Reformed denomination commissioned to start a church in the new suburbs of Orange County, California.

Sister Aimee's creative illustrated sermons were the focus of her services; Robert Schuller made plain messages about the power of positive thinking the focus of his preaching and services. Early in his career, Schuller found that the message of Norman Vincent Peale hit the mark with his congregation of Orange County suburbanites. The music ministry of the church was intentionally eclectic, favoring traditional choral and organ music while popular entertainers also offered special music. Like Sister Aimee, Schuller made a mark with architecture. His first sanctuary was contemporary by the standards of the early 1960s. But his second building, completed in 1979, is one of the most distinctive church buildings ever built. The Crystal Cathedral, which seats nearly three thousand, is built in the shape of a star and enclosed entirely by more than two hundred thousand panes of glass. A row of fountains occupies the center aisle, and as the service begins a giant door to the right of the sanctuary opens to outdoor fountains and a view of palm trees and the southern California hills in the distance. A massive Jumbotron television screen allows attendees to see the speaker and others on the platform.

The Crystal Cathedral was the first American church to make extensive use of marketing and church growth techniques as a centerpiece of its mission. Schuller's famous door-to-door survey helped him shape his service and message for the audience of 1950s suburbanites. He does not use the term *seeker*, but he does consider his services geared to the unchurched. Schuller's target audience is affluent Orange County executives and entrepreneurs who are skeptical about the relevance of Christianity and its practical benefit for their lives.[12]

Following in the footsteps of the Crystal Cathedral, Willow Creek Community Church is the most recent and probably the most successful current version of revivalist worship. Founded in the mid-1970s as an outgrowth of a youth ministry led by Bill Hybels, the church has mushroomed into one of the largest in the United States. In the 1990s, approximately fifteen thousand attended one of five services held on Wednesday, Thursday, and Saturday evening as well as Sunday morning. Each service is a creatively and thematically planned and tightly scripted presentation of music, drama, multimedia, and message. This approach places Willow Creek, and the thousands of churches that view it as a model for their worship service, squarely in the tradition of revival worship developed by Charles Finney.

The Church Growth Movement

The seeker service movement also owes much to the Church Growth movement, founded by Donald McGavran in the 1950s. Studying growing churches in India, McGavran noted several important sociological factors, which he described in his early works on Church Growth. One of these factors is cultural adaptation of worship and preaching. Another factor is what he called the "homogeneous unit principle," the observation that people are more receptive to the gospel in the company of their peers. As McGavran put it, "People like to become Christians without crossing racial, linguistic, or class barriers."[13] McGavran's student C. Peter Wagner discovered that many of the mentor's principles worked in a North American setting as well. Church Growth theory uses the social sciences of sociology, ethnography, and demographics to understand how people live, think, and feel.

The movement is influential and controversial. Wagner has taught and mentored many of the leading seeker church pastors in his courses at Fuller Theological Seminary, notably the late John Wimber, Rick Warren, and Walt Kallestad. As the megachurch became more prominent in the 1980s and 1990s, the church growth movement's practical focus attracted many pastors and church leaders to conferences and courses on how to build a growing church.

Church Growth theory does not endorse or discourage any particular liturgical or musical style for worship, but it does have a lot to say about what goes on during a service. Because the service is for the unchurched a front door into the congregation, it's important that the service be carefully planned and confidently executed. Relying heavily on sociology and demographic research, Church Growth experts offer guidance on how well many aspects of the service connect with a given group of people, a target audience—from the parking lot to the nursery, from the architecture to the style of music.

As we will see shortly, Church Growth theory has its weaknesses when it comes to worship. But the seeker church movement reveals at least two important contributions of the Church Growth movement to the worship awakening. First, Church Growth advocates helpfully emphasize the importance of the visitor's experience of a service. It is easy for a pastor or church member to overlook aspects of the service that are obvious to a newcomer. Wagner uses the term *church growth eyes* to refer to the ability to see things about our church as visitors see them. Kennon Callahan underscores the importance of valuing a visitor's perception of the service. "The first major component of corporate, dynamic worship is a service that is warm and winsome, welcoming and hospitable, gracious and encouraging."[14] A visitor-friendly service is the mark of a hospitable and welcoming congregation.

Second, Church Growth theory challenges pastors and church leaders to pay attention to the "environmental factors," the details and aspects about a church that are not directly related to worship but that determine how user-friendly a service is. Many ministry experts recommend a congregational study and diagnostic tools to help the pastor and church leaders identify areas of strength and weakness. This begins with the campus, including the parking lot, buildings, signs, and accessibility; it goes on to examine the people worshipers meet on the way to the service (parking lot attendants, greeters, ushers, and others); then there is the architecture and furnishings of the sanctuary, and the ability to hear and see in it; the bulletins, hymnals, and other worship aids; the kind of people on the platform leading the service, and how they look and lead; and finally, child care and children's ministry programming. Ministry experts also remind the pastor and church leaders about the importance of quality in ministry. Like it or not, a worship service has plenty of competition for people's time and attention. The quality of the environmental factors is often the reason a newcomer decides whether a service is worth attending.

Seeker Service Issues

Since the mid-1980s, the seeker service strategy has generated hope and enthusiasm among its adherents, and criticism from its detractors. But why do seeker services seem to succeed at attracting unchurched people?

To begin with, a seeker service works because the seeker church has a clear commitment to reaching seekers, a characteristic even the critics acknowledge and applaud. Gregory Pritchard notes that "the idea of a seeker service is a modern adaptation of Wesley's open-air meetings, Paul's discussions in the Ephesus town hall, or Jesus' hillside parables . . . the concept of creating a public forum for presenting the gospel is a wonderful idea."[15] A church that succeeds with seeker service has a laserlike focus on connecting with the unchurched. Outreach and evangelism is not one program among others; it is *the* program.

Second, advocates claim seeker services work because they offer clear communication about Christianity in a culturally relevant way. As Willow Creek's Pastor Bill Hybels explains, people can expect to hear the gospel in a way they can understand. This culturally relevant "creative persuasion" is aided by a commitment to avoid confusing language, symbols, and gestures. Related to this is the multisensory environment a seeker service creates. Architecture, sound, and sight combine to communicate a clear theme at a number of levels. The arts, in particular, play an important role in connecting with the seeker at an affective, or emotional, level. The seeker church works hard to understand the likes, dislikes, and spiritual state of the people it tries to attract. It is a sophisticated student of human nature, and a savvy marketer that understands consuming patterns, TV, movie and music interests, and the local community and its worlds of work and leisure. Not surprisingly, people who attend a seeker service usually find it easy to understand and user-friendly.

This helps us understand how a seeker service draws a crowd, but how well does it achieve the stated aim of leading unbelieving and unchurched people to a commitment to Christ, and then to commitment to fellowship and ministry in the church? On the first part of the question, there can be little doubt that seeker churches have done remarkably well in presenting Christ to unchurched people, and presenting a way for them to respond. The second part of the question is more difficult to answer because no studies have been done to measure how effectively converts are assimilated into a church or how deeply rooted their spirituality becomes. The general consensus among ministry experts and seeker church staffers, however, is that seeker churches face a significant challenge in moving people to deeper discipleship.

Some of the reasons for the ongoing problems the seeker church faces are reflected in four issues raised by the movement's critics: the focus of the seeker service, use of popular culture and electronic media, the prioritization of evangelism over worship, and performance versus participation in worship.

Worship for Whom?

Critics of seeker services complain that they are more focused on a target audience than on God. The service does not preserve the centrality of God in worship and the integrity of Christian truth in preaching. In *Room for God?* Pastor Robert Wenz worries that some churches have moved beyond being sensitive to unbelievers, to "accommodating them at the cost of violating biblical truth."[16] This problem is particularly acute for seeker-sensitive services, which seem to be both worship and an evangelism event.

How is God sidelined in a seeker service? Critics point to several aspects of the seeker strategy that make the unchurched, rather than God, the focus of worship and preaching. First, the emphasis on popular and commercial media has a distorting influence on the Christian message and worship. Use of media and the arts is not direct enough; Pritchard worries about "the potential lack of willingness to upset or confront [the seeker]. If a high priority is placed on providing entertainment rather than on communicating a message, the method will distort the message."[17] In the effort to be interesting, the seeker service emphasizes entertainment over content.

Again, the critics are anxious about the overemphasis on psychological language and concepts, another aspect of the focus on the seeker rather than on God. Unchurched people understand little theology, but they do understand some psychology. Yet by adopting the language and thought-world of popular psychology uncritically, the seeker church trades theological tradition for temporary human trends and opinion. Pritchard argues that "making the gospel relevant can easily compromise it. The unintended consequences of this approach are that Hybels incorporates large chunks of the American psychological worldview into his basic teaching and teaches that fulfillment is a consequence of the Christian life."[18] By relying so heavily on popular psychology, the seeker service runs the risk of confusing the Christian message with the message of secular social science. A focus on the audience instead of God and the willingness to change the content of the Christian message seem to go hand in hand.

Selling Jesus?

Relying on marketing strategies to determine the preferences, tastes, and interests of unchurched people to design relevant services that connect with the seeker is likewise a human-centered quality. Both Schuller and Hybels began their ministries by going door to door, surveying their neighborhoods. Pritchard believes that marketing methods inevitably distort the Christian message: "Willow Creek's use of marketing language and reasoning has been adopted wholesale from the marketplace. The problem is that the marketing perspective of needs, research, target markets, market share, target-audience profile, and product inevitably modifies any human endeavor to which it is applied."[19] To capture the attention of the unchurched, critics claim that the seeker church chooses style over substance and entertainment over serious theological content, in a misguided belief that these are what the seeker really wants. Marva Dawn questions the assumption that musical style determines church growth: "What is faulty is churches' assumption that if we choose the right kind of music people will be attracted to Christ. It is idolatry to think our work makes the difference. . . . Worship music is used to proclaim Christ, not to advertise him."[20]

Pritchard further claims that the marketing mentality produces two consequences that are dangerous for a church. First, it exposes pastors and church leaders to the temptation of manipulation; "the ability to identify and massage the target audience's emotions is a large part of the marketing strategy."[21] More than one critic has claimed that seeker service is guilty of bait-and-switch, the unethical business practice of advertising one thing to draw customers and offering another in its place. A church should not stoop to the world's hard and ruthlessly cold way of influence to communicate its message. The second danger of the marketing mentality is what Pritchard calls "fulfillment theology." Because marketing is based on identifying needs and developing strategies to fulfill those needs, those who use it to help shape the Christian message end up distorting the message. American consumer fulfillment, he argues, is vastly different from biblical and traditional theological understanding of personal fulfillment.

Evangelism and Worship

Critics point out that because of its deep roots in revivalism, aided recently by the Church Growth movement, the seeker service movement is bound to confuse the relationship between worship and evangelism. In *Worship Evangelism*, Sally Morgenthaler highlights a problem with how the church responds to the seeker church movement: "It is becoming more and more difficult for seeker-driven churches (those who have adopted the seeker-event approach) to establish or maintain worship as their number one priority."[22] Many seeker churches offer a midweek worship service for believers in addition to the weekend seeker service. But many regular attendees and new members usually prefer the weekend service and skip the worship service, thus missing the opportunity to participate in congregational worship.

As long as emphasis on the priority of evangelism continues, churches are likely not only to distort the purpose of worship but also to continue to "deprioritize" worship, as Morgenthaler puts it, treating worship as just another program among others. This confusion about the priority of worship will have a serious effect on a church over the long haul; "Christian maturity and long-term commitment to outreach are ultimately dependent on the worship life of a congregation. What is gained in the short term may ultimately be forfeited when worship is allowed to slip into a number-two or lower position."[23]

Another sign of the confusion about worship is the growing belief among laity (and even some pastors and worship leaders) that a seeker event is a worship service. In the 1980s and 1990s, Willow Creek went to great lengths to emphasize to its members and attendees, as well as to the rest of the Church, that its seeker events are not worship service. They scrupulously avoided using the word *worship* to describe a weekend service and used a variety of means to communicate the contrast between "new community" worship services and weekend events, and stress the importance of attending worship for Christians. Yet the confusion between worship and seeker event continues among many attendees at Willow Creek.

Other seeker churches add to this confusion by calling a seeker service worship.[24] As a result, they are open to critics who worry about "dumbing down" worship service simply to draw a crowd, and who see a confusion of means and ends of evangelism and worship. Unfortunately, many churches view a new service first in terms of numerical growth and only secondarily in terms of spiritual growth. Church leaders often say, "We need a new service to reach the young adults in our neighborhood." To Morgenthaler and others, this is confusing the purpose of worship. Regardless of its liturgical or musical style, worship is not for us; worship is for God. Evangelism is a natural by-product of worship; a new service adds new people to a church, but this is not reason enough to add a new service.

Performance or Participation?

The last set of challenges for the seeker service movement concern the issue of performance and participation. A seeker event requires little, if any, active participation from the congregation. This is not a problem for seeker events like Willow Creek's, which are not offered as worship service. But for a church that attempts a seeker-sensitive worship service, the issue of participation is critical. A key assumption of seeker service advocates is that seekers don't want to participate actively in worship. They are uncomfortable enough just showing up, it is argued; to ask them to participate in unfamiliar activities could put a seeker in an unreceptive attitude. Authenticity and honesty are also a concern. Why have seekers say, sing, or pray things they don't believe yet or aren't sure of?

Clearly, many in our society are ambivalent toward traditional Christianity, and this forms a barrier to active participation in worship. In the past, they have dealt with it by dropping out of church. Seeker service has attracted many by lowering the barrier, removing confusing words and symbols and translating Christian teaching into familiar concepts.

As we see in later chapters, this apologetic approach will probably be less necessary in the future as the postmodern generations—Generation X and the Millennials—mature to adulthood. Since

1995, there has been a slowdown of interest in seeker service, for a couple of reasons. First, apologetic seeker services work well with formerly churched people who have been turned off by church in some way, but less well with people who have no history or connection with a church. Seeker service is most meaningful to those with a residual impression of Christianity. Those who have never attended church do not appreciate the accommodations seeker service makes because these people have no residual experience by which to evaluate it.

Because few members of Generation X and the Millennial Generation were raised in church, there are fewer people with residual experience of Christianity, an important factor in seeker service. At the same time, the number of truly unchurched people—that is, people with no previous experience of Christianity—grows as immigration continues. There is some regional difference at work here; the percentage of adults who dropped out of church is higher in the Southeast and Midwest, and apologetic seeker services will continue to be effective in those regions for some time. The percentage is lower on the coasts, and in large urban areas. Pastors and worship leaders in those areas must take into consideration the needs of those who have little or no exposure to Christianity.

Another reason for the slowdown of seeker service is a rethinking of the assumption that seekers and believers don't mix. Many are questioning this "benign apartheid" approach. Several books on worship and evangelism offer a strong biblical, theological, and practical approach to authentic worship that can also be attractive to the unchurched.[25] Even at the flagship seeker churches, attitudes about seekers and worship seem to be changing. At Willow Creek, for example, the barrier between seeker and worshiper is breaking down. The emphasis has been shifting more toward active participation in worship. According to Curt Coffield, who became the worship leader for New Community services there in early 2001, this new strategy reflects awareness of the changing needs of the seeker: "Willow knows that seekers have changed over the past thirty years, and so our approach to connecting with them has to change with them. People aren't coming as much to be convinced of the relevance of Christianity as they are coming with a hunger for God."[26]

There is no conclusive evidence to suggest apologetic seeker services are doomed to fail in the future, but as we shall see later, the experience and participation orientation of the post–Baby Boomer generations raise serious questions about a service that limits active participation.

The Praise and Worship Movement

Contemporary worship is often viewed as a product of the charismatic movement partly because much of the new worship music has come from charismatic churches. The number of Pentecostals and charismatics has grown rapidly in North America since the 1970s and is expanding quickly in the rest of the world. Although their music is familiar to many, few know much about charismatics and where they've come from. A look at their history and ethos helps us understand their contribution to worship today.

Pentecostalism and the charismatic movement is a touchy subject for many Protestants. Even in our ecumenical and open-minded times, some mainline Protestants view the groups skeptically and are suspicious of their liturgical and musical contribution. Many older members of mainline churches still view Pentecostalism as mostly a working-class phenomenon. Others still harbor hurt and anger over the activities of speaking in tongues or healing introduced by charismatics into the mainline church in the late 1960s and early 1970s. Whatever the cause, it is time to set aside prejudice against Pentecostals and charismatics and appreciate their contribution.

The Roots of the Praise and Worship Movement

Pentecostalism and the charismatic movement did not simply materialize; they have deep roots in the soil of American popular religion, especially in Methodist revivalism, the Holiness movement, and African American churches.

Methodist Revivalism

As we have already seen, the Methodist movement represented a significant renewal of worship in America in the late eighteenth and early nineteenth centuries. In England, John Wesley's passionate preaching and his brother Charles's soul-stirring hymns reached those who were turned off by the stiff formalism of the Church of England in the seventeenth century.[1] Among those most alienated from the established religion were the urban poor, who flocked to Wesley's large evangelistic meetings and joined his "societies," or small prayer groups.

Wesley did make some changes to the Anglican (Episcopalian) Book of Common Prayer, but the movement is better known for its great hymns than its liturgical texts. Charles Wesley wrote more than six thousand hymns, many of which are now found in nearly every Protestant hymnal, notably "Come, Thou Long Expected Jesus," and "O for a Thousand Tongues to Sing." These songs were a breakthrough in seventeenth-century Britain; for the previous two hundred years, Anglicans in England and Presbyterians in Scotland had sung mostly psalm tunes composed during the Reformation. Charles Wesley's hymns matched plain words with winsome melodies, encouraging congregational participation in worship. Worship historian James F. White observes that "the hymns gave the people much active participation in worship and punctuated every service. Familiar tunes were used to make them as singable as possible." Methodist worship did not feature choirs, service music, and solo instruments, since Wesley believed these elements did not promote "joint worship," as he put it. For Wesley and the Methodists, "music was a form of active participation rather than passive listening."[2]

As we saw in the previous chapter, frontier or revival worship was simple, participatory, and usually evangelistic in focus. White points out that "Methodism learned to adapt worship to the un-churched people on the frontier, who, first of all, had to be brought to Christian faith itself. Certainly no prayer book could appeal to largely illiterate people, but simple songs could. For frontier people, freedom was important and structures not. So the frontier devel-oped forms of worship that were demonstrative and uninhibited, abounding with shouts and exclamations and fervent singing."[3] The Methodists were not alone in the effort to adapt worship to the fron-tier; the Baptists were also very successful, and—to a lesser degree—so were the Presbyterians and Congregationalists, though not without controversy and even division. The Lutherans and Episco-palians, with a more formal approach to worship, found the frontier less inviting. An old saying goes, "the Methodists and Baptists came on horseback, the Presbyterians came by wagon, and the Episco-palians came on the train."

The early Methodists justified their simple and demonstrative worship by appealing to the example of the early church and to the power of the Holy Spirit. They pointed to the absence of forms in the New Testament as a warrant for their simple service and argued that they had recovered the apostolic practice of the early Christians in their evangelistic preaching and altar calls. Like John Wesley, the American Methodists also stressed the importance of the inward work of the Holy Spirit, accepting outward physical manifestations of shouting, shaking, and falling down as signs of the Spirit's presence in a person. Preachers often described these phenomena as "baptism of the Holy Ghost," an outpouring of grace that could accompany saving faith or be an experience of grace that came after conversion. This early Methodist emphasis on personal and physical experience of the Spirit in worship is an important starting point for later Pen-tecostals and charismatics.[4]

The Holiness Movement

As the nineteenth century progressed, the Methodist move-ment branched out in several directions, of which the Holiness movement was an important one. The chief characteristic of the movement was its emphasis on personal holiness, or "sanctification," displayed in moral and ethical conduct and also in a life of prayer, worship, meditation on the Bible, and fellowship with other believers. Holiness people viewed personal moral character and conduct as the best measure of the Spirit's presence in one's life.

The Holiness movement continued the revivalist practice of large gatherings, or camp meetings, which lasted a week to ten days with services in the morning, afternoon, and evening. The worship featured new gospel songs, composed by songwriters such as Fanny Crosby and others, that used popular song forms with a refrain, or chorus. Usually a camp meeting featured several ministers preaching at length on various subjects of personal holiness, described by one reporter as "earnest, soul stirring." The pastor also often encouraged physical expression in worship—shouting, shaking, swaying, and falling as a response to the influence of the Holy Spirit.[5]

The "tarrying meeting" became an important feature of worship in a Holiness gathering or church, when Christians would gather to pray earnestly for the gift of the baptism of the Holy Spirit and for entire sanctification.[6] The origins of this sort of meeting go back to the "Tuesday Meetings for the Promotion of Holiness," hosted by Sarah Lankford and Phoebe Palmer in New York City beginning in 1835. In his *Guide to Christian Perfection* (1839), Timothy Merritt argued that the purpose of worship was to call the converted Christian to complete consecration to God (or entire sanctification, as the Methodists termed it). Tarrying meetings often gathered on a Sunday afternoon or evening after the main service to wait (or "tarry") on the Holy Spirit. When the Spirit "fell upon them," as they described it, the responses might include weeping, laughing, shaking, passing out ("slain in the Spirit"), and—especially at the turn of the century—speaking in tongues.

This view of worship as an experience of the Holy Spirit brings us to the threshold of Pentecostalism as it emerged in the twentieth century. Donald Dayton describes Holiness teaching and worship as "a sort of pre-Pentecostal tinderbox awaiting the spark that would set it off."[7]

African American Worship

Along with the Holiness tradition, the early Pentecostals were also strongly influenced by African American worship. Worship scholar Melva Costen points out that black worship draws on four important sources: African worship practice, the American experience, Christian heritage, and Western cultural tradition. Slaves blended these sources, creating liturgical and musical styles in the process that were carried on in the black churches following the Civil War. This distinctive practice and attitude toward worship among many African Americans is rooted in the peculiar institution of slavery.

Because it was dangerous for slaves to worship God, they gathered in clandestine meetings held in cabins or outdoors that often lasted all night. The call to worship went out long before the meeting began, as slaves passed word of the gathering to each other in the code found in songs such as "Steal Away to Jesus" or "Get You Ready There's a Meeting Here Tonight." Gathering together was for slaves a deeply spiritual act, but also an important social activity since they were on separated plantations. The services featured singing, prayer, preaching, and shouting; the slaves worshiped vigorously and used the whole person to encounter God.

Slave worship was frequently emotional and exuberant. Costen tells us that "shouting in worship, including involuntary physical movements, is one way that a person responds emotionally to the encounter, movement, and enabling power of the Holy Spirit. Such physical response, described as religious ecstasy or 'getting happy,' also may have involved uncontrollable screams, yells, and vocal utterances called 'speaking in tongues.'"[8] Slave worship was thus highly participatory. The service was a community event; clergy were virtually nonexistent and slaves led the service and preached by virtue of their call from God and the approval of other slaves.

The distinctive characteristics of African American worship involve imports from Africa and their careful cultivation among slaves and in black churches following the Civil War.[9] The primal worldview of Africans is a rich part of the slave worship expression. For one thing, Africans share an intuitive belief in the nearness of God. All life is connected to the spirit world and to God. Second, Africans do not embrace the Western division of life into sacred and secular realms; rather, they view life as a whole. Third, Africans stress connection to each other in family, extended family, and tribe. Personal identity is formed in the context of community, and worship takes on added significance for Africans as a community act.

These characteristics helped to shape early Pentecostal worship. William Seymour, a black preacher from Houston, was among the early leaders of the Azusa Street revival in Los Angeles in the early years of the twentieth century. As we have already seen, Aimee Semple McPherson's encounters with blacks in the early 1920s strongly shaped her attitude about worship. Virtually alone among the white evangelicals and Pentecostals of her day, Sister Aimee promoted "Negro music" in her church, including spirituals and jazz. Although white Pentecostals embraced many of the worship practices and attitudes of African American Christians, they were reluctant to embrace blacks as brothers and sisters in Christ. By the 1920s, the multiracial character of early Pentecostalism gave way to segregation; white Pentecostals gravitated toward the Assembly of God or the Church of God, while black Pentecostals joined the Church of God in Christ. Only recently have these groups started closing the breach.

Pentecostal Worship

Pentecostal Worship to 1950

Most scholars trace the beginnings of Pentecostalism to the Azusa Street Revival in Los Angeles in 1906. Reports of speaking in tongues had circulated among Holiness people for some time before this, particularly in 1904 at a Bible school in Topeka, Kansas, led by Charles Parham. William Seymour studied with Parham in Houston and took his message of the baptism of the Holy Spirit to

Los Angeles, where he began preaching and leading meetings in a house on Bonnie Brae Street. The congregation later moved its meetings to a black Methodist church on Azusa Street that had been converted into a stable.

From Los Angeles, the Pentecostal movement spread quickly, first up the West Coast and then to the Southeast. Soon the movement went international; English Methodist evangelist and pastor T. B. Barratt visited Azusa Street and took the Pentecostal fire to Oslo, Norway. Before long, Pentecostal churches sprang up in Africa, India, Brazil, and Chile as well.[10]

By all accounts, the early Pentecostal meetings were more fervent in terms of spiritual intensity and emotional and physical expression than anything even Holiness people had previously encountered. The Holy Spirit fell on nearly everyone in attendance, leading to speaking in tongues; prophesying; physical healing; and uncontrolled shouting, weeping, and laughter. Many would shake violently under the Spirit's control and roll around on the floor, earning the early Pentecostals the derisive nickname "holy rollers." At the beginning, Pentecostal worship was an inclusive affair that attracted working-class and poor people who felt shunned by middle-class churches. Harvey Cox notes that Pentecostalism has thrived among the poor around the world.[11] It also attracted worshipers from diverse racial and ethnic backgrounds, though this did not last long. Women were also prominent in leadership in the early days of Pentecostalism, but in less than twenty years—despite such well-known exceptions as Aimee Semple McPherson and later Kathryn Kuhlman—men took over preaching and pastoral leadership in most congregations.

The Pentecostal movement that emerged from the Azusa Street Revival was a singing revival, adapting familiar worship music and creating new songs. Edith Blumhofer writes that the "Pentecostals sang the gospel songs of their day, some of the better-known hymns of the church, and choruses billed as 'given' by the Holy Spirit. In many places, they kept singing songs they had sung before, adding some to express new dimensions of religious experience."[12] Yet the Pentecostals went beyond their revivalist and Holiness forerunners in the way they used music. Chuck Fromm notes their "services were characterized by fervent singing undirected and often unaccompanied. Sometimes, however, the lively congregational chorus would be joined by the beat of drums and tambourines, and the blare of trombones and coronets in the manner of a Salvation Army street band."[13] Twenty years passed before Pentecostals published a hymnal.

From the beginning, Pentecostal worship has been exuberant and expressive. Services are full of upbeat, hand-clapping songs, as well as slow, mournful songs of lament and longing. Pastors and song leaders encourage the congregation to dance and move to the music, and shouts of "Amen" and "Hallelujah" punctuate the service. The congregation kneels and weeps as well. Pentecostal preaching—even in white churches—borrows heavily from African American preaching and builds on the "call and response" interaction with the congregation. Robert Duvall's film *The Apostle* (1997) captures many aspects of classical Pentecostal worship that live on to the present.

Pentecostal Worship from 1950

For the first half of the twentieth century, Pentecostalism was an underground movement, largely ignored by the mainstream churches and secular media. McPherson was an exception to this rule, and an important transitional figure in the maturing Pentecostal movement. We have already seen how her evangelistic emphasis led to featuring miraculous healing in her meetings and to embracing popular musical styles and the radio, which were innovations in mass evangelism. But McPherson was also an innovator in Pentecostal worship. She was clearly Pentecostal in her theology of baptism of the Holy Spirit, speaking in tongues, and healing, but the creative preaching and polished choir performance in worship service at the five-thousand-seat Angelus Temple in the 1920s and 1930s looked quite different from the boisterous meetings on Azusa Street only twenty years earlier. The focus of the service was no longer the congregation, but the platform.

Edith Blumhofer says that McPherson "represented a style that gained increasing favor among Pentecostals, a style which featured one or more performing stars. She altered the nature of individual participation, which she professed to value but at the same time insisted on controlling. In many ways her style was the trend of the future."[14] McPherson was thus the first in a long line of Pentecostal stars extending to TV personalities such as Oral Roberts and Kathryn Kuhlman; and to the present in such well-known Pentecostal celebrities as Jimmy Swaggart, T. D. Jakes, Benny Hinn, and Reinhard Bonnke.

The form of early Pentecostal worship continued in many smaller congregations that cherished the songs of the movement's early years and attempted to stay faithful to the original form of Pentecostal worship. As often happens, the further away in time from the original Pentecostal impulses these churches grew, for pastor and churchgoer alike, the more it felt like going through the motions. By midcentury, many Pentecostal churches needed revival.

Beginning in the early 1950s, three developments helped to inject new life into Pentecostalism and put that worship experience within reach of most Protestants: the "Latter Rain" movement, television, and the charismatic renewal movement.

The first of the three was an important revival and renewal movement within Pentecostalism in the late 1940s and early 1950s known as the Latter Rain movement; it became an important source for the charismatic renewal in the mainline churches in the 1960s. At the time, the revival was hailed as the blessing from God that would come to the Church shortly before the return of Christ. For many Pentecostals, it was welcomed as a renewed focus on a personal experience of God, instead of theological and political squabbling in and among denominations. The Latter Rain movement saw introduction of several worship innovations, among them the heavenly choir, or singing in the Spirit. This was spontaneous singing, often in tongues, for several minutes accompanied by a single chord sustained on the organ, or by the repetition of a simple two-or-three-chord progression. One participant described the worship as "praise flowing up and down like rhythmic waves of gentle ocean breezes and then rising to a crescendo of melodious praises."[15] Other observers have noted the dronelike quality of this singing, which resembles chanting in other religions.

The Latter Rain movement also popularized the singing of short worship songs, known as scripture songs or praise choruses. The composers of many of these songs are unknown, since they did not file copyright on their compositions. The movement also introduced dance to Pentecostals, both formal choreography with a dance troupe and informal, spontaneous movement on the part of the congregation. D. L. Alford writes that "it is not unusual [to see] Charismatic worshipers singing, shouting, clapping hands, leaping, and even dancing before the Lord as they offer him sincere praise and thanksgiving."[16] The Latter Rain movement represented a maturing and consolidating of Pentecostal worship practice and theology. Although it was primarily an intra-Pentecostal development, the movement served to shift the focus of worship onto an encounter with God and away from doctrinal differences. This revival would soon spread beyond Pentecostalism to the rest of Protestantism through the charismatic movement. But before we come to that, we have to consider another phenomenon that helped to put Pentecostals in front of millions of Americans: television.

Pentecostals were among the first to discover and develop the potential of electronic media—radio and television. Mainline churches, which had sufficient financial resources, had surprisingly little interest in the new communication media when they first appeared. As we have already seen, McPherson became a pioneer Christian radio broadcaster when she started KFSG from her church in Los Angeles. Such Pentecostals as Rex Humbard, Roberts, and Kuhlman were quick to recognize the potential of television for their ministry. In the 1980s and 1990s, Jim and Tammy Faye Bakker, Paul and Jan Crouch, and other personalities developed ministry that depended exclusively on TV. Cox observes that the primal spirituality of Pentecostalism is well suited to the media: "television is a modern technology that has a curious similarity to shamanism. The shrinking of distance, the larger-than-life-presence, the compression of time, the sense of belonging suggested by the congregation's response, the appeal to the emotional rather than logic—all integral to the topography of television—are also elements of shamanism."[17]

For its first fifty years, the Pentecostal experience had little direct impact on other Protestant denominations. But around 1960 the "Pentecostal blessing," usually initiated by speaking in tongues, began to appear in the mainline Protestant church as well. For many established churches, the charismatic renewal movement was a breath of fresh air. People welcomed the focus on personal experience of God through worship and prayer, the openness to the miraculous, and the pastoral concern in healing because they felt the experience of God had been underemphasized in their own church. In fact, most charismatics in mainline churches had no interest in leaving for a Pentecostal one; these mainline charismatics believed their experience added a living experience of God to the theology of their tradition.

Other mainline Protestants did not view the charismatic renewal favorably. Many pastors secretly feared loss of control as charismatics met without their leadership in small groups for prayer and Bible study, and to practice the spiritual gifts. Lay leaders and members feared an outbreak of charismatic activity in the worship service, and the takeover of adult and youth education by charismatics with questionable theology and motives. By the mid-1970s, thousands of Presbyterian, Lutheran, Baptist, and Methodist congregations found themselves in the midst of serious internal conflict over charismatic activity.

The ongoing influence of Pentecostal teaching in the charis-matic movement was another reason to be suspicious of charismat-ics. This included the controversial doctrine of the baptism of the Holy Spirit, which charismatics called "the full gospel."[18] Mainline and conservative evangelical Protestants had two major problems with this teaching. First, they found it difficult to square charismatic teaching on the full gospel with traditional Protestant interpreta-tion of key Bible passages, particularly Acts 2 and Acts 19. Second, full gospel teaching seemed to create two classes of Christians: those who have received the full blessing of God, and those without it. This implied to many Protestants that their theology and experi-ence was only a partial gospel. Thus, however well-intentioned their motives, charismatics found it hard to avoid creating an impression among the rest of their congregation of a different theology and spir-itual elitism. Unlike Pentecostals, who viewed speaking in tongues as a necessary validation of baptism in the Holy Spirit, charismat-ics downplayed its importance. Nevertheless, the practice was an important part of the charismatic experience and its teaching. For many Protestants, speaking in tongues was viewed as excessive and out of control; some even labeled it demonic.

Other charismatic practices made their way into the Protestant church with less controversy, among them worship in small groups and emphasis on healing. By the mid-1980s, small groups and a reg-ular (monthly or quarterly) healing service were fairly common among mainline churches. Many of them also adopted a number of worship songs rooted in charismatic circles, and during the ser-vice worshipers occasionally raised their hands in devotion to God.

The controversy over charismatic activity in the mainline Protestant church crested in the late 1970s. Since then, pastors and lay leaders seem to have made their peace with the charismatics in their midst, either by accommodating their practice and theology in small groups or by forcing them to leave for another church. Since the 1980s, a number of independent charismatic churches have started throughout the country and are linked to similar ones around the world. This new movement among charismatics is known as the "third wave" or the "new apostolic church movement."[19] One charismatic group, the Vineyard Association of Churches, is typical of this movement. The late John Wimber, founder of the Anaheim Vineyard Fellowship, was previously a member of the Yorba Linda Friends Church, an Evangelical Quaker congregation, and then a pastor in the Calvary Chapel movement. His charismatic practice and theology led him to start a new church, which later became the spearhead of a new denomination.[20] As we will see shortly, Wimber's attitude toward worship has been influential in many Protestant churches.

Understanding the Praise and Worship

Charismatic worship music and liturgical style has been highly influential in Protestant churches, yet few understand the difference between Pentecostal and charismatic worship on the one hand and traditional Protestant forms of worship on the other. It stems from the use of music and the structure of worship, as well as the role of popular music.

Worship Rhapsody: Creating Musical Flow

Protestants from established churches who visit a charismatic praise and worship service are bound to notice that its structure differs greatly from the traditional Protestant service. Charismatics value a smooth flow in the service and avoid the start-stop feel of Protestant worship, often by eliminating or combining many of the elements of the service. Thus a praise and worship service often has only three or four discernible sections: twenty to forty-five minutes of congregational singing, prayer and announcements, and the sermon, sometimes followed by a "ministry time" of prayer and charismatic activity.

The use of music appeals to Protestants since the songs themselves and how they are combined seem to be effective in facilitating congregational worship. Musician and theologian Barry Liesch
uses the term *free-flowing praise* to describe this first section of twenty
to forty-five minutes of congregational singing, usually conducted
by a worship leader and accompanied by a band. Songs are often
stitched together into a medley by improvisational playing and
modulation to create a sense of seamlessness, of one song flowing
into the next. The worship leader pays attention to the thematic as
well as musical order and sequence of songs.[21]

Liesch identifies two approaches constructing free-flowing praise:
the model developed by Wimber and commonly used among Vineyard churches, and the neo-Pentecostal model that has emerged in
charismatic churches more closely aligned with classical Pentecostalism. Despite differences in how the two models explain worship theologically, both emphasize progression in worship, from a
beginning point as the congregation gathers to a desired objective,
whether "intimacy with God" (Vineyard) or "the holy of holies"
(neo-Pentecostal).

The Vineyard model uses five distinct phases or moments in
free-flowing praise: (1) invitation, (2) engagement, (3) exaltation,
(4) adoration, and (5) intimacy.[22] In this model, the first three to
five songs are often upbeat and focus on gathering to worship God
and then attending to the nature and attributes of God in exaltation. The music often shifts at this point to a softer and mellower
sound that permits the worshiper to acknowledge God's presence in
adoration. The worship leader may invite the congregation to sit.
Thematically, the adoration and intimacy sections feature songs that
address God personally. The final intimacy phase is the quietest. In
many Vineyard churches, songs rich in biblical and nonbiblical an-
thropomorphic language predominate; many songs describe a relationship with God in physical terms (seeing, hearing, touching,
holding, kissing). As biblical justification for this, Vineyard worship

leaders emphasize a meaning of a New Testament Greek word for worship (*proskuneo*), "to turn toward to kiss," which they take to mean intimacy or closeness to God.[23]

The neo-Pentecostal approach is likewise a five-stage process, drawing on an understanding of worship in the ancient Jewish tabernacle and temple: (1) "outside the camp," (2) "through the gates with thanksgiving," (3) "into His courts with praise," (4) "onto the Holy Place," and (5) "in the Holy of Holies."[24] The service begins with the gathering of the people outside the dwelling place of God, rejoicing in the encounter with God about to take place with upbeat and energetic songs. Psalm 100:4 is a cue for the next two stages: "Enter his gates with thanksgiving and his courts with praise." The songs celebrate the greatness of God and offer thanks for God's goodness. The mood changes as worshipers move into the Holy Place and finally to the Holy of Holies. Liesch notes that in these two phases, "all attention is now directed solely to God, Jesus, or the Holy Spirit."[25]

Musical leadership is an important feature of free-flowing praise; a worship leader leads congregational singing with verbal and visual cues, and by directing the band and other singers. The role of the worship leader is often misunderstood in the Protestant churches, which is familiar with a music director and song leader. The worship leader often fills those roles by overseeing the church's worship ministry and by leading congregational singing, but there are some important differences in how the worship leader interacts with the congregation in a praise and worship setting.

Worship leaders think of themselves first of all as worshipers. Their primary focus in the service is on God, not on the music to be presented or on the congregation's singing. This difference is more than semantic; it is a new view of the role of leadership in worship. One worship leader described his philosophy to me this way, "I'm here to worship God, and if that's what you want to do too, then I'll make it easy for you to follow me." As a result, the worship leader often pays less attention to musical issues than the traditional music director in preparing for worship and has another kind of relationship with the congregation during the service than the traditional song leader does.

The worship leader is generally given more latitude in the service than is a counterpart in a traditional church. The pastor frequently delegates selection and arrangement of songs to the worship leader, who then makes important decisions during the free-flowing praise, such as whether to add or drop a song, or repeat a song again or cut it off and move to the next song, when to invite the congregation to sit or stand, and when and how long to encourage singing in the Spirit. The worship leader is also expected to lead in other elements of the service, such as spoken prayer, giving liturgical instruction, and exhortation. Above all, the leader values the ability to understand and shape the spiritual mood and atmosphere of a service as it happens.

The Distinction Between Praise and Worship

The praise and worship label also points to a theological perspective about how Christians experience the presence of God in worship. Mainline and conservative evangelicals usually view praise as an element of worship, along with adoration, thanksgiving, confession, and the like. But for many neo-Pentecostals and charismatics, *praise* and *worship* refer to different moments in the progression of free-flowing praise.

Neo-Pentecostal pastor and writer Bob Sorge draws six points of distinction between praise and worship.[26] First, God does not need our praise, but he does seek worshipers (John 4:23). Second, "praise can be sometimes distant, but worship is usually intimate. Relationship is a requirement for worship because worship is a two-way street, involving giving and receiving. It is possible for praise to ascend one way only, but worship involves communion and fellowship."[27] Third, praise has an external quality to it; it is visible and audible. Worship, on the other hand, is inward and "not always evident to an observer."[28]

Fourth, "praise is largely horizontal in its purpose, while worship is primarily a vertical interaction. Praise is often preparatory to worship. . . . Praise can be conceived of as the gateway to worship."[29] Another way to look at this is to see praise as primarily corporate and worship as primarily individual. Fifth, praise is generally more exuberant, while worship is more reflective and quieter; "the mood of slower songs is more conducive to worship, and faster songs lend themselves more readily to the activity that characterizes praise."[30] The last difference between praise and worship can be found in the struggle between the flesh and the spirit. Sorge says "it is often necessary to stir up our flesh and our soul to praise the Lord. But worship does not seem to involve human effort to the same degree. It is more often characterized by a quiet and unassumed basking in God's presence."[31]

We have more to say about the neo-Pentecostal theology of worship in the next section, but some comments now may be helpful. To begin with, Sorge (and most other neo-Pentecostals) do not mean to make this distinction between praise and worship absolute or imply that the two are mutually exclusive. Sorge goes on to say that praise and worship could be happening simultaneously: "When I lift my hands, am I praising or worshiping? Obviously I could be doing either, or even both."[32] Second, it is important to remember that charismatic theology is largely experiential, or praxis-based. That is, charismatics tend to work from their experience of God toward scripture to find patterns and principles that help them understand the experience. Several of Sorge's explanations of how praise differs from worship seem to have a just-so quality to them, appearing to work backward from experience to theological rationale. But before we write this off as mere subjectivism, we should remember that this method of theological reflection has a long history in the Church, going all the way back to the apostles themselves. More than one theologian has noticed a striking similarity between theological perspectives in charismatic writing and the New Testament books of Luke and Acts as well as the letters of Paul.[33]

The Holy Spirit in Worship

Neo-Pentecostals and charismatics are known for their emphasis on the Holy Spirit and the gifts of the spirit (*charismata*) in worship. An expectation of an encounter with God the Holy Spirit fuels the service. The pastor and worship leader make space for the Spirit to move among the congregation through the miraculous gifts (speaking in tongues, interpretation of tongues), prophesy and words of knowledge (special insight given to some about others), and healing. These activities can happen at any time in a service, though most often during musical worship at the beginning or the extended period of prayer frequently known as ministry time. Worshipers are invited to come forward to pray with the pastor and lay counselors, who lay hands upon them and anoint them with oil. In many churches, the worshipers are encouraged to pray with and for one another in the pews.

Charismatic pastors and worship leaders expect to be guided by prompting from the Spirit, or by a "word of knowledge," an insight given by the Spirit to a person or the congregation. In some churches, for example, the leader appears to put the service on hold while waiting for direction from a word of knowledge. This direct communication can lead to another song, a topic for prayer or ministry, or a time of singing in the Spirit in which worshipers may pray melodically in tongues.

Participation in Worship

The praise and worship style of service is liturgy in the original sense of the word, namely, the work of the people. This is clearly demonstrated in two important elements of Charismatic worship: participatory worship music and emotional and physical expression.

Praise and worship service is highly participatory; worshipers are expected to sing, clap hands, raise their hands in adoration, and even sway and dance. The pastor or worship leader evaluates the effectiveness of a song by how easy it is to learn and how well it allows the worshiper to express praise and worship to God. Other elements in the service, such as prayer and the sermon, also allow participation.

Praise and worship services encourage a range of emotional and physical expression in worship. Charismatic worship is afraid of neither exuberant celebration nor tearful repentance and contrition. Some say that praise and worship services engage the right brain extensively, that is, the affective dimension of the human personality, while traditional Protestant worship has typically been cerebral and intellectually oriented, or left-brained. Until recently, most Protestant churches avoided emotional extremes for fear of offending or manipulating some participants. There is always the danger of group dynamics damaging an individual emotionally or spiritually, and possibly even physically. Insensitive or manipulative worship leaders have sometimes encouraged the congregation to do things that are harmful.

Unleashing human emotion in worship can be healthy or destructive. It is true that many Pentecostals and charismatics try to manipulate the emotional state of the congregation by suggesting what worshipers should feel or how they should respond. In fairness, it should be pointed out that charismatics are not alone in this; many Protestant churches also attempt to control expression by suggesting the kind of emotional state that is appropriate (it is acceptable to feel reverent and thankful, but not joyful and celebrative; fine to be humble and contrite, but inappropriate to reveal brokenness and pain).

Praise and worship services make space for physical expression. To be sure, some Pentecostals and charismatics have gone to excess with physical expression of worship. Yet, as with emotional expression, it is also true that in traditional Protestant worship freedom of physical expression is restricted to standing, sitting, and in some cases kneeling. Other kinds of physical activity are frowned upon (raising hands, clapping, dancing), even though these are explicitly encouraged in the Bible.

The Role of Popular Music

Pentecostals and charismatics have made two important contributions to music in worship. First, they have enriched the canon of worship music with hymns, scripture songs, and choruses. The charismatic experience has motivated many musicians to compose songs, expanding the range of musical styles to include folk, jazz and gospel, rock and pop, and country. As we shall see in Chapter Three, the praise and worship movement has heavily influenced the industry of contemporary worship music.

Second, the praise and worship movement has introduced new ways of using music in worship. For charismatics, music serves a utilitarian function as a means of facilitating congregational participation. Singing in the Spirit, as we have seen, is just the most extreme form of participation in musical worship. This helps us understand why charismatics favor popular music genres rather than classical European styles. Praise and worship advocates are not against hymns so much as they are for participation; thus they favor music that is more accessible to their worshipers.

Issues for Protestant Worship

Mainline Protestants can learn from the praise and worship movement, and many pastors and church leaders quietly admit it exposes a profound weakness in Protestant worship. Charismatics are strong where many of us are weak: in one's confidence before God in worship. Protestants may seem ambivalent about God, unsure of what they believe and uncertain of God's presence in worship; many simply do not expect to encounter God in worship. A service is an opportunity for fellowship and inspiration.[34] Protestants may be good at talking *about* God, but less comfortable talking *to* God. As a result, it is often difficult to move an established church beyond inspiration and information to offer a deep encounter with God by encouraging participation in corporate worship.[35]

The praise and worship movement has had a significant impact on nearly all Protestant churches, from Anglican to Wesleyan. It started with a trickle from the early 1960s through the 1980s, as charismatic Protestants met in small groups and attended special healing services. But the momentum has increased dramatically since 1990, as churches express more interest in using contemporary worship music and opportunity for free-flowing praise, whether in the existing service or adding a new, contemporary-style service.

Experiencing God in Worship

The praise and worship emphasis on the Holy Spirit troubles and attracts many other Protestants. A Presbyterian pastor reported his experience of a charismatic activity: "At the close of one of the sessions, we were invited to gather in small groups—varying in size from two or three to seven to ten persons—and engage in prayers for healing. It was to be preceded by a time in which anyone and everyone could pray in their own way, including speaking in tongues, which was understood to be a kind of chant or humming. I sat through some of this and then left, believing that much of this was manipulative and misguided." This is a typical response for many Protestants on first encountering charismatic worship; it reveals the nervousness and discomfort many feel about the Holy Spirit and charismatic practice.

Much of this uneasiness is rooted in denominational culture, or ethos, which governs attitude and feeling about worship. Presbyterian pastor and theologian Sheldon Sorge (the brother of Bob Sorge, quoted extensively in this chapter) observes that when it comes to worship, mainline Protestants bring different expectations from those of charismatics; Presbyterians think of worship "almost entirely in terms of our response to God. Leitourgia is our work, and it is up to us to do it with integrity." For charismatics, on the other hand, "the chief purpose of worship is to bring us into an encounter with God. Corporate worship is the arena where the Spirit goes to work amongst God's people."[36] Sorge elaborates: "Given this variation in understanding of what is going on in worship, we can see a bit more clearly why Pentecostals more likely long for 'Spirit-filled' worship than do Presbyterians. In one paradigm, the chief question is, 'Did God show up?'; in the other, it is 'Did we appropriately honor God?'"[37]

Experiencing God in worship is the key issue confronting Protestants. They have a hard time responding to people who come asking, "Will we experience God here?" It is not a question that mainline Protestants usually ask of themselves.

Importing Praise and Worship Practice and Theology

We should be discriminating when it comes to borrowing from the praise and worship movement. In *New Harmonies*, Lutheran worship leader Terri McLean offers mainline Protestants helpful guidance on choosing contemporary music for worship. She recommends a four-stage filtering process of song selection: (1) theology, (2) mission, (3) songwriting, and (4) the service. The theological fit is probably the most critical for her mainline Protestant audience. "Lyric content," she writes, "is the single most important factor in determining which songs we use in worship."[38] Charismatic songwriters inhabit a different theological world than most mainline Protestants do, and this is evident in their frequent use of individual, personal expression; King James–style English; Biblical metaphors and images that the mainliner now chooses to avoid, such as *Lord* and *King*; and above all their heavy use of masculine pronouns for God.[39] Retrofitting existing songs is a partial solution. Amy Grant's song "Thy Word" can be changed to "Your Word," and Rick Founds's "Lord I Lift Your Name on High" can be changed to "Lord, We Lift Your Name on High" easily enough. Adjusting songs that use the masculine pronoun for God is trickier; in some cases, the difficulty can be overcome nicely by changing "he" or "him" to "you" and "his" to "yours." Thus Tommy Walker's song "He Knows

My Name" becomes "You Know My Name" in a way that fits with the lyrics of the song. In other cases in which such changes alter the lyrics too much and create confusion, it is best to continue looking for other songs. The long-term solution to these theological problems is emergence of contemporary style songwriters whose theological outlook better matches the needs of the mainline church.

The pastor and worship leader in an established Protestant church badly needs the kind of discriminating guidance that McLean offers. A Presbyterian congregation in California began a contemporary style service in the early 1990s. The congregation hired a worship leader away from a Vineyard church, but the pastor and elders offered no guidance or expectation about the shape or style of the service. Instead, the leadership of the church turned the young man loose to do whatever he thought best. The result, not surprisingly, was identical in every respect to a Vineyard service. Not surprisingly, conflict rooted in different understanding between Reformed and Vineyard worship began to emerge, creating an unnecessary leadership headache for the pastor and the elders.

Shifting to a New Worship Ministry Structure

Failing to appreciate the difference in how a Charismatic service is prepared and led is another danger in attempting to emulate Charismatic worship in a mainline or conservative evangelical setting. As a pastor of a mainline Protestant church in the mid-1980s, I found planning and leading traditional Presbyterian worship to be a relatively simple affair; I picked three hymns and told the choir director and organist my selections by Wednesday afternoon. I also controlled the rest of the service, including the sermon, the prayers, and other liturgical elements. It was simple and straightforward.

Things began to change, however, when we added contemporary worship music to the first service. Now I had a worship team to work with, and choices to make about which songs to use and in which order. How would we transition between songs? What kind of guidance could we give the congregation? Suddenly, the simple service became complex; I learned that what seemed easy on the platform at the Anaheim Vineyard when I visited there was actually hard to do at our small Presbyterian church.

Many pastors and church leaders are making the same discovery: what works with apparent ease in a charismatic setting doesn't transfer all that well to a mainline one. Four barriers are often in the way. The first is the pastor, who must believe in the process of worship renewal and support it. The senior pastor of a large church in Texas once remarked that the day his church sang contemporary worship music on a Sunday morning would be his last. A few years later, the church started a new, contemporary-style worship service; the senior pastor does not preach at it, nor does he attend it. Not surprisingly, attendance remains weak because the congregation does not view it as a real worship service.

The second obstacle is ministry style. Most established Protestant churches don't use a team ministry model. George Cladis notes that "the late twentieth century has been marked by a severe decline in the influence and effectiveness of traditional churches and a sharp rise in new, entrepreneurial congregations" which use teams in ministry.[40] By contrast, the praise and worship church is usually team-oriented, and the worship department is made up of multiple teams led by a volunteer or staff leader.

Space is a third barrier; older sanctuaries are not designed for the kind of music and congregational participation that happens in a praise and worship service. The latter works better in a space congenial to popular music rather than traditional church music. It also works better in a space that focuses on congregational participation rather than performance by the preacher and the choir. Pastors and leaders in a church seeking to adapt the praise and worship style have to think about space, sound, and visual display.

A final obstacle is the musical leadership. Music directors in established churches report difficulty in adjusting to the praise and worship style of service. Some resist contemporary worship music for aesthetic reasons; they think it is boring, repetitive, or musically uninteresting. Others view free-flowing praise as an affront to decency and order in worship. Still others trained in traditional church music have a hard time playing music that requires improvisational skill or the ability to follow a chord chart and melody line rather than a full piano score. A growing number of resources are available to help traditionally oriented musicians cope with contemporary worship music, but there are still few programs that train a traditional church musician to be a worship leader in a free-flowing praise and worship setting.

3

The Contemporary
Worship Music Industry

M usic has been an important feature of Protestant worship from
the earliest days of the Reformation. Since 1970, worship
music influenced by popular musical styles has steadily gained acceptance in churches of all denominational backgrounds. In this
chapter, we chart the rise of contemporary worship music (CWM)
and the industry that has stood behind much of the innovation in
worship music since 1970.[1] For our purposes, CWM refers to worship music in the genres of popular music produced over the past
thirty years by North American Protestant recording and publishing companies, churches, and individuals.

In the minds of many, *contemporary* means new music, while *traditional* means old (and old-sounding) music. Contemporary is probably not the best term to use in describing the new music of the
worship awakening. It comes from the Latin and means "with or at
the time." When used regarding music, the broadest sense of the
word *contemporary* includes anything composed recently. But in the
worship awakening, it has acquired another meaning, one identifying as contemporary certain musical styles: rock, folk, pop, gospel,
R & B, reggae, country, and hip hop. Thus it is possible for a song
composed in 1970 to pass itself off as contemporary in this second
sense of the word.

As we see in this chapter, traditional is somewhat misleading
when it comes to describing other kinds of worship music. The root

meaning of *tradition* refers to the process of handing something on from one generation to the next. Thus traditional worship music is rooted in the history of the Church's praise, which we receive as our legacy. In the current discussion and debate about worship music, traditional covers a spectrum of styles and songs composed over a long period of time. Sadly, it has gained a negative overtone suggesting music that is dusty and worn out. As we shall see, the matter isn't quite as simple as that.

So, what is remarkable about CWM? For one thing, the origins of CWM and its main producers are outside the orbit of most Protestants. CWM comes from a world other than that of denominational agencies and publishers, and it is the product of a commercial production "culture," that is, a network of songwriters, artists, producers, publishers, and distributors. Their assumptions, beliefs, and goals have shaped not only the sound of CWM since the early 1970s but also its theological content and attitude toward worship. To understand the worship awakening, it is important to understand this production culture.

Many pastors and church leaders are suspicious of CWM because they don't know that much about its parentage, nor about the people who write, publish, record, and distribute new worship music. Some of these attitudes are shaped by denominational provincialism. Some church leaders have never ventured musically beyond what is known and used in their denominational circle. Lingering doubt about charismatics also play a part. Pentecostals and charismatics, for example, were once looked down upon by most Protestants, yet today those churches are the source of a significant portion of CWM. Many pastors and lay leaders still wonder if anything good can come from those once known as the holy rollers. Can Presbyterians sing Pentecostal worship songs? Can a Lutheran let a charismatic put words in the mouth of the congregation? Such questions lead to an important discussion about how worship music shapes congregational identity.

Since the late 1990s, a few denominations have become involved in producing new worship, but most CWM comes from commercial recording companies, not church-sponsored agencies. This is an important shift. Until the 1970s, most Protestant churches received their congregational worship music—the hymnals—from their denomination, or at least from a denominationally approved publisher. A few nondenominational songbooks from groups such as Young Life or Youth for Christ began appearing in the pews as early as the 1950s, but they supplemented rather than replaced existing hymnals.

Since the 1970s, things have changed dramatically. The Presbyterian Church USA (PCUSA) is a good example. In 1972, the northern branch of Presbyterians produced *The Worshipbook,* the first new hymnal since 1955. It was not popular among the churches, however, and in the 1970s and 1980s a large number instead purchased a commercially produced hymnal, *Hymns for the Family of God,* edited by the late Fred Bock.[2] For many churches, it was their first experience of going outside the denomination for something as important as a hymnal. This happened in several other groups as well, and it effectively ended the worship music monopoly that the denomination held over its congregations. Despite this, many Presbyterian churches are still nervous about using materials produced outside the denomination. In many cases, the denomination has contributed to this sense of discomfort by either ignoring CWM or offering blanket criticism of it. In 2000, two presbyteries issued "cautions" to congregations about contemporary worship music. Pastors and lay leaders secretly wonder if it's all right to use songs from a commercial publisher, particularly when denominational officials are pushing them to purchase their own new hymnals. This has not deterred commercial publishers. Word Music developed two successful hymnals that included traditional hymnody and CWM, the *Hymnal for Praise and Worship* (1986) with Maranatha! Music and the *Celebration Hymnal* (1992) with Integrity Music. The *Renew!*

hymnal appeared in 1999 under the guidance of Robert Webber, an advocate of blended worship.[3]

A Song for Us: CWM in North America

The contemporary worship music industry has roots in several historical antecedents, notably revivalist worship, music from parachurch youth ministries after World War II, and the Jesus music of the late 1960s and early 1970s.

Revivalist Worship Music

One important source of today's CWM is revivalist worship, in particular the music publishing companies that sprang from the work of such evangelists as D. L. Moody and Billy Sunday, and their enterprising musical companions Ira Sankey and Homer Rodeheaver. Historian Laurence Moore notes that "as a shaper of popular/commercial culture [Moody] was as important a figure as P. T. Barnum. No one understood better than he did that religion had to become a business in the nineteenth century and that success in religion depended on sound and innovative business practices."[4] The music of turn-of-the-century revivalism was a mix of classical hymnody and new gospel songs, composed with an ear to the musical tastes of American popular culture of the day. Song leaders used both congregational singing and performance music to prepare people for the message. This approach to music, developed in revivalistic churches, still shapes the approach to music in many Protestant churches now, and it has been refined even further in seeker service.

Youth Music

The post–World War II era was a time of innovative youth ministry, particularly in the use of music. New parachurch ministry groups such as Youth for Christ (YFC) concluded traditional church music no longer appealed to teenagers and turned to other kinds of music instead. Donald Hustad, a musician who worked with Billy Graham in those years, writes that "Youth for Christ activity was the first twentieth-century emphasis on special worship/evangelism styles for a specific age group."[5] The idea of worship music intended for a single generation stuck with Protestants—especially evangelicals—for the rest of the century. Sunday School songs such as "I've Got the Joy, Joy" and "Deep and Wide" emerged at this time. The chorus—the refrain of a gospel song sung without accompanying verse—was also popular. Hustad observes that "when YFC congregations sang traditional gospel songs, frequently the stanzas were omitted completely. In addition, many independent choruses were composed and collected in a proliferation of 'chorus books.'"[6] Later, popular song tunes were used along with hymn and chorus lyrics. A favorite in the late 1960s was "Amazing Grace" sung to the tune of the folk hit "The House of the Rising Sun."

Kids and youth group leaders also frequently changed a few words of the lyrics to give them a Christian spin. Songs with upbeat, positive lyrics such as "I'd Like to Teach the World to Sing" and the Holland-Dozier-Holland hit "How Sweet It Is" often got the Christian treatment. Bill and Gloria Gaither, composers of popular gospel songs, were also important transitional figures. Their use of current musical genres (Broadway show tunes, pop ballads, or standards) helped reduce the resistance to a secular music style by demonstrating that hit sounds didn't cancel out Christian lyrics.

"Youth musicals" began to appear in the mid-1960s, designed for youth choirs and a pop band accompaniment. Such projects as *Good News* (1967) and *Tell It Like It Is* (1969) were message-oriented and featured songs of testimony, encouragement, and challenge to commitment. Yet, according to Chuck Fromm, it was taboo at the time to mention Jesus or use traditional language for God because of the controversial nature of the music.[7] Producers thought they had to avoid provoking traditionalists who viewed rock and roll as too worldly for worship. Nevertheless, the music caught on; to cite one example, "Pass It On" (from "Tell It Like It Is") eventually became a favorite for youth and college groups in the 1970s.

Youth musicals had a significant impact on young Christians in the 1960s. For one thing, they validated the popular musical styles kids were listening to on the radio, at least for youth meetings and evangelism. Although such composers as Buryl Red, Ralph Carmichael, Jimmy Owens, and Kurt Kaiser were not rock and rollers, they did encourage kids to use their instruments and their music. For another, youth musicals established the commercial music recording and publishing companies as a vehicle of innovation in worship music, a role they would play with considerable impact in the next twenty years. The youth musicals were an important step, one that did much to prepare for the next step, known as Jesus music.[8]

Jesus Music

Youth musicals were written for Christian youth; but as popular as they were with church kids, they did not fully capture the music of the new generation. In the late 1960s and early 1970s, a large segment of American youth became disillusioned with traditional Protestantism and dropped out of church. For them, the sixties meant unlimited personal freedom, sexual liberation, and mind expansion through drugs and alcohol. The journey to self-discovery, however, often ended in personal tragedy. Addiction, unwanted pregnancy, financial ruin, crime, and broken relationships were all that many had to show for their adventure in the new counterculture.

The Los Angeles and San Francisco areas became a magnet for hippies looking to tune in, turn on, and drop out. Although many churches resisted the youths who came for help—unable to look past their beards, beads, and jeans—some did try to reach out to the kids who came to them looking for something authentic in the Christian message. Some counterculture youths became Christians and began writing songs to Jesus, about Jesus, and about their personal encounter with Jesus in their own rock and pop musical style. Pastor Chuck Smith of Calvary Chapel of Costa Mesa recalls how four recently converted young men in a club band known as Love

Song came to him with a request to share a new song in church; they sang "Welcome Back" for him in the church parking lot. Smith invited the group to share the song at Bible study that evening. Soon young people with new songs took over the musical leadership of Thursday evening Bible study, which packed the fifteen-hundred-seat sanctuary. Later, groups performed at football stadium festivals. To respond to the demand for recordings of these new artists, the church started Maranatha! Music, and before long it was a self-supporting business headed by a former assistant city manager from Yuba City, California, named Chuck Fromm.[9]

The attempt to make worship music relevant in the context of the sixties counterculture gave Jesus music both a negative and a positive perspective. The negative one was antitraditional and antiestablishment; many believed that traditional church music wasn't meaningful for the young Baby Boomers. The Jesus movement felt strongly that if Christian worship were to be meaningful, it had to be freed from the baggage of 1950s' "culture Protestantism." The old music of their parents' church, both the classically oriented mainline church and the Billy Graham crusade clones of conservative evangelicalism—and even the youth musicals of the midsixties—simply would not work.

The positive perspective was their high esteem for authenticity and simplicity. This attitude came partly in reaction to the perceived hypocrisy and conformism of culture Protestantism, and partly in response to the counterculture's value for individual expression. Jesus music came to be characterized by its simplicity and personal expressiveness, as contrasted with the perceived obscurity and cold objectivism of traditional hymn lyrics. Boomers also linked their own musical styles with authenticity. Young people identified with emerging rock and roll, and to a lesser degree with the folk music of the sixties.[10] As Larry Norman sang in his anthem "Why Should the Devil Have All the Good Music?" "I ain't knockin' the hymns. / Just give me a song that moves my feet!"

Looking back over the early Jesus movement and its music, I find it remarkable not how much youthful Baby Boomers gave away to the counterculture but rather how much of the substance of Christian worship they preserved in a new format, especially in their emphasis on biblical preaching, prayer, and congregational participation. Critic Ken Myers writes that "the Jesus People were essentially Christian hippies, an unorganized assortment of relatively new believers who were adamant in their eagerness to construct their fellowship and worship according to the sensibility of the counterculture."[11]

Myers describes the Jesus people accurately, but he misses the mark when it comes to their motive. Having studied many churches that grew out of the Jesus movement, USC religion professor Donald Miller concludes "[these] churches appropriated elements of contemporary culture without accommodating all its values."[12] This is particularly true of worship music. For one thing, as John Frame discerns, Christians raised on Jesus music learned how to praise. Despite what its critics have said about it, early CWM was, for the most part, both God-centered and biblical in content.[13] They also stressed a variety of worship themes (adoration, praise, confession, humility before God). Despite widespread negative feelings about traditional church music, many of these new churches used hymns regularly, though with new arrangements.

Two new features, however, signaled a different function for music in worship. First, the songs were a personal expression of worship and faith. They were usually written in the first person singular, unlike many hymns that are statements about God. Some critics point to this as a sign of surrender to the individualism of the counterculture, but it is probably better viewed as a reaction against the formality and conformism of the 1950s' culture Protestantism.

Second, the songs were short and intended to be repeated frequently—again unlike hymns and gospel songs, which develop complex thoughts over several verses. Brevity and simplicity were a virtue for the new worship song since its lyrics often had to fit on a single overhead transparency. Repetition allowed worshipers to sing with the emotions, or from the heart.

The Sources of Contemporary Worship Music

Now that we have some sense of the history of CWM, we can turn to the producers who make it available to the Church today. There are five main sources of CWM: the big four worship music companies (Maranatha! Music, the Vineyard Music Group, Integrity Music, and WorshipTogether), minor worship music labels, the contemporary Christian music industry, the growing number of independent producers, and denominations.

The Big Four

Having originated at Calvary Chapel in Costa Mesa, Maranatha! Music was the first record company to specialize in CWM, though it stumbled upon the style almost by accident. In the early days of the Jesus music movement, there was no clear distinction between worship music and message music (that is, between music to be sung in worship and music for evangelism). Groups and artists sang songs to God and about God indiscriminately in a variety of settings. Artists affiliated with Calvary Chapel visited many churches and led worship. Before long, such songs as "Seek Ye First" (Karen Lafferty), "Father, I Adore You" (Terrye Coehelo), and "Open Our Eyes" (Bob Cull) found their way into many worship services. The "Maranatha! Praise" album, released in 1974, is generally acknowledged to be the first CWM project.

By the late seventies, Maranatha! faced the challenge of continuing to produce and promote contemporary Christian music as well as worship music. Fromm, the president at the time, later wrote that "at Maranatha! Music in 1979 we had a full roster of popular contemporary Christian artists, each requiring substantial recording and promotional budgets to continue their 'ministries.' Fewer artists were receiving greater attention with diminishing results. At the same time, the branch of Maranatha! Music involved with simple songs of worship, called Praise Music, was flourishing. Our mandate seemed clear: by 1980 we had released from contractual obligation all of our artists and began concentrating our efforts on a program of equipping young music ministers for active roles in local communities."[14] By this time there were several CCM labels (among them Word and Sparrow) that focused on message music, but Maranatha! elected to produce and publish worship music exclusively.

Mercy Publishing was begun as a personal venture by John Wimber, as we have noted the founding pastor of the Anaheim Vineyard Christian Fellowship, in the early 1980s. Wimber's musical roots went deep in rock and roll, having been a sideman and arranger for the early pop group the Righteous Brothers. After a dramatic conversion in the late sixties, Wimber eventually became pastor of the Anaheim Vineyard church. Because of his musicianship, contemporary worship music was a leading feature of the new church, and before long the church attracted several songwriters and many musicians. The first album, *Hosanna!*, was released in 1984. As a nonprofit arm of Vineyard Ministries International, the company now focuses almost exclusively on worship songs emerging from more than eight hundred Vineyard congregations around the world. As a result, Vineyard songs reflect the theology and philosophy of worship taught in the Vineyard.

By the mid-1980s, CCM and CWM were firmly established in at least some parts of the evangelical Protestant world, in particular among independent charismatic churches, which had already embraced popular musical styles for their services. Songwriters were active in these churches but generally unable to get their songs published and recorded at Maranatha! or Mercy, which worked with a relatively small number of songwriters. To address this problem, a group of pastors met to form a new company, called Integrity Music, in 1987. Collecting songs from around the country and connecting with leading independent songwriters and worship leaders, the company began releasing a steady stream of projects in a variety of musical styles, among them pop, country, Hebrew-style folk, and gospel. In 1994, Integrity became a publicly traded company, and by 1998 it was ranked the number two label for sales in Christian music, according to SoundScan.[15] Many attribute Integrity's initial success to an infusion of songs from new songwriters, many of whom were well-known in independent charismatic circles. The company also solidified its place in the market with effective marketing and distribution, and a popular subscription program that delivered the latest cassette or CD to the customer by mail.

The newcomer among the big four is the EMI Christian Music Group and its CWM label WorshipTogether. Started in the late 1990s, WorshipTogether emerged quickly as a platform for a new generation of younger worship leaders and songwriters from the United Kingdom such as Martin Smith of Delirious?, Matt Redman (no biological relation to the author), Stuart Townend, and Noel Richards, along with twentysomething Americans such as Chris Tomlin. The worship awakening in Britain found an early advocate in worship leader and songwriter Graham Kendrick, along with John Wimber and Vineyard artists such as Andy Park and Brian Doerksen, who visited the country frequently. Large youth gatherings added momentum to new ways of worship: the Spring Harvest festival is the oldest, going back to the mid-1970s, while the Cutting Edge and Soul Survivor events emerged in the 1990s as popular platforms for new worship leaders and their songs.[16] These events, along with their American counterpart Passion conferences, are loud and raucous events that encourage energetic participation through singing, dancing, and shouting.

Musically, WorshipTogether is strongly influenced by the alternative rock sounds of bands like U2, REM, the Red Hot Chili Peppers, and Phish. Theologically, the lyrics of many songs are steeped in biblical imagery and personal expression of praise. In addition, the emphasis on confession of sin and personal brokenness, and the forgiveness of Christ through the cross, are interesting aspects of many WorshipTogether songs.

Usability is an important production value of the big four. They record songs written primarily for congregational singing, rather than just for listening. Songs are generally selected on the basis of the songwriter's relationship to a local church and the setting for which the song was composed. Usability affects decisions about how a song is produced, and preference is given to keys, tempos, and arrangements that facilitate, not deter, congregational participation. Maranatha! Music's Promise Keeper songs, for example, are intended for use at men's conferences. As a result, the songs are arranged as much as an interval of a third lower than originally composed to help men sing them comfortably.

Some music critics describe some of the big four's recordings as "vanilla" and "safe," meaning the arrangements and performances are bland and uninteresting. But this criticism misses an important assumption the big four make about their role in selecting and recording music. Artistic decisions about which songs to record and how to arrange them are usually made, we have seen, on the basis of usability. Big four producers are generally wary of doing too much to a song because of how production and performance can limit its usability in a church. As one producer put it, "A song that is too flashy says to a worship leader in a church 'You can't do this song unless you have the resources we had to record it.' That's not what we're about. We want to present a song in such a way that a worship leader can say, 'We can do that.'"

The usability value means that the big four are each fully committed to sheet music publishing and other worship ministry resources (workshops, instructional videos, manuals). Each company publishes many songs in a variety of formats—words and melody, piano score, and arrangement for band (called a chart). It is probably fair to say that because of the emphasis on usability, music publishing and worship leader and musician training is at least as important as record production.

The impact of this business philosophy on the worship awakening should not be underestimated. The big four are not in business just to sell CDs but rather to equip the church with a range of products and services designed to help people use their music in worship. The companies see themselves as agents of worship renewal by giving a church new songs to sing *and* a new way of doing worship ministry. Company leaders are also helping to stir the pot by creating a forum for discussion of worship issues through workshops and conferences, by using the Internet, and, perhaps most important, by means of *Worship Leader* magazine. Launched as a joint venture between Maranatha! Music and CCM Communications, *Worship Leader* grew to a paid subscription of more than forty thousand in just eight years.

Minor Labels

In addition to the big four, a number of smaller companies and divisions of larger companies also record and publish contemporary worship music. They are minor only in the output, producing fewer than ten to fifteen projects a year (each of the big four releases between twenty and forty per year) and focusing on a few songwriters or artists. For example, PDI Records is the recording and publishing arm of People of Destiny International, a small evangelical denomination; it features primarily songs written and performed by just a few songwriters. Rockettown Records, led by songwriter Michael W. Smith, is an example of a CWM label begun by a larger record company, in this case by secular giant EMI's Christian music division. BMG, another industry heavyweight, also has a Christian music division made up of the labels Sparrow, Myrrh, and Birdwing.

The connection with larger secular labels has generated concern among some that I address shortly. Other smaller labels produce songs for specific uses in church. Whole Hearted Worship, led by veteran worship musician Gerritt Gustafson, produces worship music for small groups. The standard of quality varies greatly among the smaller labels, depending on mission and production values. Some labels are artist-driven, featuring songs that are worshipful but not necessarily usable for congregational worship because of personalized lyrics, idiosyncratic melodies, and vocalizing. Others offer music that is entirely suitable for congregational use. Production quality and musicianship vary from adequate to outstanding. Because of their small size, some minor labels are often unable to produce the accompanying resources on their own—sheet music, for instance— and so they may work with a larger music publisher.

Contemporary Christian Music

Since its rise in the seventies, contemporary Christian music has helped to create a desire for contemporary musical styles in worship. The line between message music and worship music was never clear to begin with, and it remains blurred today. Several CCM artists have written and recorded worship music, notably Twila Paris and Michael W. Smith, and artists such as Petra begin concerts with worship that typically includes new worship music and hymn arrangements, prayer, and a brief meditation on a passage of scripture.

In the early 1990s, the CCM scene was rocked by corporate buyouts of the Christian labels Word and Sparrow. As a result, some began to wonder about the mission of CCM and the spiritual integrity of the artists. Was CCM about ministry or making money? In its first years, many agreed that the mission of CCM was music for witness and evangelism. Later, people began to wonder whether artists were serving Christ or their careers. In the middle and late 1980s, a number of artists began to get airplay on secular radio stations with songs that intentionally avoided any explicitly Christian references. People then wondered about the spiritual integrity of CCM artists as reports surfaced of adultery and financial misconduct. One way many artists have responded is by recording personal devotion music and worship music.[17] It is now common to find songs addressed to God alongside message songs directed to Christians or unbelievers.

According to CCM insider Charlie Peacock, conformity is the main problem with the industry. The go-along-to-get-ahead mentality among artists and producers is harmful for individuals and for the Church because "conformity produces legalism, performance-based acceptability, and stunted, uninspired imaginations. It is a conformity that breeds apathy and complacency. Wherever there is an abundance of this type of conformity, there is little chance for diverse, faithful, and imaginative business, music and ministry."[18] Peacock chastises the industry for its narrow, groupthink conformity, and the tendency simply to mimic popular musical styles.

Many seeker churches use CCM's message songs effectively in the service when the lyrics can open the door to a sermon or help reinforce it. But pastors and worship leaders should be selective in considering a worship song recorded by a CCM artist, and bear in mind some features of CCM worship music. For one thing, CCM recordings are generally artist-oriented. The songs are usually written for artists, not congregations, and meant for solo or ensemble performance, not congregational singing. Moreover, CCM artists give their version of a song an idiosyncratic and personalized treatment. Music may be performed in a key or tempo that is comfortable for the artist, but such a setting doesn't always work for a church. Occasionally, a company will produce a split-track version of songs; however, they usually work better for soloists, groups, and choirs than for congregational singing. Finally, most CCM companies gear product sales to individuals, not to churches, and thus do not generally produce resources such as sheet music for use in a church.

The Independents

Although the big four and other commercial producers dominated production of CWM for the past twenty years, their monopoly has ended. The creative energy in CWM is no longer exclusively with the established recording and publishing companies. Because of changes in song publishing and record production and distribution that create direct access to churches, independent record producers are now emerging as an important source of new music and a fresh approach to worship. Until recently, a CWM song needed the industry for three main reasons: publication, recording, and distribution. Since 1990, however, a trio of important developments have broken down the barriers for an independent project.

First, creation of Christian Copyright Licensing, Inc. (CCLI), in 1991, effectively democratized music publishing. Until that time, a church wanting to avoid copyright infringement had to write directly to the copyright holder for permission to reproduce lyrics in a bulletin or on an overhead. Most congregations ignored this requirement, but those that did attempt to stay legal found the publishing companies unable or unwilling to help them. Chuck Fromm (who was then president of Maranatha! Music) agreed to support creation of an independent company that would monitor usage, collect fees, and pay royalties to the copyright holder. Today, CCLI offers an umbrella usage fee covering nearly all CWM publishers, including most minor and independent producers.

By this process, CCLI also allows individuals or smaller groups of songwriters into the music publishing business. Previously, the only way to publish a song with any hope of recognition was to submit it to a major publisher. The big four, for example, are selective. Vineyard Music Group usually publishes songs written only by members of a Vineyard congregation, while Maranatha! Music stopped accepting unsolicited submissions for a time. Integrity Music does record and publish material from new writers, but it generally uses material from a stable of writers under contract. Thanks to CCLI, however, a church is now able to use a song from a writer working with a growing number of minor and independent labels.

Second, low production costs democratize the recording process. The cost of recording a CD is now a fraction of what it was ten years ago. Previously, only a well-capitalized record company could afford professional musicians, studio time, and production expenses. In

1990, the bill for a typical project was at least $30,000. By 2000, in-expensive and easy-to-use recording technologies reduced the production costs to the point where a church can record its own CD of worship music for around $5,000. The means for recording the work of new songwriters is within the reach of many a congregation.

Third, the low cost of Internet marketing and sales has opened up the process of marketing and distribution. Business writers Joseph Pine and James Gilmore use the term *disintermediation* to describe the strategy of companies that "go around retailers, distributors, and agents to connect directly with their end buyers."[19] Until recently, independent producers could not afford to advertise and sell a project themselves. Only an intermediary, an established distribution company, had the resources to pay for the high cost of advertising, maintaining inventory, and shipping because all this required staff and infrastructure. But since the mid-1990s, the Internet has changed the rules of commerce by leveling the playing field for all producers. By establishing a link with an Internet distributor such as Amazon.com or Christian Book Distributors (Christianbook.com), an independent label with a Website does not need the large distribution companies, who generally prefer to work only with established recording companies.

The benefits of these three trends are significant. For one thing, independent projects are expanding the stylistic range of worship music and releasing creativity. Independent artists are experimenting with newer sounds and instrumentation (alternative rock, Latin music, rap and hip hop, world music). Traditional sounds and instruments are also making a comeback (big band, Dixieland). The mass-appeal strategy of the big four companies may have restricted the range of musical styles in the past, but on a self-supported independent project the songwriter and arranger have artistic control over their own music.

Tommy Walker, the worship pastor of Christian Assembly in Eagle Rock, California, is a forerunner in the local-church-based independent recording movement. By 2001, Christian Assembly's

label Get Down Records had released five CDs, four of which feature original compositions from Walker and other songwriters in the
congregation. A fifth project, entitled *Acoustic Hymns* (1998), features arrangements of classic hymns and gospel songs. At the same
time, many of Walker's original songs and hymn arrangements have
been recorded and published by various CWM and CCM labels. His
song "Lord, I Believe in You" was nominated for a 1998 Dove award
for best female vocalist for CCM artist Crystal Lewis, and his
arrangement of "A Mighty Fortress Is Our God" was a best-selling
choral octavo for Word Music in the same year. Although Walker
is pleased that commercial versions of his music are well received,
the artistic freedom of his own label allows him to select and
arrange songs as he sees fit.

Second, an independent project permits a congregation to customize and vigorously pursue the freedom to capture sounds that are
unique to their specific setting. For example, the Worship Band at
Mars Hill Fellowship in Seattle released *Tension*, a CD of alternative-
rock-style worship music in 1998 that a commercial record company would have been reluctant to do unless it changed the band's
sound and style. By recording their own CD as an independent,
this team can explore the full range of their own congregational
voice without having to adopt alien production values. As a result,
a worship leader can discover important clues about how to find
the congregation's own worship voice by hearing expression of musical worship in a congregation without the filter of commercial
production.

Third, a worship leader can use an independent project to teach
new music to the congregation. Each summer at the Covenant
Church of Pittsburgh, Denise Graves and her team produce a CD
of new worship music, called *Songs of the Season*. Released in the
fall to coincide with a new sermon series from Pastor Joseph Garlington, each CD typically includes a mix of original compositions
and "covers" of previously recorded CWM. The project allows the
team to record new material and also give its interpretation to other

music. Another purpose for each project is instructional: to teach the congregation new worship music without taking up time in the service to do it.

Independently produced CWM also has some potentially negative features. For one thing, an independent project often lacks the quality control of commercially produced CWM. Most indie projects rely on amateur musicians and producers, and the results can be mixed. Even though digital recording technology can produce quality sound for a lot less money, it cannot do anything to help poor singing and playing. Production quality also depends a great deal on the producer and the engineer. Only a few independent projects can match commercial CWM for quality of musicianship or technical production.

The source of independent projects is another issue. Buyers of commercial CWM generally know who stands behind the project they buy, so they know generally what to expect in terms of theology and approach to worship. The same is not always true with an independent project. Some indie producers (Tommy Walker is an example) are already well known; others are not. Because producing and distributing a CD is relatively easy and cheap, there are people with projects who are almost completely unknown. Some independent producers are accountable to a church board and pastor, or to a group of churches; others are not. Nor is it always easy to tell the nature of a project's connection to a local church or its theological perspective by reading the liner notes or viewing the producer's Website. The lesson here is let the buyer beware; a pastor or church musician needs to do homework before using any CWM, but especially independently produced CWM.

Denominations

Although the Southern Baptist Convention helped produce the groundbreaking youth musical *Good News* and the follow-up hit *Celebrate Life* in the mid-1960s, not until much later did other denominations step into recording or publishing CWM. Most mainline denominations have committed themselves to the Liturgical Renewal movement (which we examine in the following chapter) and are thus either generally unaware of CWM or hostile toward it. It is not uncommon to hear mainline church leaders complain about bad theology expressed in many CWM songs, or about the failure of many writers to embrace gender-inclusive language, for example. At the same time, few are encouraging musicians and songwriters in their denomination to come up with acceptable alternatives. Smaller conservative evangelical denominations have had another set of theological objections, stemming from their suspicion of the Pentecostal and charismatic roots of much of CWM. But even among groups open to new worship music, a smaller denomination often lacks the resources to engage in publishing very much and thus relies on independent evangelical music publishers.

Some denominations are preparing collections of new worship music:

• The General Board of Global Missions of the United Methodist Church has produced several CDs of current worship songs from around the world, though they are more folk than pop in style.[20] The General Board of Discipleship of that church, on the other hand, has championed CWM with a variety of resources for pastors and worship teams and is preparing a hymnal and songbook.[21]

• The Presbyterian Church (USA) has also produced a songbook of CWM, *Lift Up Your Hearts*, that mixes worship songs from around the world with such CWM favorites as Bob Fitts's "Blessed Be the Lord God Almighty."[22]

• The Evangelical Lutheran Church of America has produced a collection of more than 160 songs called *Worship and Praise*, which includes pop worship songs by Lutheran songwriters and contemporary arrangements of older folk hymns.[23]

• In 2001, the Christian Reformed Church published *Sing! A New Creation*, a supplement to their hymnal that includes a large selection of CWM.[24]

These projects are likely to produce growing acceptance of CWM among mainline Protestant churches. By publishing and producing CWM, the denominations are sending an important signal to their churches that CWM is acceptable for corporate worship and suitable for use. There are also resources available to help a church select and use CWM, and it is easier than ever to find training events to help the pastor, worship leader, or team member.[25]

Issues for the Contemporary Worship Music Industry

The CWM industry has played a leading role in the growth and development of the worship awakening, though not everyone is happy with this development. Some critics see CWM as rooted in a secular worldview of modernity. In their view, CWM is tainted by the consumerism and secularism of commercial culture.

CWM as a Business

It is frequently argued that the business practices of a CWM company inevitably turn worship music into a product. The commercial process creates a conflict of interest between God's values and human values, between spiritual things and the ways of the world and the flesh. The tension has been heightened in recent years as CCM companies that produce CWM have been bought by secular recording giants EMI and BMG. Can a worship song be a commodity? Does the commercial process of composing, arranging, producing, marketing, and advertising a song damage it or make it unsuitable for Christian worship? Is the worship song as a product compatible with the purpose of worship music?

Some critics of CWM point to the consumerism of American culture and complain that CWM is tainted by its association with the forces of greed and materialism. A church should not entrust production of worship music to a company whose bottom line is profit instead of the needs of the congregation. By adopting the marketing and advertising strategies of the commercial culture, CWM is secularized and therefore corrupted.

CWM as a Product

Does the commercial recording and publishing process affect the quality of new worship music? Does all commercially produced worship music lack artistic or theological integrity? Calvin Johansson worries that mass culture, *kitsch,* and commercialization of worship music have "lowered standards, encouraged musical tastelessness, and promoted artistic inertia."[26] He argues that to be commercially successful, a composer must sacrifice musical integrity. This kind of complaint about commercialization of popular music is valid, as far as it goes, and there is some value in Johansson's critique. To be sure, the commercial process has produced inferior products from time to time. But this is not the fault of the commercial process per se. Denominational hymnal and liturgical resource committees have a mixed record as well. To suggest that there is something inherently wrong with CWM because it is produced by commercial enterprises reflects a misguided belief about the marketplace.

It is no secret that the industry has produced an overabundance of CWM in recent years. By 2000, the CCLI catalogue had grown to more than two hundred thousand worship songs. Worship leaders complain that they can't keep up with the new music released by the big four, let alone from other sources. This situation has created a feeling among many that songs are beginning to sound alike or aren't adding anything to the range of worship themes. In a column in *Worship Leader,* Pastor Randy Rowland, whose church in Seattle uses CWM almost exclusively, complained that praise and worship music seems to be stuck in a stylistic ghetto: "There is something disturbing about the Christian church, purportedly led by the Holy Spirit among whose characteristics one would assume would be creativity, whose art is mainly imitative. Where is the spiritual creativity in the midst of songs that all sound the same?"[27] The growing quantity of CWM has not necessarily produced an increase in quality.

Yet as strange as it may sound, the church needs more new worship songs, not fewer. The solution is not a moratorium on writing new worship music; rather, pastors and church leaders should encourage songwriters to explore a wider range of themes and emotions for worship music. For example, songwriters have not mined themes such as lament or confession of faith and sin as thoroughly as others. They should also explore using more scripture in their songs. Many typically include a line or two, or just an allusion; recently, some songwriters have attempted to work with longer sections.

Recent developments in recording technology and product distribution point in a promising direction, addressing Johansson's concern about the sacrifice of artistic integrity and the lowering of musical quality. If anything, artistic control and musical quality are on the rise as the cost of recording and publishing music drops dramatically. The impact of this on the worship awakening can be significant as songwriters mature in their craft by leading worshipers into an authentic encounter with God through familiar musical idioms.

The CWM Industry and the Church

Some worry about the control of music production that resides in the hands of a relatively small group of artists, producers, and executives who are not accountable to any church or denomination. It is no secret that a record company's production values—the artistic decisions about repertoire and presentation—are often defined by the needs of the recording and marketing process (projected revenue and expenses, available musical talent, advertising, and so on) instead of the needs of the congregation for worship music people can sing with theological integrity. Most producers and executives would admit they have sometimes thought more about the bottom line of a CD than its potential impact on a congregation or the individual. But these concerns can be overstated, and they do not apply equally to all CWM producers. Vineyard Music Group/Mercy Publishing is a nonprofit venture completely accountable to Vineyard Ministries International, which is, for all intents and purposes, a denomination. Maranatha! Music and Integrity Music are for-profit corporations, but they have pastors on the board. Minor labels and CCM-sponsored projects do vary in their church relationships. Some are operated by church associations, while others are secular record company subsidiaries. Churches often sponsor independent projects, the fastest-growing and most innovative source of CWM. Denominations, which at first were skeptical of CWM, are now accepting and endorsing songs with their own projects and resource guides.

A stronger link is needed between the CWM industry and the churches. Each side must take the initiative to connect with the other, and to get involved in one another's world. CWM companies should invite and receive more direction and leadership by way of pastors and church leaders on their boards. Companies can invite church leaders and denominational worship and music staff to participate in its artist and songwriter gatherings.

For their part, church leaders and denominational officials have to be more understanding and accepting of CWM and its production culture. The representatives and advocates of CWM continue to be excluded from many denominational gatherings where worship issues are discussed. Church leaders must demonstrate they are serious about dialogue with CWM by inviting their leaders and advocates to participate in developing hymnals and worship resources, and to contribute to their journals.

Perhaps it is time for a summit conference, or a series of meetings between CWM leaders and denominational leadership to explore common ground and issues that need clarification. Together, churches and CWM companies have an opportunity to develop a fresh theology and philosophy of parachurch ministry.[28] They can put into practice the kind of partnership that already exists between the Vineyard Association of Churches and the Vineyard Music Group. VMG's mission is to be an outlet for songwriters and worship leaders within the Vineyard and a resource to the wider Church. The company also partners with the denomination in offering workshops. Other CWM companies can partner with denominations similarly to create a lasting contribution to the worship awakening.

In my estimation, CWM will carry on its leading role in the worship awakening, for a couple of reasons. For one thing, CWM keeps on growing in popularity. Product sales are climbing, and such events as Promise Keepers, Women of Faith, and the Passion Conference continue to expose more churchgoers to new styles of worship music. Mainline and conservative evangelical churches are adapting and adopting CWM as a way to help close the gap between the church and the surrounding culture. All this adds up to a bright future for the CWM industry. For another thing, the CWM industry will work hard to stay popular. It adapts quickly to shifts in popular culture. As a market-sensitive industry, CWM continues experimenting and evolving along with developments in popular music. This flexibility and eagerness to stay fresh is undoubtedly going to help keep CWM songwriters and producers at the forefront of the worship awakening for the foreseeable future.

The CWM industry represents one influential and largely successful shaping of the role of music in the worship awakening in North America. The Liturgical Renewal movement, which emerged from Roman Catholicism and mainline Protestant denominations, represents quite another approach, though it has many points of common concern and emphasis. That movement is the subject of Chapter Four.

4

The Liturgical Renewal Movement

Protestants today are more aware of their historical roots in the ancient Catholic church than any other generation has been. The ecumenical movement, which emerged in the twentieth century, has highlighted the common elements of faith and practice that unite all Christians. At the same time, scholars in Europe and North America from many Christian denominations have studied ancient liturgical texts and current worship practices. These studies raise important questions about the nature of Christian worship and how it is prepared and led in churches today.

This group of liturgical scholars and reformers is known as the Liturgical Renewal movement. Although it began in the Roman Catholic Church, it spread quickly to Anglican and Lutheran churches, and from there to other Protestant groups. As we shall see, now conservative evangelical and even Pentecostal churches are learning about worship from the movement.

This chapter examines the work of this group of worship scholars, looking at their aims and goals for the reform of Protestant worship. We also assess the strengths and weaknesses of the movement and suggest important lessons we can learn from it. But to understand the movement better, we should briefly survey its development over the past 150 years.

The Liturgical Renewal Movement

In the two sections that follow, we trace the development of the Liturgical Renewal movement from its origins in the Roman Catholic Church and its adaptation by Protestants in the years after the Second Vatican Council.

Liturgical Renewal in the Roman Catholic Church

The Second Vatican Council (1962–1965) introduced sweeping changes into the Roman Catholic Church, especially in worship. Although to many Protestants at the time these liturgical reforms seemed to come out of nowhere, in fact, they were nearly a hundred years in the making. In the mid-nineteenth century, the Roman Catholic Church experienced a quiet but important renewal; several of the monastic religious orders were reestablished and grew, and monasteries that had been destroyed or secularized during the Napoleonic period were rebuilt or taken back. Many priests, monks, and scholars turned their attention to the spiritual life of the parish church, in particular daily prayer offices and weekly celebration of the mass.

The next generation of church leaders and scholars, notably Pope Pius X and Dom Lambert Beauduin, added more energy to the growing liturgical reform movement in the early twentieth century. In 1903, the pope issued *Motu Proprio*, a document on church music that opened the way for more congregational participation in worship; two years later another decree was released, encouraging Catholics to receive communion frequently, rather than once or twice a year as was often the custom. The papal bull *Divino Afflatu* (1911) brought further reforms to the Breviary (the manual of daily prayer), the liturgical calendar, and the lectionary (the cycle of scripture readings for each week).[1]

Beauduin's 1909 address on "The True Prayer of the Church" sought to address the problem of excessive individualism and privatism in Catholic religious life. John Fenwick and Bryan Spinks observed that for Beauduin, "piety was no longer based on corporate liturgy, but had become a private matter. The answer was renewal of the liturgical life. He proposed two practical lines of action: a translation of the Latin Missal was to be put in the hands of the Catholic laity; and use of the Daily Office should be encouraged."[2] Although two world wars put much of this work on hold until the 1950s, the movement continued to gain ground among scholars and the hierarchy.

In 1962, Pope John XXIII convened the Second Vatican Council and appointed a commission to work out the reform of worship. The fruit of their work was the *Constitution on the Sacred Liturgy* (CSL), promulgated by Pope Paul VI in 1963. Seen in historical perspective, the CSL was a breakthrough. Fenwick and Spinks comment that "in seven chapters of 130 paragraphs the whole worship of the Roman Catholic Church, more or less frozen since the Council of Trent in the sixteenth century, was put into the melting pot."[3] It is difficult to understate the paradigm shift in worship that the CSL represents for Roman Catholic worship. Language was just the most noticeable reform; now Catholics could use the vernacular, or local, language for worship. Other reforms also had a profound impact on churches, with emphasis on congregational participation and use of popular hymnody, relevant symbolism, and biblical preaching.[4]

The CSL was actually only a first step in what is still an ongoing process, though it has been the crucial blueprint for reform intended to shape the texts it has inspired. The next step came in early 1964, when the pope established a *consilium* (council) of bishops and liturgical scholars to oversee the production of liturgical texts, which in 1969 became the Congregation for Divine Worship. A number of working groups were appointed to various aspects of Catholic worship. As each group completed its work, the new texts—in Latin—were then sent for approval to the entire *consilium* and to the pope.[5] These official versions (*editio typica*) were then sent to the bishops for authorized translation in their countries.

The effect of the reforms inspired by Vatican II has trickled slowly down to most congregations. For example, the pope did not authorize a new missal (the first since 1570) until 1970, the first authorized version in American English did not appear until 1975, and the International Committee on English in the Liturgy (ICEL) finally produced its own version in 1997.

Many congregations in North America have enthusiastically embraced the liturgical reforms of Vatican II, although there has been scattered resistance among some clergy and laity to the reforms of Vatican II since the mid-1960s. As a sign of compromise, in 1984 the Vatican began giving permission for a church to celebrate the old Latin mass under certain circumstances. Nevertheless, scholars generally agree that the liturgical reforms of Vatican II have been successful, particularly for churches in North America and in the "two-thirds world," where the need for relevance in the surrounding non-Catholic cultures is felt by many to be great.

The impact of CSL was heightened by the other documents promulgated by Vatican II, especially the *Constitution on the Church*. Vatican II envisioned a church that is open to the world. In worship, this means liturgy that is "inculturated," that is, relevant to the cultural context in which it takes place. Pre-Vatican II liturgy was uniform; the Mass was said the same way everywhere. CSL saw the need not only for the vernacular in worship but also for flexible liturgical forms; it encouraged use of nonverbal symbols, gestures, and musical styles.[6]

Vatican II also envisioned participatory worship. CSL addressed the need for regular and faithful attendance and participation in worship. This perspective was rooted in a view of the church that emphasized the whole people of God, not just the priests and the hierarchy. German Martinez observes that "from this paramount ecclesial perspective important liturgical understandings evolved: the baptismal priesthood of the faithful, [and] the full participation of the people at both tables."[7] A visible example of this is the relocation of the altar in many Roman Catholic churches. Prior to Vatican II, the priest faced the altar with his back to the people. As a result of CSL, in most churches the altar has been pulled closer to the congregation and the priest now faces the people during celebration of the mass.

CSL also stresses the importance of informed participation in worship. Because many rank-and-file Catholics still do not understand the basics of the liturgy, bishops, priests, and educators are giving greater attention to liturgical participation as a part of catechetical instruction, especially in the Rites for the Christian Initiation of Adults (RCIA).[8]

Liturgical Renewal in Protestant Churches

The liturgical reforms of Vatican II have had a significant impact on mainline Protestants. The influence can be attributed to a growing spirit of ecumenical cooperation and appreciation for the scholarship of the Roman Catholic Liturgical Renewal movement.

The ecumenical movement took root in the years following World War II. The World Council of Churches (WCC) was formed in 1948 as a kind of United Nations of Protestant denominations. Since then, several Eastern Orthodox churches have joined, making the WCC less exclusively Protestant. Although the Roman Catholic Church did not formally recognize or join the WCC, it did send observers, who took an active role in discussion. In response, a number of observers from Protestant denominations in Europe and the United States attended Vatican II and participated unofficially and informally in its work. Protestant liturgical scholars studied the work of their Catholic counterparts and sought to adapt their conclusions and recommendations to Protestant settings.

The first fruit of this dialogue among Protestants was the statement on the Eucharist issued by the WCC General Conference held in Montreal in 1963. This document is a broad consensus on the form and the content of the Eucharist, clearly inspired by the Liturgical Renewal movement in the Catholic Church.[9] The ecumenical "convergence" in worship led further to the Baptism, Eucharist, and Ministry (BEM) document drafted in Lima, Peru, and released in 1982, with its consensus eucharistic liturgy, known as the "Lima liturgy."[10]

Beginning in the 1970s, most mainline denominations began to incorporate insights from the Liturgical Renewal movement into production of new worship resources. David Newman notes that among these groups "the convergence extends to almost all areas of liturgy, including the Eucharist, Christian initiation [baptism], calendar and lectionary, daily prayer, and other services such as ordination, marriage, the funeral, and a wide range of pastoral liturgies."[11] Other aspects of worship have been affected: church architecture and furniture, vestments, service music, the role of laity in worship, and use of liturgical texts such as unison and responsive reading and prayer.

Fenwick and Spinks note that the paths to liturgical renewal have differed somewhat for Catholics and Protestants. For their part, Roman Catholic liturgical reforms generally involved "streamlining and restoration," a kind of liturgical housecleaning. But for most Protestants, liturgical renewal meant a "radical reshaping" of existing worship practices.[12]

The experience of the Presbyterians is an example of the influence of the Liturgical Renewal movement among mainline Protestants, in particular through changes in architecture, vestments, and the order of service.[13] Traditional Presbyterian architecture featured a central pulpit with a communion table placed directly in front, with no candles or open Bible upon it. Beginning in the 1950s, Presbyterians began to build and remodel their churches to include a split or divided chancel, after the fashion of the Catholics, Anglicans, and Lutherans, with a lectern and a pulpit on either side of the altar. Second, in the traditional Presbyterian service the pastor wore either a black Geneva gown or a business suit. In the 1970s, however, many clergy began to wear a cassock with a stole whose color depended upon the liturgical season and matched fabric covering the pulpit, lectern, and altar. Finally, the order of Presbyterian worship changed significantly.

Traditional Presbyterian services generally included a prayer of confession at the beginning, a pastoral prayer, and one or two scripture readings, followed by a sermon. The offering and a concluding hymn and benediction rounded out the service. Under the influence of the Liturgical Renewal movement, services began to change. The offering was moved to a place before the sermon, and the prayers of the people were placed after the sermon. The most notable change, however, was the frequency of the Lord's Supper, or communion. Traditional Presbyterian churches celebrated quarterly communion (four times a year). But beginning in the 1970s, many church leaders and pastors began encouraging their church to adopt monthly celebration as a stepping stone to weekly.

The *Presbyterian Hymnal* (1990) and the *Presbyterian Book of Common Worship* (1993) represent the full flower of influence from the Liturgical Renewal movement. They are ecumenical in their approach, adopting the convergence form of worship advocated by BEM and the ecumenical movement, and freely borrowing liturgical texts, practices, and musical forms from other Christian traditions. A similar approach to worship influenced by the Liturgical Renewal movement can be found among other mainline denominations—Methodists, Congregationalists, and Lutherans.

Conservative evangelicals have been slow to appropriate the insights of the Liturgical Renewal movement, for several reasons. First, evangelicals have historically been suspicious of Roman Catholic liturgical theology. Theologically, most view Roman Catholicism in terms of the Reformation critique of medieval Catholicism. As a result, the reforms of Vatican II are often poorly understood and dismissed as superficial. Among evangelicals, however, historian and theologian Robert Webber has been a leading advocate of the Liturgical Renewal movement. His approach calls for convergence, the blending of aspects of the Liturgical Renewal movement agenda with some of the central concerns of evangelical Protestantism and the charismatic renewal movement.

A keen observer of evangelical church life, Webber believes the convergence movement began in the mid-1980s, led by evangelicals who were moving toward the liturgical church or who embraced a more liturgically oriented approach to worship.

Webber identifies six elements of worship that exhibit this convergence phenomenon.[14] The first is restored commitment to the sacraments, especially the Eucharist. As Webber sees it, the sacraments are becoming more than a badge of our obedience to God in worship; they "are seen as holy and sacred unto the Lord, a symbol with true spiritual meaning used as point of contact between man and God. The Lord's presence and power are released in these acts as the worshiper encounters God through the elements."[15]

Second, the convergence phenomenon expresses the desire of many evangelicals to know more about the early church. Historic practices capture mystery and the transcendence of God in a way that more modern forms of Protestant worship do not. Third, convergence worship stresses the unity of the church and a desire to overcome division. As Webber writes, "convergence churches appreciate the gifts that each stream of the church provides to the whole."[16] Using the historic liturgical forms of the ancient Catholic church bears witness to the fundamental unity of all Christians. In this regard, the convergence movement represents a belated evangelical embrace of the ecumenical movement.

Fourth, Webber's approach embraces diversity and inculturation. The convergence church, like most evangelical churches, is strongly congregational in organization, in the sense that it is only loosely affiliated with denominational structure and makes nearly all of its own decisions about church life at the local church level. It generally enjoys significant freedom to adjust traditional liturgy or even create new forms to suit local needs.

Fifth, the convergence church seeks to integrate form and freedom in worship. Among liturgical theologians, Webber has demonstrated a sincere desire to engage charismatics about worship and willingness to incorporate charismatic worship practice in the convergence service. He sees the exchange between historic liturgy and charismatic passion moving in both directions. Charismatic renewal is taking place among Roman Catholics, Anglicans, and Lutherans; and charismatics are discovering traditional liturgical elements, such as the creeds, the Eucharist, and historic hymns and chants.

Sixth, convergence worship holds a greater role for ritual gesture, symbol, and visual art in worship. The convergence church is at the forefront of recovering the arts in worship (visual art, crafts, and symbols); "signs and symbols," Webber says, "point beyond themselves to a greater truth and serve as contact points for apprehending inward spiritual reality."[17]

Webber understands that many evangelicals are still skeptical about the Liturgical Renewal movement and its evangelical counterpart, the convergence movement. They worry that key theological insights may be compromised (biblical authority, the uniqueness of Christ's atoning work, the authority of the local church). Such fears are often rooted in stereotype or negative personal experience. Yet Webber sees convergence in terms of what is gained for evangelicals, rather than what is lost: "The convergence movement is definitely not the abandonment of a stream but a convergence of streams. The work of God is inclusive, not exclusive, bringing forth from each tributary those things which he has authenticated. Such issues as evangelism, mission and the work of ministry by the power of the Holy Spirit continue to be released in marvelous ways in people's lives, bringing about conversion, healing, release from bondages, and change in the direction of life."[18]

The Aims of the Protestant Liturgical Renewal Movement

The overall goal of better appreciation of the church's historic worship practice enjoys nearly universal support among advocates of the Liturgical Renewal movement, however much they may disagree about the details. The main aims include restoring the centrality of Christ to worship; restoring the centrality of the Bible to worship; introducing the Christian year and the lectionary; encouraging richer sacramental practice; and promoting fuller congregational participation in worship, particularly in music.[19]

The Liturgical Renewal movement seeks to restore the centrality of Christ to worship. The primary target of the movement is the worship practices of 1950s American culture Protestantism, the legacy of mainline Protestant accommodation to the values of middle-class America in the post–World War II years. Worship in the 1950s magnified the values and preferences of the surrounding society and culture more than of God. A secondary target for the Protestant Liturgical Renewal movement has been revivalist worship, which crept into many Protestant churches in the twentieth century. Both removed Christ from the center of worship and replaced him with other concerns; American culture Protestantism replaced Christ with a celebration of the American way of life, while revivalist worship made the spiritual state of the worshiper the center of worship.

According to the Liturgical Renewal movement, worship should focus God in Jesus Christ. James F. White writes that "Christian worship is rejoicing in what Christ has done for us, a form of God's self-giving in which the historical events are again offered to us. In worship, we experience anew the events of salvation history in terms of our own lives."[20] This ecumenical concern emerges also out of historical studies of worship practice up to the fifth or sixth century A.D. The primary result of this research has been an emerging scholarly consensus about the classic fourfold order of early Christian worship, the *ordo*. This simple order comprises the Gathering, the Word, the Table, and the Dismissal.

The Protestant Liturgical Renewal movement also seeks to restore the centrality of the Bible. It may seem unnecessary to advocate this; after all, Protestants are supposed to believe in *sola scriptura*, scripture alone. In fact, there has long been erosion of the use of scripture in Protestant worship. This is not limited to theological liberals;

conservative evangelicals have also been using less and less of the Bible in worship. According to White, "Scripture functions in the worship of thousands of Protestant churches only as a means of reinforcing what the preacher wants to say."[21] The Liturgical Renewal movement advocates more Bible in worship in the form of several scripture readings in each service—generally an Old Testament text, a Psalm, a passage from the epistles (letters), and a gospel reading. The lectionary arranges readings in a three-year cycle on the basis of the first three gospels.

The strength of this approach is its focus on scripture in worship. Multiple readings shift the focus away from the pastor's pet ideas to the Bible. Similarly, the lectionary establishes a broad biblical basis that is larger than the "preacher's private canon," as James White puts it. The primary assumption behind the Liturgical Renewal emphasis on scripture thus runs counter to other approaches to scripture in worship, especially revival worship and the seeker service movement. There is oftentimes no clear theme shared by all four readings. This might be seen as a weakness, but Liturgical Renewal advocates consider it a benefit.

Despite this, the benefit of multiple readings and the lectionary can be undercut in practice a couple of ways. First, it is diminished by a pastor who either fails to explain the purpose of multiple readings or who spends too much time in the sermon trying to find a hoped-for golden thread connecting all the readings. These efforts may be due to lingering expectations on the part of clergy and laity for thematic clarity, the legacy of both liberal topical preaching and evangelical expository preaching. Second, an unimaginative preacher undermines the aim of the lectionary by gravitating to the gospel passage and preaching on nothing else. In this case, the preacher's canon is replaced by a "gospels-only canon," which is hardly an improvement.

The next reform concerns the importance of the Christian year. Most mainline and evangelical Protestants have historically observed Christmas, Good Friday, and Easter. Many have marked Pentecost as well as the seasons of Advent and Lent. Yet civic and commercial cultural holidays, such as Martin Luther King Day, Valentine's Day, Mother's Day, Father's Day, Memorial Day, and Thanksgiving have become as important in many churches as specifically Christian occasions. In response, the Liturgical Renewal movement advocates a fuller Christian calendar.

At the heart of the concern for the Christian year is renewed emphasis on Lent and Holy Week, in particular the *Triduum*, which in essence is a single worship service spread over Maundy Thursday, Good Friday, and the Easter Vigil on Saturday night. As a result, many mainline churches and even some evangelical ones now observe Lent, beginning with Ash Wednesday, in a creative way that encourages deep prayer, discipleship, and service. Although Protestants have traditionally celebrated Palm Sunday and Good Friday, many also now have services for Maundy Thursday and the Easter Vigil.

The strength of this emphasis on the Christian year is its insistence on a Christian calendar that counts for more in planning and leading worship than the civic or commercial cultural calendar. Creating an alternative understanding of Christian time is crucial, because commercial culture cannot be the source and norm for Christian worship; pastors and worship leaders must not let civic and commercial cultural occasions coopt the service. At the same time, Protestants have observed their special occasions, including World Communion Sunday, Reformation Sunday, the National Day of Prayer, and the International Day of Prayer for the Persecuted Church.[22] To date, Liturgical Renewal advocates have shown little interest in including these observances in the Christian calendar, though they do not prevent a church from including them either.

The next concern of the Liturgical Renewal movement is recovery of meaningful sacramental practice for both Baptism and the Eucharist. Baptismal practice has been sorely in need of reform among mainline Protestants for years. Liturgical Renewal advocates criticize indiscriminate infant baptism as a legacy of the culture

Protestantism of the 1950s. Baptism is about initiation into God's covenant community, not simply a rite of passage that acknowledges a birth and the blessing of a new life. Related to this is the Liturgical Renewal movement's critique of the practice of confirmation. Because the act of incorporation into Christ's Body is complete, not partial, at baptism, it is argued that there is no need for a later act to "confirm" it.

Many Liturgical Renewal advocates are taking the lead in developing baptismal rituals for use in a post-Christian context.[23] The Church sees more adult baptisms because fewer people were baptized as infants. This is an opportunity that those who practice believer's baptism have taught us we ought not to miss. The Roman Catholic Rite of Christian Initiation for Adults demonstrates a shift from an individualistic way of thinking about conversion to an experience shared in community; it even included baptism by immersion(!).

Weekly celebration of the Eucharist is an important goal of the Liturgical Renewal movement. Until recently, many Protestants celebrated the Lord's Supper, or communion, as few as three or four times a year. Calvin's efforts at a weekly celebration (not well-publicized) were defeated by the elders of Geneva, who worried that taking communion too often would somehow cheapen the occasion. Except for Lutherans, the Disciples of Christ, and Churches of Christ, who celebrate communion weekly, most Protestants participated in communion no more than five times a year.[24] In the past twenty years, however, there has been a trend in many mainline churches to celebrate the Lord's Supper monthly. A few conservative evangelical churches have tried this, including a number of seeker churches that celebrate communion monthly at a midweek believer's service.

In addition to more frequent communion, the Liturgical Renewal movement also aims to improve the quality of the celebration. In both mainline and evangelical churches, communion often seems tacked on to the service, with little creative preparation and leadership. White points to two elements in need of special attention: the Eucharistic prayer offered prior to distributing the elements, and the method of distribution. Like others, White is particularly critical of the common Protestant practice of distributing small crackers and thimbles of grape juice to people seated in the pews.[25]

In recovering a healthy sense of sacramental practice, the Liturgical Renewal movement has broken out of the grip of Enlightenment rationalism. Protestant sacramental practice, on the other hand, still seems to be captive to rationalism. As a result, Protestant sacramental practice is not nearly as strong as Protestant sacramental theology. There is much Protestants need to learn from others at the practical level of preparing and leading a service that includes baptism and the Lord's Supper.

The Liturgical Renewal movement's view of the role of music in worship is difficult to describe briefly, since there are competing perspectives. Nearly all advocates agree on a functional view of music in worship; in other words, it should facilitate congregational participation. They are sharply critical of how the traditional Protestant church has used choral and instrumental music as performance, entertainment, or, worse, "traveling music" (or background music).

Although the movement in principle endorses all forms of congregational singing, including hymns and contemporary worship music, its advocates have special enthusiasm for two forms of worship music, Psalms and ritual music. The Psalms have been around a long time in Christian worship. They were chanted in Roman Catholic and Anglican services and metricalized and paraphrased in Reformed and Methodist hymnals. In the nineteenth century, the practice of Psalm singing faded. Now new versions of the Psalms are making it easier for the congregation to sing. Ritual music, known to some as service music, comprises shorter pieces of music sung at various points in the service, particularly the Eucharistic liturgy, such as the "Glory to God in the Highest" (Gloria in Excelsis), the "Lord Have Mercy" (Kyrie Eleison) or the "Lamb of God" (Agnus Dei).[26] The "Doxology," sung after the collection of the offering, is a remnant of ritual music found in many Protestant services, while a few churches still sing a "Gloria Patri" (Glory to the Father) after the Assurance of Pardon. Many Liturgical Renewal churches are now giving the congregation new settings of the service music that was traditionally reserved for the choir.[27]

The Liturgical Renewal movement is divided on the issue of appropriate style for worship music. Many prefer traditional European and western musical forms for worship. They believe that recovering traditional liturgical forms includes recovery of traditional musical styles as well. Others advocate a more open approach to the style of music for worship, which could be called "musical pluralism." Drawing on ethnomusicology (the study of music in cultures), scholars such as Michael Hawn observe the process of music making in various cultures and relate it to the use of music in worship. As a result, they encourage pastors and worship leaders to use musical styles that are best suited to their cultural setting and to include musical styles from the world Christian church in their worship.[28]

Issues for the Liturgical Renewal Movement

The Liturgical Renewal movement challenges Protestants to think biblically, historically, ecumenically, and pastorally about worship, which is not something they've done well in the past. Indeed, the failure to think critically allowed Protestant worship in the 1950s to degrade in many places into a weekly rally boosting the American dream. The failure to think theologically about worship has led to practices more focused on people than on God. The failure to prepare and lead worship pastorally has meant that people leave worship without encountering and experiencing the presence of God. So the challenge to think critically, theologically, and pastorally about worship should be welcomed by Protestant pastors and lay leaders.

This is not to say, however, that the movement is right about everything when it comes to worship, or that its recommendations are a magic formula with all the answers for every church. Even the movement's most ardent advocates would not claim so much. To benefit fully from the Liturgical Renewal movement, we must assess its weaknesses as well as its strengths.

The first weakness of the Liturgical Renewal movement is its shaky relationship with the church. The main advocates are scholars and denominational officials. With the exception of the evangelical convergence movement, the movement is anything but grassroots renewal. At best, it is viewed by pastors and lay leaders as an academic and denominational agenda for the whole church. At worst, it comes across as top-down, patronizing interference in the worship life of the churches. Some of this perception is rooted in the academic origins of the movement. Viewed from the pew, the greatest asset—scholarship—is the greatest liability. Ordinary pastors and average churchgoers are suspicious of ivory-towered intellectuals who recommend sweeping change but who do not know, and do not seem to care, what things are like in the local church.

In some ways, this kind of criticism is unfair; many of the leading advocates of the Liturgical Renewal movement are pastors, and many of the scholars are active in their churches. In other ways, though, the perception is justified. In the 1970s and 1980s, denominational officials effectively coopted the Liturgical Renewal movement, investing heavily in production of hymnals and other liturgical aids designed by the movement's advocates. The effort produced mixed results. Some churches found the new resources helpful, but the enterprise also produced a number of damaging unintended consequences. Among them was a shift in the locus of liturgical planning. Many pastors and church leaders got the message loud and clear that the denominational bureaucracy thinks it knows better; innovation in worship is too risky for the local church. Bureaucracy and committees are better suited to manage change because they are inclusive and representative.

In her book *Christian Worship and Technological Change*, Susan White identifies the deficiency of bureaucratically managed liturgical reform: inability to connect with the local church, failure to connect with worship history and tradition, and a tendency to depersonalize worship.[29] In organizational theory, the purpose of a bureaucracy is to manage change. This expectation is appropriate for business, government, and other enterprises, but White asks us to consider the unintended consequences for worship when a bureaucracy manages liturgical change: "Can worship that is bureaucratically conditioned serve the spiritual and liturgical needs of diverse congregations and individuals?"[30]

First, bureaucratically driven worship innovation often fails to connect with the grass roots. In many cases, worship innovation is not developed in a congregation but in a setting far removed from the local church, namely, in academia or a denominationally sponsored liturgy committee. Even though the products of the process are often extensively field-tested in the local church, the focus of innovation and development is not the church but an academic symposium or conference or a denominational committee meeting.

The development of the PCUSA *Book of Common Worship* (BCW) is typical of this approach. The BCW is the product of extensive scholarship and many hours of meetings. During the 1980s, the committee produced the seven-volume *Supplemental Liturgical Resources*, a kind of first draft to be tried out in churches; it incorporated the feedback into the final version, released in 1993. Although many churches have embraced the BCW enthusiastically, the overall response of the denomination to the BCW has been lukewarm at best.

By guiding the innovation process as it does, the liturgical bureaucracy often manages to stifle creativity emerging from the local church. Because such innovation cannot be categorized, filed, and easily referenced, the liturgical committee often ignores it. The consequences of this mind-set are obvious to Susan White: "Because any bureaucratic system tends to suppress creative energy . . . to the extent that a denomination or congregation values worship that is open to the spirit of creativity it will be less than satisfied with liturgies that have been strained through bureaucratic structures."[31] The committee preparing the BCW did surprisingly little research on the worship practices of Presbyterian churches, or on trends in worship outside the denomination. As a result, there is no awareness in the BCW of the seeker service and praise and worship movements, which were rapidly emerging at that time.

Second, bureaucratically driven worship innovation often fails to connect with worship history and tradition. As White makes clear, a bureaucracy is supposed to manage change, not preserve a denomination's worship heritage. As a result, denominational liturgical innovation often cuts a church off from its worship tradition: "Bureaucratically produced liturgy carries with it a sense of discontinuity with the past, rather than a sense that it is the product of a natural evolution from previous forms of worship."[32]

Again, development of the BCW illustrates the problem. In preparing the resource on baptism, the Presbyterian Joint Liturgy Group heard papers from a number of scholars, including one on the development of Reformed baptismal theology and practice in the sixteenth century. In then end, however, the baptismal liturgy of the BCW includes little of this heritage.[33]

Finally, bureaucratically driven worship innovation often alienates worshipers. According to White, bureaucracies are usually more interested in numbers than in people. Bureaucrats approach problems abstractly and consider solutions anonymously. Similarly, because ideas or agendas matter more than people do, bureaucratic innovators have a hard time resisting ideological influence. This approach is alienating to the end user in the local church for two reasons. For one thing, it can be emotionally restrictive. White notes that a bureaucracy "imposes control on the spontaneous expression of emotion."[34] The worshiper is being told how to feel and which emotional states are appropriate in worship. Effective worship leadership might minimize some of this, but pastors often find themselves swimming against a strong current flowing down from the bureaucracy.

This is because, next, bureaucratic worship resources carry a strong hidden curriculum designed to reinforce expert scholarly knowledge and bureaucratic competence. As White observes, "the worshiping community has become simply a passive receptacle into which liturgy (and also theology) is poured from above, and the authority of its liturgical experience is discounted."[35] This patronizing approach is disempowering to the church, which finds itself liturgically dependent on the denomination.

As a result, it should not be surprising to learn that many churches in the PCUSA and the United Methodist Church do not use the hymnals and worship aids produced by the denomination, or use them only sparingly. The movement may remain out of touch with the grass roots in the future unless it can connect itself to the local church and to the other sources of worship awakening (such as the contemporary worship music industry) that have found greater acceptance in the local church.

To be sure, not all innovation from the Liturgical Renewal movement is bureaucratically produced. There are interesting examples of grassroots worship innovation at the Taizé community in France and the Iona community in Scotland. Many churches in North America have adopted some of their liturgical practice and music. Churches in the two-thirds world are another source of liturgical innovation. There are some encouraging signs that the Liturgical Renewal movement is getting its message out apart from denominational liturgy bureaucracy through talented speakers and worship leaders, notably Webber, Iona community leader John Bell, and music composer and producer Marty Haugen.

The success of Webber, Bell, and Haugen in connecting with churches at the grassroots level highlights a second weakness of the Liturgical Renewal movement: its general failure to come to terms with the contextual factors of American society and culture. The movement's advocates typically display their intense distaste for aspects of American life the rest of us enjoy (or at least tolerate) every day: TV and movies, popular music, and technology. Despite good intentions about globalization, the narrow and Eurocentric preferences of most Liturgical Renewal advocates give the impression of discomfort in contemporary culture. Many (though of course not all) resort to reverse ethnocentrism, a kind of any-culture-is-betterthan-ours argument; although it is appropriate for liturgical elements to be adapted (inculturated or contextualized) in other cultures, it is inappropriate to adapt them to cultural forms in North America because its society and culture is uniquely antithetical to the Gospel.

Third, the movement is having a hard time shaking the perception that it cares more about liturgical texts and performance of symbolic and ritual action than about an authentic encounter with God in worship. Some movement advocates readily fall into the trap of thinking that real worship happens when the right liturgical element is done the right way. This kind of magic-formula approach to worship is bound to strike Protestants as odd. At the same time, it is easy to discern anti-individual and antiexperiential attitudes lurking behind the emphasis on community and shared experience. This can create insensitive and personally damaging moments in worship. There is real danger in such a strong focus on liturgical performance; the traditional Protestant critique of formalism should be taken seriously. Ritual action and symbolism do not explain everything about Christian worship. It is possible to distinguish too sharply between outward form and inward attitude, but it is equally mistaken to equate the two.

Finally, the Liturgical Renewal movement is biased against Protestant worship practices and carries a thinly veiled hostility toward anything derived from evangelical revival worship. Too often, the movement's criticism of revival worship is marked by caricature and assertion, with little firsthand experience and limited understanding of its motivation and aim. In one widely quoted article, a Lutheran liturgical scholar tastelessly compares evangelical megachurch worship with the medieval fascination with relics. Painting with quite a broad brush, he portrays all megachurches as focusing exclusively on individual decisions and ignoring the historic elements of worship.

Another example of this high-handedness is the movement's failure to engage Pentecostal and charismatic worship. Fenwick and Spinks think that the Liturgical Renewal movement has been a "seedbed" for the charismatic renewal that swept through the traditional liturgical church in the 1970s: "The Liturgical Renewal movement did not give birth to the Charismatic Movement, but it provided an incubator for its early development."[36] There may be some truth to this for Roman Catholics, but it misses entirely the complex relationship between charismatics and the Protestant churches. This kind of liturgical provincialism does not help Protestants achieve better understanding of the process of worship renewal.

The kind of worship services recommended by the Liturgical Renewal movement are not a one-size-fits-all formula for every Protestant church. Even the movement's most devoted adherents admit that pastors and worship leaders must use their judgment in preparing and leading a service. Yet as we survey the other main sources of the worship awakening, it is apparent that the movement has not accounted for the range of liturgical and musical options available. Pastors and church leaders have much to learn from liturgical scholars and their painstaking research into the history of Christian worship and the variety of worship expression around the world. Yet we must continue to test their recommendations for the reform of worship by the standard of scriptural authority and the pastoral needs of our congregations.

Part II

Contours of the
Worship Awakening

5

Ethnicity, Culture, and the Worship Awakening

In the 1960s, Bob Dylan sang "the times, they are a-changin'." Peter Drucker puts these changes in historical perspective: "Every few hundred years in Western history there occurs a sharp transformation. Within a few short decades, society rearranges itself—its worldview; its basic values; its social and political structures; its arts; its key institutions. Fifty years later there is a new world. And the people born then cannot even imagine the world in which their grandparents lived and into which their own parents were born. We are currently living through just such a transformation."[1] The social and cultural changes we experience affect churches and worship powerfully and profoundly, yet few pastors and church leaders understand this impact.

In the next four chapters, we take a look at several aspects of this social and cultural transformation as the background of the current worship awakening. In this chapter and the next, we explore the changes in American society brought about by ethnic and racial diversity, and shifts in generational dynamics. In Chapters Seven and Eight, we consider changes in contemporary culture—particularly the emerging postmodern worldview, an experience orientation, popular culture, and electronic media and information technology.

The Changing Face of American Society

North America is populated by a wondrous variety of people, nearly all of whom are immigrants or descended from immigrants. In recent decades, however, more and diverse kinds of immigrants have arrived on our shores. In the Los Angeles public school system, for example, children speak more than eighty languages. North Americans are more generationally diverse as well. Thanks mostly to advances in health care and living conditions, there are now five living generations, surely for the first time in human history.

Immigration and birth rates tell a revealing story of change in the American population. According to the U.S. Census Bureau, the total number of Americans will increase from 249 million in 1990 to around 392 million by the year 2050. But the net growth rate (births plus immigrants minus deaths) within various ethnic groups will not be the same. For many years, whites have been the majority and blacks were the largest minority. This is changing. Over the next fifty years, the white population is projected to decrease by 30 percent, while other ethnic groups will increase by 92 percent. The bottom line is this: by 2050 no one ethnic group will be a majority; whites will be the largest minority in a nation of minorities.[2] Among other minorities, the proportion of African Americans—now at 12 percent—is expected to grow to just over 14 percent by 2050.[3] However, Hispanics will replace African Americans as the second largest minority in the United States by 2010, and Asian Americans will continue to be the fastest-growing group.

Demographer Mike Regele points out that changes in the ethnic makeup of American society will have an enormous impact on mainline and conservative evangelical Protestant churches, which are mostly white in membership and aging: "Many [churches] have become White religious ghettos in the midst of racially diverse communities. . . . So while the general U.S. population is backfilling its declining Anglo-European population with diverse peoples and cultures from around the world, the church is choking on the change."[4]

Churches with a worship service that reflects European culture and tradition generally are finding the congregation growing smaller, and discovering—belatedly in many cases—that their services do not appeal to immigrants from the rest of the world with their own worship expectations and values.

Let's briefly survey the worship perspectives and practices of these two prominent groups, African Americans and Hispanics.

African American Worship

The first important characteristic of African American worship is its roots in African culture and religion, and its development under the institution of slavery. Without understanding these roots, it is difficult if not impossible to understand African American worship today. The cultures and rituals of Africans were (and are) diverse, but there are some common elements enabling us to speak of an African perspective that shapes worship for African Americans. To begin with, Africans have a holistic view of life and worship. Pedrito Maynard-Reid states, "of all the cultures which make up the pluralistic society of the United States, the African American may capture best the holistic view of worship."[5] There is no dichotomy between sacred and secular among blacks, as there frequently is among European Americans.

As a result of this holistic worldview, Africans are highly experiential. To know the world as a spiritual place is to experience it through the subjective and intuitive aspects of the human personality. Again, African culture places a high value on relationships and community. Maynard-Reid notes that "African culture is profoundly tribal and communal in its essence."[6] Hence African American worship celebrates individuality in community; worship is a highly relational and participatory event, and everybody contributes in his or her own way. "It is understood," says Maynard-Reid, "that everybody fashions his own offering of praise to God in his own way. That is what one is supposed to do. One is supposed to know the theme well enough to use it in the fashion that befits one's spirit."[7] Finally, the African religious heritage includes distinctive forms of communication and uses of music that African Americans have developed into unique styles of preaching, prayer, and worship music, as we shall see.

The slaves brought many African cultural and religious practices with them, which they maintained after converting to Christianity (often in secret). Some slaves worshiped with their owners in white churches, usually seated in the balcony. Many worshiped secretly at a gathering in their cabin, or more commonly out in the countryside at a "brush arbor." In such a meeting, slaves devised a new form of worship. Worship scholar Melva Costen comments:

> Over the period of time from the arrival of Africans in Virginia in 1619, new verbal language forms had evolved. In the process, however, basic symbols, symbolism, and manners of expression used in traditional African communication had been retained. Exposed to new ways of life and means of livelihood, they had been made aware of the meaning of marginalization, oppression, and degradation, all of which affected their psyches. In an effort to find freedom and understanding, traditional beliefs and practices, Christian beliefs and practices, and the reality of existence merged. As a result, a unique African American Christian faith was shaped.[8]

Getting ready for the brush arbor meeting, known as the "the invisible institution," was an important part of worship, as slaves passed the word in songs such as "There's a Meetin' Here Tonight" and "Steal Away to Jesus."[9] The meetings were a social event as well as religious, since for African Americans the two are closely linked. As the slaves gathered from various farms and plantations in the area, they exchanged greetings and news of relatives and friends. A preacher usually officiated at the service, though the congregation usually required little direction and prompting to participate in songs and prayers. The slave preacher, like his traditional African counterpart, was viewed as a holy man who spoke for God to the people, from his experience with God; the familiar African call-and-response enabled the congregation to participate in the preaching with shouts, affirmations, and encouragement. As Costen observes:

> The Invisible Institution was not an accident of a few rebellious people. It was a divine necessity for a people for whom religion was integrally related to all of life. The hypocrisy of a distorted gospel, heard under the influence of slave masters who desired to keep slaves in check, forced slaves to identify time and space where they could freely be in communion with God and with each other. Hearing the words from the Bible interpreted in the light of their oppressed condition freed the slave worshipers to pour out their sufferings and needs and express their joys in their own sacred space.[10]

We would not know much about worship in the invisible institution were it not for the "praise houses," the African American churches on the Sea Islands, off the coast of South Carolina and Georgia, which were settled by freed slaves long before the end of the Civil War. Costen notes that "for generations these people of African descent had been isolated and were, therefore, able to preserve African and newly shaping African American practices longer than in other places."[11] Since the Civil War, black churches have evolved with a variety of worship styles, ranging from highly expressive service to one with all the elements of European liturgical tradition. Church leaders also debated whether African practices and beliefs could be allowed in worship.

Over the years, African American churches have further developed many distinctive worship perspectives and practices, which are really a fusion of African and European American tradition and practice. The music of African American worship is a good example of such fusion. C. Eric Lincoln and Lawrence H. Mamiya conclude that it "is in essence a study of how black people 'Africanized' Christianity in America."[12] Music is a vital feature of African American life as a whole, and it often reaches fullest expression for blacks in worship.

A casual observer of an African American service will notice several features of African American worship music.[13] First, it is participatory; most of the music is intended to encourage the congregation to sing. There may be anthems or solos, but even these allow worshipers to clap, sway or dance, and sing along. Freedom of spontaneous personal expression, or improvisation, is a high value in many black churches. Unlike white musicians, who rarely stray from the printed sheet music, many African American musicians play worship music by ear, even if formally trained in music. Vocalists and instrumentalists—as well as the worshipers in the congregation—are encouraged to give music their personal stamp.

Second, African American worship music is textually and musically passionate. The lyrics of African American worship songs capture a broader range of emotion than traditional hymnody or contemporary worship music. The songs of joyous celebration are upbeat and celebrative. They encourage physical participation through clapping, swaying, and even dancing. Spirituals and gospel music—perhaps the only musical style developed in the church specifically for worship—are known for their vibrant tempo and energetic rhythm. But African American hymns and worship songs are not afraid to address profound emotions such as sorrow, grief, lament, and anger. Many of these songs, the forerunners of the blues, capture pain and suffering in a poignant way that leads many worshipers to tears. Because African American music reflects its African musical roots, rhythm stands out as the distinctive feature in black worship.

Preaching is another such feature of African American worship, functioning like music because it emphasizes primarily the emotional, affective side of understanding, rather than the cognitive and intellectual. This does not mean that the cognitive is ignored, but it is not made the primary or exclusive mode of understanding, as in much white preaching. Because African culture is primarily oral, Maynard-Reid observes that "gifted black preachers particularly appeal to the sense of hearing." He goes on to quote Wyatt Tee Walker: "Black preaching is aimed primarily at the ear as the route to the heart, as over against being aimed at the eye as the route to the mind."[14] The musical aspects of black preaching can be heard in the repetitive cadences and rhythmic delivery of black preachers. Dr. Martin Luther King's "I Have a Dream" speech and the Rev. Jesse Jackson's "I Am Somebody" address to the 1984 Democratic National Convention are good examples of effective cadence and repetition. In many black churches, the preaching becomes musical as the preacher chants or sings the message, often accompanied by the organ. Preaching is also a congregational activity; rather than sitting passively and listening, African American worshipers participate in preaching through spoken affirmation and encouragement, in effect entering into a dialogue with the preacher.

Hispanic Worship

Hispanics are a large and rapidly growing group, and also quite diverse. The term *Hispanic* includes a number of nationalities and cultures: Mexican, Central American, Cuban, Puerto Rican, other Spanish-speaking Caribbean people, and South American. Hispanics are as religiously diverse as they are nationally and culturally diverse. Hispanic popular religion is usually a mix of European, African, and Native American sources.[15] Though there is no such thing as a typical Hispanic, just as there is no such thing as a typical Anglo, there are some common elements among Hispanics that allow us to describe Hispanic worship in general.

First, Hispanic worship is characterized by fiesta. "Latino worship is a fiesta," writes theologian Justo Gonzalez.[16] Significantly,

Hispanics do not distinguish between sacred and secular fiesta, or religious and nonreligious fiesta. As Maynard-Reid points out, fiesta "pervades the life of the Hispanic person and community."[17] This blending of sacred and secular things and events strikes many Anglos as foreign, accustomed as we are to distinguishing sharply between sacred and secular, religious and nonreligious. Thus folk and popular Hispanic music, dance, traditional arts and crafts, and family celebrations can be freely woven into Hispanic worship. Moreover, fiesta does not mean just a party. As Michael Hawn puts it, "it is a celebration amidst struggle. There is always joy and hope in a fiesta no matter the circumstances."[18]

Second, Hispanic worship celebrates *familia* and *comunidad* (family and community). Maynard-Reid observes that "when Hispanics come to worship, they come to a family fiesta. Hispanic worship is a festive celebration when the extended family gathers together to praise God and celebrate having one another as family."[19] Hispanic worship is strongly corporate, unlike much Anglo worship with its emphasis on personal and private religious experience. The worship service is often the high point of the week for Hispanics, gathering extended family, friends, and neighbors. In North America, the importance of gathering the *comunidad* is underscored by the realities of racism and language barriers. The Hispanic church is an important reminder of cultural and ethnic identity in a foreign and often hostile new country.

Third, Hispanic worship encourages passion and participation, which a visitor notices right away. Services are upbeat; rhythmic music and a friendly, joyous, colorful, and festive atmosphere prevails even in a church in the poorest barrio. In cultures that prize fiesta, it is not surprising that Pentecostal and charismatic churches are growing rapidly, because they encourage what Hispanics value most: an opportunity to express themselves before God. As Maynard-Reid says, their "worship is consonant with the fiesta spirit. [They] gain ready acceptance with their indigenous, spontaneous, emotional and enthusiastically festive worship services."[20] In Hispanic cultures, a fiesta is an event in which all participate. It is not a performance put on by some for the benefit of others, as in traditional Protestant worship service. Gonzalez notes that "in most cases the differences between our worship and that of the dominant culture is that we think in terms of planning a party more than rehearsing a performance."[21]

Music is perhaps the most revealing element of Hispanic worship because it captures much of Hispanic identity; roots in many cultures; the challenges of survival; the joy of life found in fiesta and *familia*; and the hope of freedom, peace, and justice in the coming of Christ's kingdom. Hispanic music is rich and varied, drawing from a variety of musical traditions, especially African and Native American rhythms, European instruments, and Spanish folk melodies. Hispanic music is fusion music, welding different styles into new sounds. For Hispanic worshipers, music functions as a cultural marker, a sound that creates a sense of identity, or *comunidad*, particularly for Hispanics in North America. Maynard-Reid emphasizes that "Hispanic music is not only meant to stimulate the emotions of the participant; it is a means by which a people recapture their rich and varied history. Through music they return to their roots. In music they express their inner and total self—their yearnings, feelings, struggles, and historical passage."[22]

Not surprisingly, music is a vital feature of Hispanic service, and an opportunity for all to participate. Surprisingly, however, Hispanic music has been rarely heard in Hispanic churches until recently. Hispanic Roman Catholic and Protestant churches alike used primarily traditional Northern European and North American hymns played on the organ or piano. In the last twenty years or so, however, this has begun to change as churches introduce Hispanic musical styles to accompany hymns, and songwriters compose a new style of worship music, the *corito*. Because of the similarity of the words, it is tempting to translate *corito* as chorus, but that is not entirely accurate. Although many *coritos* are short, some are longer. Like North American contemporary worship music, there are a variety of lyrical themes, ranging from scripture passage to personal testimony, proclamation, expression of personal devotion, and intimacy with God. Like CWM, *coritos* frequently emerge from a conservative evangelical community and reflect its theological concerns. Musically, *coritos* are usually set to contemporary folk and popular musical styles.

In many Hispanic churches, bands with guitars, bass, keyboards, drums, lots of percussion, and other instruments usually accompany congregational singing. The worship bands encourage people to play along regardless of ability, so it is not uncommon to see quite a few people on the platform, especially youths and children, several guitar players and percussionists, and numerous woodwind and brass instruments. In one church in southern California, the worship leader considers worship service a rehearsal for his band: "We say, 'If you want to play with us next Sunday, bring your instrument and join us. Our songs are not hard, and we'll make room for you.' But I also make sure I have a core of strong musicians who know the music. It makes it better for everybody."

Hispanic preaching has not attracted the attention of scholars as African American preaching has, but it is a lively tradition that flourishes in a variety of settings. For one thing, Hispanic preaching is biblical. Among Protestants, including Pentecostals and charismatics, the preacher is expected to stick close to the text. He or she needs to make a passage come alive with meaning for the worshiper, and to make it relevant in application to the listener's everyday life. As a result, the preacher usually speaks from forty-five minutes to an hour or more. As with African American preaching, though in a less ritualized manner, the Hispanic congregation enters into a dialogue with the preacher through affirmation and encouragement.

In keeping with the spirit of fiesta and *familia*, Hispanic worship is social and relational; it also is quite tactile, with lots of touching, hugging, and holding hands, including the men. The time of greeting and the celebration of communion are important elements in each service when worshipers exchange the *abrazo*, an embrace or hug. *Testimonios*, personal words of testimony from worshipers, are an increasingly common element in the Hispanic church. During these moments, worshipers share joy and concern, needs and answers to prayer to encourage others and receive encouragement from them.

Issues for the Worship Awakening

Worldviews and Worship

Immigration from other parts of the world has increased dramatically in the past twenty years, most notably from east Asia (mainland China, Taiwan, and Korea) and south Asia (India and Pakistan). But the majority of immigrants came to the United States from Africa, mostly through the forced relocation of the slave trade in the eighteenth and nineteenth centuries, from the Caribbean, and from Latin America. A couple of important features of non-Anglo culture have significant implications for the future of Protestant worship.

For one thing, immigrant cultures bring their own worldview to North America, differing sharply from the traditional Western, European frame of mind. As we will see in later chapters, European culture is strongly influenced by Enlightenment rationalism, which separates natural and supernatural, rational and emotional, spiritual and physical. This dualistic worldview has shaped how whites worship for generations. In an increasingly diverse culture, however, white culture is losing its dominance. This diversity of worldview puts a question mark beside time-honored liturgical practice and musical style. Other cultures, however, do not make such distinctions, particularly those from Africa, Latin America, and the Caribbean. Their worship reflects a holistic approach, meaning they do not draw distinctions between sacred and secular, spiritual and physical, rational and emotional elements in the service.

Fusion of Liturgical and Musical Styles

One example of this is the popular music scene. Forty years ago, popular music was dominated by white artists such as Frank Sinatra and Tony Bennett, playing mainstream jazz and swing music. African Americans, by contrast, listened to other styles, particularly be-bop jazz, blues, and R & B. The fusion of musical styles by artists such as Elvis Presley, Chuck Berry, and others introduced a new era of music that blurred the lines between white music and black music. The fusion continues with the addition of Latin sounds from such artists as Gloria Estefan, Carlos Santana, and Ricky Martin.

White response to increasing ethnic diversity ranged from avoidance and flight to acceptance and embrace. Most major urban areas experienced white flight, as Anglos moved from downtown neighborhoods to newer suburban communities. Suburban Protestant churches often reflect their neighborhoods; many have few or no minority members, and the few they have are often upper-middle-class families. The predominance of whites in the suburbs gives little incentive to adopt a liturgical or musical style that might attract minorities.

Beginning in the 1990s, however, North American suburban communities began to change as more immigrants, particularly better educated and better paid workers in technology and medical fields, arrived from the far east and south Asia, primarily China, Korea, India, and Pakistan. One woman told me that her cul-de-sac in an upscale Seattle suburb is "a mini-UN. Next door is a couple from Korea, on the other side is a family from Taiwan, across the street is a family from Turkey, and next to them is a family from Colombia. We're the only whites on the block."

Cultural Imperialism and Worship "Balkanization"

How can there be one right way to worship for all the many cultures we see in our society today? Does one size fit everyone, regardless of ethnicity? Some believe that there is such a worship norm, but others point to the growing diversity of North American society and culture and conclude that inclusion and integration is hopeless. Interestingly, those who prefer uniformity can be found in all camps: the seeker-service movement, the praise and worship movement, and the Liturgical Renewal movement. Many worship scholars call for an inclusive community in worship that welcomes all persons. African American worship scholars such as Costen and Brenda Aghowa encourage white pastors and church leaders to watch and learn from the black church, and also to begin working together for a more inclusive approach to worship.[23]

Immigration further raises the stakes of inclusion. James White sees the growing influence of non-Western worship traditions on North American Protestants: "African, Asian and South American cultures and peoples will be major forces in shaping new Protestant traditions of worship."[24] The experience of Pentecost and John's vision of worship in heaven color the New Testament understanding of the worshiping community, events that bring different people together. Yet some ministry experts do not think this notion of one big happy family in worship is possible, or even desirable. Some African American and Hispanic leaders would affirm the goal of an inclusive worshiping fellowship but also warn against loss of cultural identity in attempting to blend their liturgical and musical styles in a melting-pot approach to worship. Church leaders acknowledge that African American and Anglo churches have much to learn from each other in worship, but they privately wonder if their worship styles differ too much to blend comfortably. Maynard-Reid, for example, has a strong sense of how different African, Hispanic, and Caribbean worship styles are from the dominant Anglo approach, but he offers little advice on how people of all kinds can come together meaningfully in worship.

So, what can white, mainline Protestants learn from their new neighbors? Can whites worship like blacks, Hispanics, and others whose liturgical and musical styles are so different? Some already do; white Pentecostal and charismatic worship at least outwardly resembles black and Hispanic worship. But the resemblance may be only superficial. Some scholars see a big contrast between black and Hispanic worship on the one hand and "white emotionalism" on the other, since, as Maynard-Reid describes it, "the mode of worship and faith articulation is derived from the experience of worshipers." He goes on to quote African American scholar William B. McClain: "the White experience in its critical essence is not the Black experience."[25]

As important as this point is, if it is taken to mean that blacks and whites have nothing in common in worship then we have gone too far. Social location is a determining factor in black worship in a way that it is not for many whites, but to suggest that whites cannot worship like blacks is wrong and harmful to Christian unity. Interestingly, many whites are attracted to a black, Hispanic, or multicultural church *because* of that experience of life, not in spite of it. Some, it is true, are drawn by the "hot" music and entertaining preachers found in that church. But many other whites, particularly young adults, are drawn by the mode of worship and faith articulation because the white experience does not fit them all that well. They are drawn by, among other things, expression of suffering and lament, by the prophetic call to acknowledge that things aren't they way they're supposed to be, and by the proclamation of justice and mercy found in Christ and his Kingdom. Thus, although the white experience is fundamentally different from the black and Hispanic, we can say that for a growing number of whites there is something in their own experience that resonates powerfully with the experience of those groups.

There is nothing about the worship of blacks and Hispanics that precludes whites from participating in it meaningfully. But should whites adopt and adapt for their own use the liturgical forms and musical styles developed in these groups? Some believe they should not. For hundreds of years, whites have held the music of Africans, Hispanics, and Asians as inferior to European, Western music. In their minds, Protestant Christianity and Western music went hand in hand. Missionaries to Africa, Latin America, and Asia took their music with them, translating and teaching converts the classic Protestant hymns along with the Bible. New Christians were taught to denigrate their own cultural practice and musical tradition and to embrace Western liturgical forms and musical style, an attitude they brought with them when they came to North America. Even black, Hispanic, and Asian church leaders have encouraged this attitude among their followers. For example, Daniel Payne, a bishop in the African Methodist Episcopal Church and a founder of Wilberforce University, rejected spirituals as "cornfield ditties" that promote "the wildest excitement amongst the thoughtless masses"; he advocated instead Western, European music among his churches.[26]

The typically Anglo prejudice against non-Western and folk musical styles continues today in many circles. I encountered it firsthand at a conference I spoke at a few years ago. During an open-mike panel discussion, a participant asked me what I thought of this formula: "melody appeals to the intellect, harmony appeals to the soul, and rhythm appeals to the flesh." I wish I could say I had a brilliant answer for this question, but I didn't. In fact, I couldn't think of anything to say, so I asked the conference host, Pastor Doug Murren, to help me out. With fire in his eyes and without missing a beat, he said, "That's the most racist thing I've ever heard." For white churches to embrace the liturgical and musical contributions of black and Hispanic churches, Anglo pastors and lay leaders need to lay aside such narrow thinking about their style of worship and music. In a moment, we shall look at some churches where this is beginning to happen.

The Homogeneous Unit Principle and Protestant Worship

The Church Growth movement has also given some credibility to the claim that whites should be satisfied with Anglo worship. The homogeneous unit principle (first mentioned in Chapter One) was developed by church growth theorist Donald McGavran; it is advocated by many church growth experts. Writing about evangelism in

India in the pioneering textbook *Understanding Church Growth,* McGavran stated that "people like to become Christians without crossing racial, linguistic, or class barriers." He went on to argue that the dynamic of like-attracts-like is a fundamental sociological principle reflected in a growing church.[27]

In fairness, most church growth advocates, including McGavran and others, do not use the homogeneous unit principle exclusively in ethnic or racial terms. What counts as homogeneous is not race or ethnicity alone because people find affinity in many other ways besides racial or ethnic identification: age, occupation, socioeconomic status, education, gender, hobbies, and religion. Church growth theologian Charles van Engen suggests that if the homogeneous unit principle is applied to race and ethnicity alone, this is contrary to biblical teaching, however illuminating it may be of actual human behavior.[28]

Unfortunately, many pastors and denominational leaders have seized on the homogeneous unit principle over the past twenty years as a rationale for an ethnically or generationally targeted church. The seeker service movement, as we have seen, assumes the homogeneous unit principle to justify targeting the kind of people it hopes to attract. Not surprisingly, many of these seeker churches are in predominantly white suburbs. It will be interesting to see whether their understanding of their target audience changes as the ethnic and generational makeup of the neighborhood changes.

Can we balance the legitimate concern of Church Growth theory to lower barriers to Christ by establishing a sense of identification with seekers on the one hand, and the reality of ethnic and cultural diversity in our society on the other? Does it automatically follow that the church landscape of the twenty-first century will be dotted with churches having narrow ethnic and generational boundaries? Is demographic segmentation the destiny of Protestant worship in North America?

Such fragmentation in worship is possible and even likely, but I am convinced that it is neither inevitable nor necessary. Ethnic and generational segmentation will continue as a worship and ministry strategy for the foreseeable future. Affinity-group churches continue to spring up across North America, particularly targeting Generation X and the rising Millennial generation. This trend is troubling because it suggests that established churches are still not able to accommodate these groups adequately.

Can Protestant Worship Be Multiethnic?

There are encouraging signs of an alternative to affinity groups or homogeneous units. Multiethnic and multigenerational churches are mushrooming across the United States; two prominent examples are Antioch Bible Church near Seattle, and Christian Assembly in Eagle Rock, California. Antioch Bible Church has grown to a racially mixed congregation of three thousand, mostly blacks and whites, but with a growing percentage of Asians and Hispanics. The most visible leaders, Pastor Ken Hutcherson and its worship leader, Stephen Newby, are both black; the style of worship music and preaching are steeped in the African American church tradition. But Antioch Bible Church strives to avoid being labeled a black church. Newby says that one reason the church attracts a racially diverse congregation is its openness to all racial groups.

Christian Assembly, in southern California, has achieved an impressive racial and generational mix that reflects its surrounding community. Interestingly, Christian Assembly has not set out to make racial and generational diversity a goal. "We're a church that worships God," says Pastor Mark Pickerill, "and he brings us the people. We don't really pay attention to race and age."

These two churches and others like them have several factors in common. First, they are generally found in older urban areas populated by younger adults and families who are comfortable in an urban environment. Studies indicate that there has been something of a return of whites to the cities over the past decade, a trend sometimes called the new urbanism. Second, these churches are fairly new and have no denominational connection, or a very loose one.

Third, these churches all strongly emphasize worship as the priority of a personal relationship with God and as the primary ministry of the church. They also feature a contemporary, urban musical sound (gospel, R & B, soul, jazz, funk, and hip-hop). Fourth, they all emphasize a personal and corporate experience of God in worship.

Many of these churches are charismatic. Those that are not at least stress a balance between the rational and emotional aspects of worship. Finally, these new churches are both multicultural *and* multigenerational. There is no comprehensive study of these churches I am aware of, but they seem to be doing better than most at drawing all ages as well as a variety of ethnic groups.

These churches demonstrate that Protestant worship can be multicultural (and multigenerational); it does not have to be ethnically (or generationally) segmented. But how does it happen? How can a predominantly older, white Protestant church embrace this aspect of the worship awakening?

The first step for a multiethnic church has been to understand its surroundings and the need to adapt worship and ministry to it. Peter Wagner points out that a church in a transitioning neighborhood has four options: (1) resist and die a lingering death, (2) adopt a mission philosophy of ministry, (3) relocate in a more congenial setting, or (4) reinvent the ministry by making a transition to a multiethnic congregation.[29] For a church choosing to reinvent itself in a changing setting, worship is the place to begin.

Christian Assembly, for example, is the product of a merger between two small, struggling Pentecostal churches. By the mid-1980s, its attendance had dwindled to less than one hundred. Pickerill began his ministry at Christian Assembly at that time with a desire to see the church reflect its neighborhood: young, urban, and diverse ethnically. At first, the church did not know what to do to attract such people. The arrival of Tommy Walker as worship leader led them to develop a musical style that fit the community. Some older members left, but many stayed to support the church as it filled with young people. To accommodate the rapidly expanding nursery and children's ministry, the adult Sunday school classes gave up their classrooms and began meeting at other times.

One last but important theme is worth mentioning here: worship is clearly the primary activity at these emerging multiethnic and multigenerational churches. Worship creates community and outreach, not the other way around; it is the core ministry of the church out of which all others flow. Worship is not one program among others, or a means to a higher goal, such as building community, attracting the unchurched, or achieving racial or generational reconciliation. These goals are important in this kind of church and are often given more emphasis than in many mainline and conservative evangelical churches. But worship towers above them as the priority of the church's corporate life and personal discipleship. Without a compelling awareness in worship of the presence of the God who draws all nations to himself, there is not enough motivation in a religious philosophy of multiculturalism to form a lasting and meaningful multiethnic Christian community. The same can be said for creating community across generational lines as well, as we see in the next chapter.

6

How Generations View Worship

Whenever worship comes up as a topic in a church board meeting, class, or small group, it seems talk about generations is never far behind. Imagine an exchange at a leadership retreat. "If we don't have music the young people like, they won't come to our church," says Sylvia, an elder and a member of Grace Church for many years. "My own kids told me that if Dick and I weren't so involved here at Grace, they'd never go when they're home from college. They tell me our services are boring, irrelevant, and there's never any other people their age."

Stu, a founding member of Grace Church when it was formed forty years earlier, starts speaking even before Sylvia finishes. "I don't know what's wrong with young people these days. I didn't care much for church when I was their age, but it didn't stop me from going."

It is common to assign attitude toward innovation in worship on the basis of age. The conventional wisdom says that older people like the old, while younger people go for the new. Not surprisingly, many advocates and critics of the worship awakening often put their argument in generational clothes: "We need a contemporary-style service to reach the younger families," and "The older folks built this church, and we should respect their wishes for traditional liturgy and music." It is easy to spot the caricature in these opinions, but it is more difficult to understand the subtle and powerful way in which a generational perspective shapes our thinking about innovation in worship. In this chapter, we look at generational dynamics and their impact on worship; then we analyze strategies for using insight about the generations in planning worship.

A Generational Perspective on the Worship Awakening

The 1950s and 1960s represented a high-water mark for North American Christianity, particularly for mainline churches. In the United States, attendance, membership, and church building reached an all-time high in the post–World War II era. Millions of GIs returned home and settled into a life of work, family, and church. By the late 1960s, however, church watchers noticed the children of this generation were drifting away. A trickle at first, the decline in membership became alarmingly large by the mid-1980s, and a large drop in membership continued well into the 1990s. During this period, church leaders and experts debated the causes of decline and what to do about it. Yet many studies of mainline denominational decline usually find generations at the root of the problem. Put simply, the membership decline of the mainline churches reflects the failure of churches built by the World War II generation to hold on to the children of the next generation—the Baby Boomers, who began coming of age in the mid-1960s and were dropping out of churches in large numbers around that time.[1]

In every generation, there are children who are raised in a church environment and who later drop out. But for the Baby Boomers, the dropout rate was unprecedented. More than one-third of all Boomers, some thirty million, left the church they had been raised in. Where did they go? Some went to a more conservative Protestant church, in particular to a new-style church with another approach to worship and ministry. Others dabbled in Eastern religion or Native American spirituality. Most, however, didn't go anywhere and became nonpracticing Protestants. Many were willing to identify themselves by their parents' faith group but when polled said they had not attended in a while.

In the late 1980s and early 1990s, many of these unchurched Baby Boomers began returning to church. The "Baby Boomerang," as it was termed, came as some Boomers began to experience a midlife crisis of relationships and family, career and material success or failure, and the death of their parents. Other returning Boomers felt it important to expose their children to faith and moral values.[2]

The Baby Boomerang caught many mainline Protestant churches off guard in several ways. To begin with, many pastors and church leaders thought the Baby Boomers were gone for good; only a few believed they would ever come back. The sheer size of the return overwhelmed many a church. During the late 1980s and early 1990s, churches that hadn't seen more than a handful of visitors in years were suddenly deluged, particularly those in suburbs and small towns that had become bedroom communities for larger cities.

Again, many established churches were not prepared to address the expectations Boomers brought with them on their return to church. Impatient with traditional worship, they came with an ear for their own styles of music and an eye for multimedia communication; they found a service still clinging to high-art church music and a traditional preaching style, and worshipers with their heads stuck in hymnals and bulletins. Obsessive about their children, they demanded state-of-the-art child care facilities in a nursery. Fanatical about convenience, they insisted on a huge parking space for their minivan or SUV, adjacent to the entrance. Not surprisingly, many (often older) lay leaders and members of established churches viewed the Boomerang as a mixed blessing. They wondered aloud, "Who are these upstarts to come here and demand changes to our church to suit their needs?"

The Boomerang also caught many churches before they were ready for a generational transition. In the mid-1980s, the men and women of the GI generation were at a late stage of their career or in retirement, but at the height of influence in church leadership.

Improvements in health care and life expectancy meant more older adults—and in better physical and mental condition—than ever before. Many suburban churches started in the 1950s still followed the same group of leaders who had founded the church. Their sense of ownership and investment in the congregation was never higher. In short, they weren't ready in the late 1980s and early 1990s to pass the torch.

Although a few churches reacted quickly and adapted to the expectations of returning Baby Boomers, most did not adjust well enough to see many visitors stay to become active members. The mainline churches had failed to keep the Baby Boom generation from dropping out in the 1960s; in the 1990s, Boomers returned to find that little had changed. So they either drifted to the sidelines or left for a new church. Thus the Baby Boomerang failed to reverse the trend of membership decline in the mainline church.

In many cases, Baby Boomers gravitated to a new and innovative church that is independent or affiliated with a new denomination such as Calvary Chapel or the Vineyard.[3] These Boomer-friendly churches grew quickly in the 1980s and 1990s, offering another style of liturgy and music, and another approach to ministry programs.

Understanding the Generations

There has always been a generation gap. Rebellious youths and puzzled parents are commonplaces of life. Yet there is more to generational conflict than meets the eye. Differences in such things as music, entertainment, dress, and politics can cover up a deeper shift in the fabric of life, for each generation shapes and expresses wider social and cultural change. Generational dynamics are all the more powerful because we experience them personally in our family, at work, and in our church. We all belong to a generation regardless of how we may feel about it; all of us are children, and many of us are parents and siblings. A generation is more than a social construct or theory devised by academics with too much time on their hands. Our experience of being part of a generation adds an emotional element that affects how we think and make decisions.

What Is a Generation?

Many historians and culture watchers define a generation as a group of people marked by birth years. The Baby Boom generation, for example, is commonly defined as running from 1946 to 1964 because over that period the number of live births in America exceeded four million per year. Generation X, the following one, is also called the "Baby Buster" generation because the birth rate sank below four million births per year from 1965 to 1983. The Millennial generation is sometimes known as the "Echo Boom" because it represents a second Baby Boom with more than four million births per year.

Birth years alone may not be the best way of determining a generation. William Strauss and Neil Howe offer another view of generations in their pioneering book *Generations: The History of America's Future*.[4] They define a generation as a group of people who share a common experience—a social moment of spiritual awakening or secular crisis—during the formative phase of their life, usually youth and young adulthood; as those authors say, "a generation is a cohort-group whose length approximates the span of a phase of life and whose boundaries are fixed by peer personality."[5] The two pieces are important. First, a phase of life (youth, young adulthood, middle adulthood, old age) lasts roughly twenty years. What happens to a generation during the phases of life, particularly in youth and young adulthood, shapes peer personality. Second, peer personality is how each generation sees itself and the world around; "a generation has collective attitudes about family life, sex roles, institutions, politics, religion, lifestyle, and the future. It can be safe or reckless, calm or aggressive, self-absorbed or outer-driven, generous or selfish, spiritual or secular, interested in culture or interested in politics. In short, it can think, feel, or do anything an individual might think, feel, or do. Between any two generations, as between any two neighbors, such personalities can mesh, clash, be attracted to or repelled by one another."[6] Because social and cultural events shape a generation rather than birth date or birth rate, generations are not necessarily identical in length, and statistical similarity or difference has only secondary importance. Thus Strauss and Howe give dates to the five living generations that differ from those assigned by conventional demographers, as this list indicates:

Generation	Conventional Dates	Strauss and Howe (1991)
GI	1900–1927	1901–1924
Silent	1928–1945	1925–1942
Baby Boom	1946–1964	1943–1960
Generation X	1965–1983	1961–1981
Millennial	1984–2005	1982–2003

Strauss and Howe offer other important insights on generations. First, a generation conforms to a basic type, or peer personality. Surveying American history from the colonial period to the present, the researchers see four main generational peer personalities: idealist, reactive, civic, and adaptive.[7] Moreover, these four generational types appear "in the same repeating sequence." A generational cycle begins with an idealist generation, moves to a reactive one, followed by a civic generation, and then concludes with an adaptive one.

Strauss and Howe go on to relate how these generational types correspond to four main social and cultural moods in American history: the crisis era, the outer-driven era, the awakening era, and the inner-driven era. There is an important connection between the generational cycle and "recurring types of historical events."[8] Using this model, they offer a number of predictions about future generations and the future of American society; as they write, "this recurring cycle of generational types and moods helps us not only to understand the past, but also to forecast how the future of America may well unfold over the next century."[9]

How does this help us understand the way in which generations interact? For one thing, we are reminded that a generation is "people moving through time," not static or isolated but rather fluid and interactive. The "generational constellation"—the living generations in their respective phases of life at any one point in time—"is always aging, always shifting, moving up one lifecycle notch roughly every twenty-two years. Whenever the constellation shifts up by one notch, the behavior and attitudes of each phase of life change character entirely."[10] Generations both shape events and are shaped by them. Millions of Americans were alive in the 1960s, for example, but age often accounts for widely divergent experience of the sixties.

Generations and Worship

Differences between generations are real; understanding them helps us think more clearly about worship. Howe and Strauss say that "one lesson of the cycle is that every generational type has its own special vision of the American dream."[11] Similarly, each generation has a distinctive view of church, of God and spirituality, and of worship. This is not to say one generation's perspectives are better or worse than those of the generations before and after it. As helpful as generational dynamics are, some caution is in order when thinking about worship from a generational perspective.

First, generational differences do not explain everything. Any description of a generation is a generalization that can reinforce caricature, comparison, and segmentation.[12] The more we pay attention to people in sweeping, abstract terms, the more tempting is the conclusion that one generation is greater or lesser than another, or better or worse. An important lesson of generational research is that each one is different and distinctive. The broader historical view of generations helps us see the strengths and weaknesses of each generation, its achievements and shortcomings. A more realistic understanding of generations can pave the way for better understanding among generations, and hopefully lead to a healthier, cooperative way of planning and leading worship.

Second, although good generational analysis helps us understand who we are, we should be cautious about using it to say who we will become. Generational dynamics are not a base for predicting the future because people don't generally see themselves in strictly generational terms. They are likely to identify themselves by other criteria besides generation: birthplace, ethnicity, profession, religious affiliation, even hobbies. Generational analysis can't answer every question about beliefs, attitudes, and behavior, particularly when it comes to worship, so we need to forecast the future of a generation carefully.

Third, too much emphasis on generations can cause us to lose the proper focus of worship on God. As Sally Morgenthaler observes, worship is primarily for God, not for a target market of any generation. With these important cautions in mind, let's take a look at how a responsible view of generations can help a church plan and lead worship more effectively.

There are several generational factors a church leader should consider in thinking and planning for worship in the church, among them the aging population of most mainline Protestant congregations and how the five living generations view worship.

Aging Protestant Churches

Most established Protestant churches are getting older; they have a higher percentage of older generations and fewer younger generations than the U.S. population in general.[13] Most Protestant denominations experienced significant numerical growth after World War II; all reached their peak membership in the early 1960s. These churches were populated by the World War II generation, seniors, and their families. Membership began to decline in the late 1960s as their children, the Baby Boomers, began dropping out of church. Sociologists Dean Hoge, Benton Johnson, and Donald Luidens write that "the downturn in membership during the 1960s and

1970s was not caused by the departure of large numbers of older adults from the churches. Rather, it was caused by the failure of the young adults within mainline Protestantism to become committed members, thereby replacing older members."[14] The resulting graying of mainline denominations since then worries many church leaders, prompting one denominational official to predict that, given the current rate of decline, the last member of his denomination will die in 2024. Some Boomers have returned to church, but most have not; the generations that follow are even less likely to attend.

Demographer Mike Regele points out that the graying is not happening in the same way to all ethnic groups: "The actual graying is a graying of the Anglo population. This trend foreshadows a potential trouble spot. The changing population dynamics will create a racial stratification based on age. The gray American of the future is more likely to be white, and ultimately female. The young are more likely to be of some other racial-ethnic group."[15] White Protestant churches are graying faster and seem to have greater difficulty attracting young adults. This dilemma has led many pastors and church leaders over the past twenty years or so to consider what can be done to attract young adults to their church.

Why do many young adults avoid the established Protestant church? There are numerous theories and suggestions. One leading factor is the increasing activities clamoring for young adults' time on Sunday mornings. Stores, movie theatres, restaurants, and other venues of activity that never used to be open on Sundays forty years ago are now open on that day, even in the morning. Sometime in the late 1980s, baseball and soccer leagues began scheduling games on Sunday morning, too. Established churches now compete with new churches offering attractive, interesting worship service, up-to-date facilities, and a more congenial approach to ministry leadership. The mainline church is no longer the only show in town; young adults have many more choices about how to spend their time.

New Expectations

Generational perspectives shaped by popular and commercial culture play a role, too. In their search for a spiritual home, many young adults are looking for something different from the churches built by GIs and Silents. Hoge, Johnson, and Luidens remind us that "the mainline [church] made few demands on those who flocked into its ranks during the 1950s. In effect, many members acquired only a thin gloss or 'veneer' of religiosity. The church 'boom' of the 1950s was an ephemeral one."[16] Many of those who dropped out in the 1960s and came back some twenty years later discovered things were the same and moved on, either to another church or back into religious inactivity.

The defensiveness and resistance to change among many GI and Silent generation pastors and lay leaders is another reason many young adults seem uninterested in an established church. Older adults are reluctant to change things, including worship, which they feel are meaningful and significant to them. Though most GI generation pastors retired by 2000, they left behind a strong and firmly entrenched legacy that many lay leaders and adaptive Silent generation pastors who followed them were reluctant to change. Many churches have had to wait for a beloved GI pastor to retire before considering addition of new liturgical and musical elements to their service. In other churches, a GI lay leader seems reluctant to embrace the necessary changes in worship and ministry styles, often adopting an attitude popularized in the old Tarleton cigarette commercials: "I'd rather fight than switch."[17]

Several worship-related areas can serve as examples; one is the preferred size of a service and openness to innovation. Younger adults generally like a crowd; GIs often prefer a smaller, more social setting and are less comfortable with worship on a larger scale. Many churches do not have the space or the resources for large services of 500 or more, and in many cases the GI lay leaders like it that way. They have a small-is-beautiful attitude about church in general and typically prefer a smaller setting for worship of fewer than 250 people, rather like an extended family gathering. In 1970, at the end of the post–World War II church boom, large churches of 1,000 or more in worship were relatively rare. But by the end of the twentieth century, the number of large churches had grown dramatically.[18]

Today's suburban or downtown megachurch is less likely to be affiliated with an established denomination and is made up of young people. Prior to 1970, nearly all large membership churches were affiliated with a mainline denomination or the historic African American denominations. Since 1970, however, most of the new megachurches are independent or belong to a conservative evangelical denomination. The average age of a megachurch attender is much lower than in a smaller church.

In a recent article in the *Presbyterian Outlook*, GI generation pastor and columnist David Steele proclaims that "mega ain't us!" In other words, Presbyterian churches should be happy with smaller settings and what he calls "micro ministry"; "one recalls that while Jesus seemed good at the mega events where the crowds gathered to hear him preach, most of his ministry was spent with a small number of disciples. That's the kind of ministry we know how to do. I wish we honored it more."[19] Steele is undoubtedly right to emphasize the relational character of authentic and transforming ministry; fascination with numbers can distract us from the importance of relationships. But resistance to larger groups is equally unhealthy because it signals to younger adults that the kind of social setting they are often more comfortable in is not valued by others.

Not surprisingly, many younger adults have sensed this resistance to the large service in an established Protestant church. One reason many young adults flock to a larger church or to a new megachurch-in-the-making is its willingness to be or become large. Does this mean that among churches the rich get richer and the poor get poorer? Clearly, a church that continues to resist numerical growth finds it hard to attract new members and possibly loses members who find a larger church more suitable. But the current size of the church does not seem to be what determines its future so much as current attitude about the size of the church among its leaders. Openness to numerical growth is not a guarantee of growth; but resistance to growth among leaders almost invariably ensures that a church does not get larger.

With size comes a different emphasis on the character of ministry and openness to innovation. Carl George points to some important things about a larger church that are often missing in a smaller church: respect for anonymity, responsiveness to felt needs, and open and flexible leadership.[20] Megachurch leaders, according to George, embrace the opportunity that comes with more people to create a sense of safety for newcomers. Newcomers find it easier to be anonymous in a crowd of 1,500 than a gathering of 150. Again, and somewhat paradoxically, a larger congregation allows ministry to be more personalized. Smaller groups lack the resources to customize; they retain a one-size-fits-all attitude. Finally, a larger church is usually more willing to allow its leadership to respond to the needs they see emerging. These characteristics are often lacking in a smaller church with established habits and traditions. In his study of churches that attract young adults, Donald Miller finds that willingness to embrace nontraditional worship is a key factor in the growth of these new megachurches.[21]

Responding to Generations

New-style worship services designed by and for the post–World War II generations are one response to the generational impasse. The seeker service makes every effort to identify with a segment of the adult population—typically Boomers—with a nontraditional or anti-traditional approach to worship that makes use of popular culture, especially music and multimedia communication. More recently,

new churches are springing up across the nation targeting Generation X, using a similar strategy of identifying felt needs and using contemporary music and media to facilitate worship and communication.

One approach to targeting a generation is nesting—starting a
group for young adults that features contemporary worship at some
time or place other than that of the main congregational service.
This church-within-a-church strategy usually assumes the group is
church for those who attend. The group's ministry is self-contained,
and little or no effort is made to encourage participants to attend
the parent church's activities. In many cases, the group is a college
or young adult ministry led by staff employed by the parent church.
The group's strong commitment to worship, however, makes many
of these groups different from their predecessors. The campus ministry of University Baptist Church in Waco is a well-known example of this approach. The Frontline and Soul Purpose ministries at
McLean Bible Church in McLean, Virginia, are also examples of
the nesting strategy. Both programs have their own services and
their own leadership teams that function with only loose supervi-
sion from the parent church.[22] Both target young adults, with Frontline aimed at twentysomethings and Soul Purpose attracting a
slightly older and more professional group of thirtysomethings.

In other cases, the desire to operate outside the box with younger
adults means that the pastor, most likely focused on connecting
with Generation X, has started his or her own church. The best
known example is New Song Church in southern California, started
by Dieter Zander. New Song began as a mission project of Alta
Loma Community Church, but it quickly grew to around twelve
hundred in services featuring contemporary worship music, drama,
and multimedia.[23] The Next Level Church, in Denver, and the
Church at the Center and Mars Hill Fellowship, both in Seattle,
are typical of many congregations oriented to Generation X that
have sprung up in the past ten years. Next Level, which meets on
Tuesday evenings, seeks to use the visual arts and crafts extensively
in its worship, along with CWM and multimedia communication.

The Church at the Center began in 1994 as an outreach to young adults in the downtown area, while Mars Hill meets in the University of Washington district. Their services feature a band playing contemporary worship songs and hymns in a variety of alternative musical styles, and a sophisticated multimedia presentation. The churches are also generationally homogeneous at their core, that is, the leadership is all about the same age, and the ministry style and attitude toward popular culture is the same. As these churches grow, however, they also attract many Baby Boomers dissatisfied with both traditional Protestant churches and seeker-oriented churches.

These churches share a commitment to reaching young adults with the gospel, and including them in worship that is culturally relevant for them. Their leaders assume that traditional Protestant worship prevents this from happening. As an icebreaker with non-Christians of his generation, Zander asked many of them why they didn't go to church. They gave him three reasons: worship is boring, the sermons are irrelevant, and there's no one there like me. To make meaningful connections, many church leaders assume that each generation should have its own distinctive liturgical and musical styles in worship. Young adults respond best in a worship environment that is energetic, vibrant, and above all loud; they also respond to a setting that is quiet, reverent, and frequently melancholy. These styles and moods are difficult to accommodate in the traditional framework of worship in most churches.

What can we make of these approaches? On the one hand, they seem to work. Church growth experts often point to the success of churches that focus on a single generation as a rationale for a strategy of generationally targeted ministry. But this can be little more than a pragmatic appeal to whatever works. In the previous chapter, we examined the homogeneous unit principle as an application of missionary strategy in a North American context. Since the 1980s, the seeker service movement has used this philosophy as the foundation for revamping services to attract Baby Boomers. In many cases, it is being adapted for Generation X and Millennials. But

there are important differences between ethnic groups and generations; they are not the same thing, as some church growth advocates often imply.

This assumption often leads them, first of all, to overemphasize
differences between generations. Another problem with overreliance
on generational targeting and marketing, as we saw in Chapter One
with the seeker service movement, is the potential for pandering. A
desire to create identification with a generation's perspectives often
becomes uncritical accommodation to its preferences. Churches that
plan and lead worship hoping to attract one generation can often
wind up saying or doing anything to keep them coming and holding their attention.

Finally, generational dynamics, unlike racial and ethnic factors,
are not permanent. Strauss and Howe say that each generation ne-
gotiates its own passage through the four main stages of its life cycle:
youth, young adulthood, midlife, and old age. Many aspects of generational dynamics are temporary and change as the generational
cohort grows older. Tastes in clothing, music and entertainment,
cars and other things differ with the stage of life. Pastors and lay
leaders need to keep in mind that generationally targeted services
must change along with the target group. What worked before may
not work in the future. As William Temple said famously, "He who
marries the spirit of the age will find himself a widower in the next."
As we saw with seeker services in Chapter One, many seeker
churches have found strategies developed in the 1980s are now out-
dated as Boomers age, and the approach must change as the needs
of the seeker change.

Is generationally segmented worship the wave of the future?
Presbyterian pastor and theologian Ronald Byars notes that "while
one possibility might be an endless proliferation of new congregations, each specifically targeted toward an emerging generational
cohort, the more likely possibility is that existing single generation
congregations will become multigenerational."[24] As churches targeting young adults eventually find themselves needing to become
multigenerational, they seek to lead their children in worship.

Can Worship Be Multigenerational?

We have more to say about strategies for worship with various generations in Chapter Ten. For now, we can point to a variety of approaches to connecting with younger adults in worship.

Many churches seem able to attract young adults without specifically targeting them. As we have seen in previous chapters, Pentecostal and charismatic churches, along with some traditional liturgical churches, seem to connect with younger adults. Just as there are multiethnic churches, so there are now multigenerational churches emerging across the country that are either charismatic or semicharismatic in worship style. In the previous chapter, we saw how churches such as Antioch Bible Church in suburban Seattle, the Brooklyn Tabernacle in New York City, and Christian Assembly in the Los Angeles area are overcoming generational and ethnic barriers through a focus on worship.

Liturgical churches, particularly Episcopalian, Roman Catholic, and Eastern Orthodox, report increasing interest in traditional liturgical worship among young adults. Taizé-style worship has become influential among young people in Europe since World War II and in North America since the 1980s, frequently among young adults who did not grow up in a church.

Young adults are also gravitating toward churches that offer convergence worship. In Texas, for example, a number of growing Episcopal churches in Dallas, San Antonio, Austin, Houston, and elsewhere are using a convergence approach that blends traditional and contemporary elements. Robert Webber is strongly influenced by generational dynamics. In his view, seeker services and early praise-and-worship-style services are primarily a Baby Boomer phenomenon, driven by their suspicion of traditional worship and by their individualistic, consumer-oriented values. He is more hopeful about Generation X, which appears to him to be more interested in both community and tradition in worship. He is optimistic about the Millennial generation. In several recent articles in *Worship Leader* magazine, Webber agrees with Strauss and Howe that Millennials are another civic generation, with a hunger for tradition and a strong commitment to community.[25]

Multigenerational worship happens in Pentecostal and charismatic churches, and it happens in the traditional liturgical church. But multigenerational worship is having difficulty in many traditional mainline and conservative evangelical churches. Most younger adults seem attracted to the extremes of the worship spectrum; they are abandoning the middle occupied by mainline churches that have little of either traditional liturgy or charismatic enthusiasm in their service.

What does this mean for Protestants? The time has already come to adapt worship to the needs of new generations of Christians and seekers. At a recent gathering of mainline lay leaders, a roomful of mostly older adults were asked, "How many of you have grandchildren?" Most of the people present raised their hands. "How many of you would sacrifice your life for your grandkids?" The same hands went up. "Now, how many of you would sacrifice your church music for your grandchildren?"

The question is more important than the answer in this case. The difference in experience and outlook among generations is significant enough to cause pastors and church leaders to ask how we can include younger people in services designed primarily to appeal to older adults.

This does not necessarily mean we should eliminate the traditional Protestant worship service. It means simply that we cannot allow the preferences of any generation to restrict a congregation's ability to minister effectively with several generations.

7

The Postmodern Worldview

Wgle live in a time of philosophical and cultural change that is closely connected to the ethnic and generational shifts in North American society. New racial and ethnic groups moving here from around the world bring their own distinctive cultural perspectives, including religion, customs, and different ways of making sense of the world. These newly arrived worldviews now challenge the older views held by previous immigrants from northern Europe. In addition, many Baby Boomers and Generation Xers have rejected the worldview of their elders for Eastern religion and New Age philosophy. The result is that contemporary culture has become a tossed salad of often-competing attitudes, values, beliefs, and perspectives.

The term *postmodernism* is sometimes used to describe this new mix of worldviews, though the movement is far from monolithic. Not everyone agrees on what postmodernism is or what it includes; academics and scholars continue to debate and discuss the nature and significance of the movement. Yet most agree that a major shift in worldviews has taken place in the outlook of most Westerners. The label *postmodern* does offer a clue about what is happening. *Post*-refers to something that comes after something else; in this case, postmodernism comes after modernism. All of the strands of postmodernism share some effort to distance themselves from rationalist modernism, which dates from the Age of Enlightenment in the eighteenth century. Rejection of modernism is the first of several characteristics of postmodernism that we explore in some detail.

The Postmodern Worldview and the Worship Awakening

It is no accident that significant renewal and innovation in worship appeared at a time of transition from one dominant worldview to another. Philosophical and cultural shifts historically have had a dramatic impact on the theology and practice of Protestant worship. One impact of postmodernism on worship is its rejection of absolute truth and the resulting emphasis on personal experience as the arbiter of truth. In this opening section, we explore how this emphasis shapes a new view of truth and the role of personal experience in worship.

The Postmodern View of Truth

The modern worldview is characterized by emphasis on objective truth and the capacity of autonomous human reason to grasp it. Modernism could be called "posttraditionalism" because it replaced the traditional worldview of medieval Europe. That older worldview understood truth as a matter of divine revelation, accessible only through the teachings of the Church. Modernists reject religion— Christianity in particular—as the foundation of human understanding and put faith in objective truth that can be known by autonomous human reason. The early modernists went on to argue that objective truth of observable fact and scientific reasoning, not the subjective conviction of religious truth, should be the foundation of society. Early modernists such as John Locke and David Hume argued that moral truth could be established by empirical observation and reasoning from general principles (or natural law), which exist independent of religious teaching. The American Declaration of Independence displays this approach with its appeal to "inalienable rights" that are "self-evident."

Despite their disagreement, postmoderns all share a rejection of modernism and its belief in unified, objective truth that can be fully known. Theologian Stanley Grenz writes that "scholars disagree among themselves as to what postmodernism involves, but they have reached a consensus on one point: this phenomenon marks the end of a single, universal worldview. The postmodern ethos resists unified, all-encompassing, and universally valid explanations. It replaces these with a respect for difference and a celebration of the local and particular at the expense of the universal. Postmodernism likewise entails a rejection of the emphasis on rational discovery through the scientific method, which provided the intellectual foundation for the modern attempt to construct a better world. At its foundation, then, the postmodern outlook is anti-modern."[1]

The postmodern view of truth is thus both radically subjective and radically relative. It is radically subjective because what is held to be true depends on who perceives it. Enlightenment modernism believed that reality existed independently of our observation; with the proper instruments, we can observe reality as it is. Postmoderns reject this assumption and argue that nothing can be known as it really exists, but only as someone observes it. There can be no objective reality, only our subjective experiences, which may be similar or different. As Grenz asserts, according to postmodernism "scientific knowledge is not a compilation of objective universal truths but a collection of research traditions borne by a particular community of inquirers."[2]

Because human knowing is severely limited and completely subjective, truth is therefore also radically relative. Many postmoderns argue that what we think is true is socially constructed, created as the result of political decisions by a group designed to achieve or maintain power over others. What passes for truth is in fact a "narrative," or "myth," constructed by groups to provide them with meaning. Enlightenment modernism believed in a universal rationality; truth is true in London and New Delhi. In the early twentieth century, scholars began to suggest all societies share a system of beliefs that maintain and support roles and relationships in the society. They also argued that the Western rationalist worldview was a similar belief system, just like a primitive tribal myth. Although modernism believed that it was the end of myths, postmoderns suggest that it is, in fact, another myth. As Grenz points out, the unique feature of the postmodern era is that modernism has not been replaced by another worldview, but rather by an "anti-worldview" that questions myths seeking to legitimize a social structure.

The Impact of Postmodernism

Postmodernism has been making steady inroads in the Protestant church since the 1970s. For one thing, the change in philosophical climate affects Protestants along with everyone else. Even if a church hasn't changed a thing in worship since 1955, the sea change in attitudes about truth changes everything around it. A 1998 survey by George Barna revealed that a majority of Americans, including those attending church, believe there is no such thing as absolute truth. Barna notes that "this has produced a nation of churchgoers who accept only portions of the teaching to which they are exposed, and literally millions who question the truth of the Bible on which their faith is based."[3] Many churchgoers apparently doubt the existence of the God they claim to worship.

As we have seen earlier, seeker churches have led the way in responding to the challenge of postmodernism by trying to make worship and preaching culturally relevant and accessible for postmoderns. But are these services merely relevant? Or have they adopted too much of the postmodern perspective they seek to address? Critics point out that by translating the Christian message into the language of contemporary, postmodern culture, seeker churches unwittingly import aspects of postmodernism that work to undercut their affirmation of Christian truth. Seeker church leaders say they have changed the packaging but not the message; however, critics point out that changing the package changes the message as well, in two significant ways.

First, critics claim that seeker churches allow subjectivism to undercut their authority by shifting the emphasis of worship and preaching from doctrine to belief. The goal of seeker church worship service is no longer to get people to agree with Christian teachings, but rather to engender trust and belief in God. A personal experience of God is more important than affirming Christian truth; the seeker service appeal to belief is largely emotional, rather than intellectual. At Willow Creek, for example, programming staff create "moments" during the service in which the emotional and intellectual aspects of the day's theme converge to move attenders, nudging them (gently or sometimes firmly) to faith in God. This subjective appeal minimizes the importance of truth. The consumer-oriented approach to marketing the gospel further encourages privatization of faith, which undermines traditional religious authority. By abandoning traditional language and concepts and by rejecting theological authority, seeker churches make it harder, not easier, to defend the Christian view of truth.

Second, critics contend that using the language and concepts of popular psychology reinforces subjectivism. Seeker churches regularly use psychology as a common ground with postmoderns. Seeker church leaders encourage preachers to be familiar with the best-selling self-help books. Seeker service themes frequently focus on relationships, parenting, work and career, and other topics related to self-help. Rick Warren urges preachers to build practical, advice-filled sermons around "felt needs." Many of his own messages begin with the common self-help formula "how to. . . ." But some people are anxious about the alliance between Christian preaching and popular psychology. They see psychology as a secular religion that replaces God with the self. Gregory Pritchard notes that "psychological categories are not neutral medical terms. They shape how people perceive and therefore live."[4]

Critics also point out that the seeker church dependence on psychology also has the effect of making Christian truth relative. Christian truth cannot be blended with other perspectives without making it relative, thereby diminishing its authority. Kimon Sargeant uses the term *secularization* to describe the process of replacing traditional Christian language with terms and concepts drawn from non-Christian, or secular, sources. By emphasizing belief over doctrine and secularizing the message, preachers and worship leaders attempting to reach postmoderns may be doing more than simply translating the gospel. They may be transforming the gospel into merely another self-help message.

The Seeker Church View of God

One way to tell the amount of damage done by postmodern subjectivism is to analyze what seeker churches say about God. Critics believe we can detect the damage in the view of God at a seeker church. Few accuse the seeker church of entirely abandoning biblical teaching about God, but many critics think it is one-sided in its teaching; the church does not accurately reflect the biblical understanding of God. Pritchard thinks that in attempting to communicate in psychological language Willow Creek "emphasizes elements of the gospel that are appealing to the typical unchurched Harry (immanent love) and a corresponding lack of emphasis on those elements that are not as attractive (transcendent holiness)."[5]

God's holiness is one aspect of biblical teaching that some think gets short shrift in the seeker service. Sargeant points out that the seeker church pastor does not avoid God's holiness but alters its character through forced analogy: "Rather than depicting God as the One who desires—or even demands—worship, seeker church pastors instead compare God to human examples of authority."[6]

This criticism that the seeker church has sold out the biblical doctrine of God may not stick as well as many think, for a couple of reasons. First, the seeker church is not as imbalanced in its teaching as the critics allege. Sargeant, who has done extensive firsthand research at Willow Creek and among churches affiliated with Willow Creek Association, agrees with Pritchard that seeker churches emphasize God's love and compassion, but not to the exclusion of

God's holiness and justice.[7] Moreover, there is little to suggest that seeker churches are so different from most other Protestant churches in their emphasis on God's love.

The critics are right to warn us about the dangers of distorting or diluting the Christian understanding of God. It is easy to find examples of a preacher who pushes the envelope too far and inadvertently misrepresents God. A quick look through the religion page in any major newspaper reveals that preachers at most churches are proclaiming a loving God. If overemphasizing the love of God is a problem, it is a common one.

As Sargeant describes it, the seeker church has opted for an accommodation strategy with postmodernism that involves a paradox. One the one hand, the church affirms orthodox Christianity and its view of God. At the same time, it asserts "that the most convincing proof of Christianity is not the historical evidence for the life, death and resurrection of Jesus but instead the practical and therapeutic benefits of belief." To gain a hearing among postmodern listeners, the seeker church begins with "what God can do for you" in order to lead people to understand and worship "God for who he is."[8]

How far can or should we go in translating the gospel and Christian worship for postmoderns? What criteria should we use to ensure that our effort to translate Christian truth for postmoderns doesn't end up transforming it instead? Few seeker church leaders have thought much about these issues; few have written down explicit guidelines. Most fly by the seat of their pants, dealing with situations as they arise from a commitment to the Bible as the final authority. This may seem unreasonably daring and scary to a Protestant in an established church, relying on decades of local tradition, or leaning on directives and resources from denominational headquarters.

There are, however, at least three resources that can guide a pastor or church leader in the task of translating Christian truth and worship in a postmodern environment. First, deep understanding of the Holy Spirit paradoxically ensures the Christian truth in worship. Protestants today are showing more willingness to trust the Holy Spirit than in previous generations. In John's gospel, Jesus says the Spirit will teach the disciples all things and remind them of his teachings (John 14:26). Many Protestant pastors and theologians are moving away from rigid, rationalist theology and embracing Trinitarian perspectives holding that the Holy Spirit ensures the truth of Christian message.[9]

Second, greater awareness of the interaction of Christian truth and the host culture in the past guides us in the task of translating Christian truth in our own day. Robert Webber and other worship scholars are giving pastors and church leaders valuable help to preserve Christian truth in worship by showing how the church has negotiated the translation in the past.[10]

Third, greater appreciation for translation of Christian truth in other cultures around the globe helps us locally. Missionaries and cross-cultural ministry experts have learned much about the danger and opportunity for Christian truth in the process of cross-culture communication.[11]

Admittedly, this is not the kind of rigid guideline and checklist that some need if they are to feel that Christian truth is adequately safeguarded. Translating the gospel into a postmodern culture is a dynamic process that involves experimentation, which almost always means some error and failure. Yet it is a reasonable step of faith to take, guided by the witness of the Spirit who speaks from Scripture, the witness of previous generations, and the witness of our brothers and sisters in Christ around the world.

Experience and Worship

The Postmodern Experience Orientation

In addition to a radically subjective and relative view of truth, postmodernism advocates a holistic and experiential approach to receiving information and perceiving the world around us. This approach is grounded in rejection of modern rationalism and its unitary view of the self. Modernism favored the cognitive aspects of the personality exclusively, downplaying or even seeking to eliminate other aspects, such as the body and emotions. René Descartes famously defined human existence as a totally mental process when he wrote "I think, therefore I am." Later philosophers such as Immanuel Kant relegated other dimensions of human personality to a secondary role governed completely by the intellect. Even religion, Kant theorized, must be carefully controlled by reason.

Postmoderns challenge the modern view of the self implied in its emphasis on rationality. Grenz observes that postmoderns reject "the Enlightenment ideal of the dispassionate, autonomous, rational individual."[12] The self is not a unitary, exclusively rational being. Drawing on psychology and brain research, postmoderns argue the self is far more complex and artificial than modernism allowed.

Walter Anderson notes four main characteristics of the postmodern view of the self[13]:

- First, the self is really a composite of selves, some of which correspond to different functions of the brain, with others constructed for social norms and expectations.
- Second, the self is changeable. The self—even the rational self—is not the stable and fixed point moderns like Descartes thought it was.
- Third, some postmoderns believe the real nature of the self is mysterious, and beyond our capacity to understand it. Radical postmoderns even go so far as to say that there is no such thing as a self; selfhood is a "social construction" designed to reinforce group identity.
- Finally, the self is relational, not isolated and unaffected by others. Postmoderns, especially feminists, argue that the self is mostly shaped by the context of social relations. A woman's way of knowing and understanding the world is not an individual and exclusively rational operation, but rather a mode of perceiving that is enmeshed in a web of personal relationships.[14]

The postmodern view of the self opens the door for new ways of receiving information and perceiving the world besides intellectual cognition alone. Postmoderns do not discount rationality; they seek instead to balance the cognitive aspects of the self with others, including the emotional, the physical, the intuitive, and the relational. Grenz writes that "postmodern holism entails an integration of all the dimensions of personal life—affective and intuitive as well as cognitive."[15] By rejecting strict modern rationalism, postmoderns relativize rationality as one mode of knowing among others. Other modes of receiving information from the world and making sense of it must be accommodated.

Narrative and Image

Postmodernism's emphasis on narrative and image is one example of a changing view of the self and modes of knowing. In rejecting rational, abstract discourse, the language of scientific observation, and philosophical analysis, postmoderns open the door to narrative and image as modes of perceiving and knowing. Narrative discourse is an ancient form of understanding the world. Preliterate cultures used stories to communicate important information about everything from the cosmos to everyday life, history and traditions, customs and morals, and religious belief. The sagas of Homer and the narratives of the Old Testament are classic examples of this discourse. The point of the stories is often to convey important information, but the manner in which it is communicated is telling.

Narrative discourse invites the hearers to place themselves in the flow of the story, either as an heir of the tradition or, in a spiritual sense, as a participant through ancestors. The Jewish Passover Seder Haggadah captures this sense of personal participation in the narrative: "In every generation let each man look on himself as if he came forth from Egypt. As it is said, 'And then shalt thou tell thy son in that day, saying, "It is because of that which the Lord did for me when I came forth out of Egypt." It was not only our fathers that the Holy One, blessed be He, redeemed, but us as well did he redeem along with them.'" From a strictly analytical and rational perspective, this sentiment is nonsense. Yet both preliterate and postmodern views see narrative discourse as a powerful way of communicating important information about personal and group identity.

Postmodernism sees narrative, or myth, as the glue in our worldview, holding information together in some way that makes sense to us. But narrative is always a human invention, or socially constructed. In *The Structure of Scientific Revolutions*, Thomas Kuhn used the term *paradigm* to describe a narrative that helps scientists explain their findings. Moderns believed natural law, which could be discovered by unaided human reason, amounted to an all-encompassing "meta-narrative" that accounted for everything. The postmodern rejects any meta-narrative, believing we do not have access to information that allows us to determine whether any paradigm or narrative is valid or invalid. Narrative may not communicate absolute truth, but it does convey important personal knowledge. It is true in the subjective sense of carrying meaning and significance, if not absolute certainty. Grenz believes this should be good news for Protestants who wonder if the Christian message can resonate in a postmodern setting; "in understanding and articulating the Christian faith, we must make room for the concept of 'mystery'—not as an irrational complement to the rational but as a reminder that the fundamental reality of God transcends human rationality."[16]

The rise of postmodernism corresponds with the rise of electronic media. To many, the modern era began with Johannes Gutenberg's moveable type printing press. In *Orality and Literacy*, Walter Ong demonstrates how the printed word both spread and shaped modernism.[17] Books were rare before the printing press, found only in monasteries or libraries of royalty. The printing press produced books cheaply, and new ideas traveled farther with greater impact than ever before. Print communication also shaped modernism in an important way. Ong writes that under the deluge of print, "orality"—the mode of thinking shaped by oral communication—gave way to "literacy." Modernism and literacy made a good match. Again, narrative oral communication is "aural," or auditory, while print is visual. By embracing print communication, modernism shifted the primary port of entry for information from hearing to seeing.

Moreover, speaking and hearing require some kind of relationship between speaker and hearer; communication by writing and reading does not. By embracing print communication, modernism shifted the context of knowledge from a relational setting to the individual. Mitchell Stephens observes that writing has the "ability to transform words into objects. Words that are written down, not just enunciated, are freed from the individual situations and experiences in which they were embedded." Preliterate people think primarily in concrete and relational ways, while literate ones are able to think mostly in abstract and rational ways. To Stephens, "our ability to find abstract principles that apply independently of situations is to some extent a product of literacy, of the written word."[18]

The new era of electronic media began with the invention of the telegraph. Through the nineteenth and twentieth centuries, speech and writing were transformed as technology improved our ability to send messages over greater distances and to more people. The invention of television in the late 1920s, however, reintroduced the image to communication. Now words could be combined with pictures, creating an audio/visual medium. This new medium has a powerful impact on how postmoderns understand their world. Image-based postmodern communication is multisensory, fast-paced, and complex.

How does image communication affect the way we think? To begin with, image-based communication is multisensory. Video engages the eyes and the ears, but new technology allows video to affect touch, taste, and even smell as well. Virtual reality games can reproduce the feel of the steering wheel of a racecar going 200 mph; soon they will provide the smell of car exhaust, too. Theme rides such as "Backdraft" at Universal Studios allow visitors to see, hear, feel, and smell a burning building. Watering holes with video game arcades such as Dave and Buster's are bringing multisensory experience into the suburban neighborhood.

Image-based communication is also fast-paced. MTV videos are famous for jump-cut editing, a technique that presents images in rapid succession. This technique has influenced everything from TV ads to shows and movies—and the evening news. Before "Seinfeld," TV sitcoms were built on a few scenes each lasting several minutes. "Seinfeld" broke the mold, building each episode on forty or more scenes, some lasting just a few seconds. Other programs were forced to pick up the pace.

Image-based communication is complex. Mixing media is common in video. We are familiar with how speech and image can reinforce each other. Our mental images of John F. Kennedy and Ronald Reagan at the Berlin Wall, for example, reinforce the words they spoke. Artists, producers, and directors also layer media (known as bricolage) to create multiple messages. Print engages the eyes, but in a linear and sequential fashion, one word after another, one thought after another. Layered postmodern communication throws several messages simultaneously at the receiver, who then connects them (or not) as he or she is able. Bricolage, particularly in video, can produce a layering of meaning and nuance that is difficult to do in speech or print alone.

The postmodern is image-oriented, but there is considerable debate over what this means. Some worry that postmodern image communication marks the end of rationality. Images are superficial and deceptive, they argue, and cannot communicate rational discourse. Critics of postmodernism see only a cultural descent into subjectivism and relativism that the church must avoid if it is to keep its message pure.

A few observations about these doomsday warnings may be in order. First, new modes of communication supplement, rather than replace, existing ones. Looking back, no new media has ever completely replaced an older one. When radio came along in the 1920s and 1930s, everyone predicted the death of the newspaper, but that didn't happen. Then everyone thought TV would wipe out radio, but that didn't happen either. The Internet hasn't diminished radio or TV, and in 1999 more books were sold than ever before. This is not to say older media survive as before; just ask anyone in the newspaper business how he or she feels about USA *Today*. New media often transform older forms and lead to new forms and hybrids, such as the cable and Internet hybrid MSNBC. It is going too far to say that image has replaced print media or will do so, though image-oriented communication is certainly transforming print media.

Second, image-oriented communication corresponds more fully to how people experience their world and receive information. Critics of image complain that it abandons analytical, abstract rationalism; it is irrational. Yet professor and writer Stephens is optimistic about image-oriented communication; "in the long term the moving image is likely to make our thoughts not more feeble but more robust, [and] it is likely to lead us to stronger understandings."[19] Print communicates abstract reasoning, one thing at a time, in logical progression. It will always be around for that kind of discourse.

The promise of image-oriented communication is its ability to go from there to engage other aspects of our personality and allow us to experience what is communicated, instead of just thinking about it. Stephens believes multimedia is particularly adept at presenting more than one point of view at a time and at grasping things for us that move too fast—a feat that is virtually impossible in print. Image-oriented communication is not irrational but includes many nonrational elements that correspond to other aspects of how we perceive and understand our world.

The Worship Experience

Postmodern culture is an experience-oriented environment that affects the Protestant church, whether realized or not. Unchurched visitors and longtime members alike approach the worship service from a postmodern experience orientation. The seeker, Liturgical Renewal, and Pentecostal and charismatic churches are the innovative ones responding to postmodernism.

The seeker church attempts to tap into the experience orientation of the postmodern, trying to create a comfortable environment that avoids being too different from the world that seekers inhabit the rest of the time. Seeker church pastors and leaders seem to understand the postmodern self, the emphasis on narrative and image. The shift from doctrine to belief mentioned earlier can also be seen as a shift from an exclusively cognitive approach to Christianity, common to modern Protestantism, to a more holistic one. Sargeant writes that the seeker service "encourages an emphasis on genuine religious experience rather than abstract doctrine. It is not that the objective reality of God is denied, but that seeker churches suggest that the best way of understanding God is via the emotions."[20]

Seeker church pastors and worship leaders understand how people are wired and strive to connect with people at other levels, particularly the emotional. At Willow Creek, service planning teams talk about a moment, a point at which ideas and feelings converge for the attender. Music and drama, in particular, help create the moment. According to Programming Director Nancy Beach, the point of a moment is identification with the seeker to help prepare the person for the message. Emotional manipulation is the danger in this approach, as several critics charge. The effort to connect with the seeker can be illusory; in Pritchard's words, "This emotional closeness is actually devoid of a true relationship. A [visitor] may actually know no one in the church and may even be sitting by himself. The emotional closeness is anonymous and can be manipulated to wrong ends."[21] In a postmodern cultural context, however, it is a risk worth taking.

A seeker church relies heavily on narrative to connect with postmoderns. Preaching uses narrative discourse extensively, though not exclusively; the service may feature a dramatic skit, a clip from a movie or television show, an interview or testimony. The seeker church plays up narrative, hoping to connect with the seekers by way of a story they know to help them see themselves in God's story, which they don't know so well. In his book *Drama Ministry*, Willow Creek's drama director, Steve Pederson, observes that good drama does at least two things. First, it establishes the theme of the service from an everyday and nonreligious perspective. At a deeper level, however, Pederson acknowledges the power of drama to tap personal experience and feeling that is difficult to talk about directly: "Believers and seekers alike come into churches all over the world, week after week, year after year, wearing smiles but with their defenses up, pretending life is better than it is. However, drama that creates identification can break through those defenses. Drama stirs our memories, probes our psyches, and exposes our pain. It has the potential to create a 'lump in the throat' kind of recognition. Perhaps something in our past, or in the present, has been buried psychologically. Done well, even a short sketch can bring that difficulty to the surface. Drama exposes us; it reveals to us afresh just how far we fall short."[22] Narrative is all the more powerful because it is nonthreatening; it places few demands on the hearer, who can engage as much or as little as he or she is able. This feature is particularly valuable when we consider the healthy skepticism many postmoderns already have for organized religion.

Seeker churches are at the forefront of using image-based communication and multimedia in the service. Ginghamsburg United Methodist Church in suburban Dayton, Ohio, has been at the leading edge of multimedia ministry, using skilled artists and technicians to produce computer-generated graphics and video for the worship service as well as for promotional ads on local TV.[23] Pastor Mike Slaughter agrees with Ong's and Stephen's assessment of the impact of image-oriented communication; churches need to understand and use video as a means of communication in much the same way Luther used the printing press to communicate the message of the Reformation.[24] The seeker church uses multimedia for many of the same reasons it uses narrative discourse—namely, to connect with the unchurched postmodern. Slaughter gives attenders at his church high marks for their understanding of image-oriented communication: "Postmoderns expect us to know how to use these tools."

Many pastors and church leaders are concerned about the financial and personal costs of multimedia technology. In the early 1990s, only the largest churches could afford computer-generated projection, and the quality wasn't very good. But the cost of equipment and software declined dramatically in the late 1990s; the quality of projectors continues to improve rapidly even as they become smaller and more affordable. Early attempts at effective media ministry also required substantial investment in people to produce and run media. In the early 1990s, a church with an extensive multimedia ministry had to hire technically trained staff. Ten years later, the situation has changed dramatically. Software makers are making equipment and software that the average computer-using church volunteer can manage. Average-sized churches are likely to begin to experiment with multimedia and shift into image-based communication.

A church aligned with the Liturgical Renewal movement also sees itself as responding in some important way to the postmodern experience orientation. Historic liturgical traditions such as Roman Catholicism and Eastern Orthodoxy never embraced Enlightenment rationalism with the gusto of Protestantism; having never been "modern" in that sense, they find it easier to operate in a postmodern environment. Modernism was hard on Catholics and the Orthodox, and high-church Episcopalians and Lutherans as well; their services were viewed by skeptical moderns as too mysterious, encouraging superstition and magic. The traditionally liturgical churches have always embraced a multisensory worship that engages the whole person. Symbols and icons foster a visually layered environment. Ritual gestures and congregational involvement require active physical participation. Weldon Gaddy and Donald Nixon, Baptist advocates of liturgical renewal, write that "each of an individual's five senses has the potential to serve God as an influential instrument of worship. Reciprocally, meaningful corporate worship appeals to all five of the senses of humankind."[25] A church that offers a rich multisensory liturgical environment finds postmoderns attracted and intrigued by it.

Advocates of liturgical renewal claim that the fourfold order of worship enshrines and enacts the grand narrative of God's salvation in Jesus Christ. As Webber puts it, historic worship "proclaims, re-cites, recounts, recreates the deeds of Christ through which its redemption was accomplished."[26] He goes on to identify two important benefits of this perspective. First, the liturgy depicts salvation as a drama played out on the stage of human history, not as a series of abstract propositions about God. Through the liturgy, worshipers find their stories fitting into the larger story of God. Second, the narrative structure of liturgical worship is participatory. The liturgy is not for people to observe, but for them to participate actively through singing and spoken response. The worshipers are players along with God in the weekly enactment of the salvation drama.

This approach to worship is resonating with a significantly large number of postmoderns. In *Ancient-Future Faith*, Webber elaborates on the call for recovery of symbolic communication: "The postmodern shift in communications from the verbal to the symbolic allows evangelicals to recover the classical Christian approach to communication and creatively apply it to worship renewal."[27] Webber observes that young adults, particularly teens, are exploring liturgical worship; "the combination of ancient forms of faith within contemporary stylings is a powerful and intoxicating combination that appeals to the young in this age of postmodernity."[28]

To be sure, this is not happening at every traditionally liturgical church. Many young people avoid a church where there is resistance to a range of emotional expression in worship. Postmoderns are less afraid of emotional expression than moderns; they seek worship where it is welcome. Second, young people avoid a church that resists multimedia technology and image-based communication. A liturgical church where the service is strictly by the book—a print-bound congregation whose members bury their noses in the prayer book or service sheet—is not likely to attract many young adults who prepare their homework with software intended for projection or Websites. A church that fuses traditional liturgical format with multimedia images and video, and new musical styles, attracts teens and twentysomethings.

Postmoderns often find Pentecostals and charismatics appeal-ing. Some charismatics make use of image-oriented communication; all have historically used narrative and storytelling as a primary mode of communication. But the most obvious common features are emphasis on personal experience and suspicion of modern ra-tionalism. Most would not endorse the postmodern view of the self, but they do embrace a more holistic approach that balances head and heart, fact and feeling.

The core of Pentecostal and charismatic worship is the convic-tion that we can experience God directly through speaking in tongues, prophesy, healing, and other manifestations of the Holy Spirit. Mainline Protestant theologian Harvey Cox notes that Pen-tecostalism succeeds where mainline Protestants failed "because it has spoken to the spiritual emptiness of our time by reaching be-yond the levels of creed and ceremony into the core of human re-ligiousness, into what might be called 'primal spirituality.'"[29] Pentecostal and charismatic experience of God can be described as unmediated immediacy. Pastors and worship leaders can lead and model worship for the congregation, but they have no role in me-diating God, in the sense of controlling how God's presence is ex-perienced. This makes Pentecostal and charismatic worship a truly democratic event, different from mainline Protestantism and even from the seeker church, which carefully controls and scripts how God should be experienced in the service. The promise of a per-sonal experience of God for anyone is likely to continue to draw postmoderns to the Pentecostal or charismatic service.

Emphasis on a personal experience of God has some drawbacks. For one thing, the stress on experience means lack of emphasis on doctrine. As Donald Miller sees it, the strength of many charismatic churches is their ability to make the sacred real to worshipers. But this "postmodern primitivism" emphasizes experience of God more than correct belief about God. In this regard, the charismatics are not much different from New Age religions.[30] David DiSabatino observes that "emotional excess abounds and the fringe elements of Pentecostalism often resemble the profaneness of a circus sideshow

[more] than anything to do with the sacred."[31] Lacking an educated clergy to interpret scripture adequately, Pentecostalism has been, as one observer put it, experience in search of a theology.

Another weakness among Pentecostals and charismatics is the frequently blurred line between experiencing God in worship and emotional release in worship. Outsiders looking in at Pentecostals and charismatics are quick to ascribe all sorts of psychological and physiological explanation to what they see. Cox finds Pentecostalism a strange brew of the physical and the spiritual, the divine and the human; the various elements are difficult, if not impossible, to sort out. Although the mixing is perhaps unavoidable (and possibly even desirable), some results are often troublesome. For one thing, emotionally expressive worship has a strangely addictive quality for many. This may lead some to worship their worship experience, rather than worship God. Moreover, many make their experience into a benchmark for others. The early Pentecostals, for example, viewed speaking in tongues as exclusive "initial evidence" of the baptism of the Holy Spirit; no speaking in tongues, no baptism of the Holy Spirit. As a result, in many churches there is pressure on the new believer to speak in tongues, and even classes to teach it. Some charismatics equate physical expression or emotional release with true worship, often trying to pressure others into some specific activity in the name of real worship.

The emphasis on the emotions in postmodern popular psychology may attract many postmoderns to charismatic worship who seek a new kind of emotional release. But the attraction quickly fades without a deep foundation in classic Christian theology and a rich worship experience that embraces the whole person and lifts the worshiper out of a solitary experience into a truly corporate setting.

In this chapter, we have only begun to probe the significance of the cultural shift from modernism to postmodernism for the worship awakening. In Chapter Eight, we explore the development of commercial popular culture, particularly popular music, as another way to understand this shift.

8

Popular Culture and the Worship Awakening

Popular culture exerts enormous influence on how we think and live. Movies, television shows, music, and ads are the stuff of conversation around the water cooler at work and around the dinner table at home. Pop culture pervasively shapes how we live and think; it puts pressure on churches, too. A preacher knows that reference to a current film, show, or song helps a point stick with the congregation. The worship leader tries to find out what kind of music people listen to during the week.

Some churches try to meet popular culture head on by adopting its sights, sounds, and feel. Others adapt or accommodate pop culture in a limited way, while still others attempt to resist it entirely. In this chapter, we explore how and why popular culture is an important context for the worship awakening. We also examine approaches to understanding and responding to popular culture, and assess their strengths and weaknesses. But first, we need to know what we mean by popular culture.

Understanding Popular Culture

The field of popular culture studies is vast, but even a brief overview can help us understand the worship awakening better. We begin with a definition of popular culture.

High, Low, and Mass Culture

Cultural expressions have traditionally been divided into two categories: "highbrow," or high-art culture; and "lowbrow," or folk culture. Until the nineteenth century, highbrow culture included the pursuits of the upper classes and the educated elite, such as classical music, refined painting and sculpture, drama and dance, and literature. These pursuits reflected the traditional and classical ideals of beauty, artistic excellence, and intellectual stimulation. The lower classes too enjoy the arts, says historian Lawrence Levine, but for different reasons from the elite. They like different styles of art as well, namely, folk styles lacking the refinement and sophistication of higher forms.[1] At best, they are merely fun and entertaining; at worst, they are immoral and degenerate.

Levine's study of drama, music, and visual art in the nineteenth century points out how the line between highbrow and lowbrow culture keeps moving. What many consider high art now didn't start out that way. Shakespeare's plays, for example, were popular entertainment until the late nineteenth century, when the cultural elite began to consider his plays high art. Charles Dickens was highly regarded in his day as a writer and was a commercial success. In the early twentieth century, George Gershwin moved easily back and forth between Tin Pan Alley songs and jazz on the one hand, and orchestral music on the other.

In the twentieth century, mass culture emerged as a result of such new technology as photography, motion pictures, and sound recording. These advances created new art forms that were neither high art nor folk art; instead, they became commercial art forms designed to make a profit for their producers by appealing to the widest possible market. Later, mass media—radio, magazine, and television—emerged, fully aimed at an even larger audience.

Because of the need to market commercial art to as many consumers as possible, mass culture was often bland and predictable. During the 1950s—the heyday of mass culture—a handful of powerful movie studios produced most of the films, a few publishers printed most of the magazines, and just a few radio and television networks controlled the airwaves. Producers and editors sought a formula that appealed to the widest possible market for their product. Many movie producers used the same actors, storylines, plot devices, and special effects precisely because the convention attracted patrons. Much popular music came to sound alike because it is essentially the same music, carefully recorded according to strict production values determined by executives.

Mass culture also includes such leisure activities as video and computer games, theme parks, and other experiences that merge entertainment and electronic media technology and offer an experience for sale. Disneyland began in the 1950s and quickly became a popular vacation destination. By the end of the 1990s, there were dozens of similar theme parks throughout the country, attracting millions each year. Theme restaurants (Planet Hollywood, Hard Rock Café) cash in on the connection with movie and music stars, and the desire of many to be part of that world (even if only for lunch or dinner). The video game rapidly grew from simple beginnings with Pong and Pac Man to such sophisticated forms as Myst, Tomb Raider, and a new generation of virtual reality games.

Popular culture is not synonymous with mass-market entertainment. Beginning in the 1970s, the uniform mass market in all forms began to fragment into many smaller subgroups in music, television, print, and movies. In 1970, there were only a handful of pop music styles, represented by the *Billboard* Top 40; by 2000, there were dozens of musical styles and stylistic hybrids to choose from, and several top forty lists. Thanks to video and cable, small film producers can afford to make movies for small audiences. The explosion of magazines is another indicator of how diverse popular media culture has become. In the 1950s, there were only a few hundred magazines, with the market dominated by a handful: *Look*, *Life*, *Time*, the *Saturday Evening Post*, and *Reader's Digest*. Today, there are thousands of magazines catering to specialized interests.

Although the mass market continues to thrive, it no longer dominates popular culture as it did in the 1950s. The movie industry was dominated by a few large production studios through the 1950s. The collapse of the studio system in the 1960s was a kind of deregulation that gave access to the market to many smaller, independent, and foreign filmmakers. Along with cable and premium movie channels, increasingly popular VHS and DVD rentals gave small-budget films an opportunity to compete with the major Hollywood studios. The 1999 low-budget independent hit *Blair Witch Project* surprised many not just because it was filmed mostly with a digital home video camera but also because its producers managed to generate interest in the movie through the Internet, without the aid of the Hollywood promotion and publicity machine.[2]

Electronic Media

Popular culture in North America is profoundly defined by electronic media: music, television, movies, computer games, and the Internet. Americans are insatiable media consumers, spending a large percentage of their disposable income on electronic hardware, CDs, movies, and computer entertainment.[3]

What makes electronic image-based media so powerful? To begin with, electronic media are stimulating and engaging. Movies, TV, and video games attract and hold people's attention. Andy Warhol once quipped that "if you show people something that moves, they'll watch it." Studies suggest that too much visual stimulation reduces brainwave activity rather than increase it, and some scholars conclude that video entertainment is making Americans dumber. Mitchell Stephens's complaint about TV is the seemingly hypnotic spell it often casts as he sits down to watch the early evening news and winds up watching "Late Night" with Conan O'Brien.[4] Despite the universal complaint of being busy, the average American still manages to spend more than three hours a day watching television. Electronic media are increasingly interactive rather than entirely passive, allowing the user to shape and direct the experience. For example, computer users "surf" the Internet for sites of interest, and programs now allow users to customize the information they receive. Many computer games heighten the engagement by making the viewer part of the unfolding action.

Again, electronic media draw us in because they reflect our lives. We see ourselves on the screen or hear ourselves in a song, and we are drawn into the story. Sometimes, these images and stories confirm what we want to believe about ourselves. Such movies as *It's a Wonderful Life* celebrated the importance of family and work, while the *Star Wars* films highlight the triumph of good over evil. At other times, movies and shows reveal things about us we don't always see or want to see. The *Godfather* movies display the human willingness to trade idealism and love for power and wealth. Reporting and documentaries show us aspects of individual, community, national, and international life we usually cannot see for ourselves. Lyrics of love songs and gangsta rap alike say things many feel but are not able to express well.

Finally, electronic media are influential because of how they shape the way we think, by changing our view of reality. Movies and TV shows are visually imaginative; creative direction and production with special effects or animation tells familiar and unfamiliar stories in a way that helps us see things anew and differently. Film and TV stories also shape our perception of the world around us, though experts disagree on the extent of this influence. The "X-Files" and "Touched by an Angel" contributed to an increase in popular belief in UFOs, paranormal activity, and angels in the late 1990s. William Romanowski calls this the "myth making" power of the entertainment industry: "As a pervasive means of communication, entertainment plays a significant role in our public discourse, both affirming and challenging prevailing attitudes and assumptions about things that matter."[5] Although electronic media are compelling and often persuasive, we must not make the mistake of thinking that this influence is always negative. The presence of Christians and other people of faith in commercial media is a reminder that these forms of communication can be used to inspire and uplift.

Characteristics of Popular Culture

Besides being highly fragmented and driven by electronic media, other aspects of contemporary popular culture are worth noting, among them its commercial nature, its emphasis on personal experience, and its focus on youth.

Commercial Culture

Advertising and electronic media go hand in hand. In *The Conquest of Cool*, Thomas Frank demonstrates the role advertising has played in defining the tastes and habits of Americans since the 1950s.[6] In the late 1950s and early 1960s, a new breed of advertisers embraced the growing countercultural movements among youth in America and effectively coopted their sound, look, and lifestyle to pitch mainstream products such as cars, clothes, and alcohol; "the enthusiastic discovery of the counterculture by . . . American business . . . marked the consolidation of a new species of hip consumerism, a cultural perpetual motion machine in which disgust with the falseness, shoddiness, and everyday oppressions of consumer society could be enlisted to drive the ever-accelerating wheels of consumption."[7]

Hip is now the official capitalist style. Advertisers watch the main outlets of youth culture, such as MTV and Miramax Studios, as carefully as their clients' earnings reports. And business is hip. Business books and magazines are big business. Consultants and personal management experts such as Tom Peters and Tony Robbins are treated like rock stars; their books top the best-seller lists, and their speaking events are a multimedia affair complete with special effects and lighting.

Advertisers use the sound, sight, events, people, and even places of popular culture creatively to get the word out about their products. Ads regularly feature eye-catching, computer-generated graphics combined with popular music. The successful Microsoft ad campaign for Windows 95 featured the Rolling Stones's hit "Start Me Up" and the slogan, "Where do you want to go today?" Product placement in movies and shows is an important means of advertising. The movies *Lost World* and *Goldeneye* featured new cars from Mercedes-Benz and BMW. Sponsorship of events is also vital to advertisers, from college football's holiday bowl games to rock concerts. Even pop culture icons have sponsors. Tennis players wear the logos of their sponsors on their shirts. (Portland Trailblazers forward Rasheed Wallace, known for his flamboyant tattoos, turned down a large sum of money to wear a tattoo bearing the logo of a corporate sponsor.) Budweiser sponsored a tour by country artist Garth Brooks, while pop legend Sting enjoyed the support of computer maker Compaq in 2000. An ad on the hood of a Winston Cup stock car for a season is more valuable than a sixty-second slot during the Super Bowl. Places help sell things, too. Companies compete fiercely for stadium and arena naming rights (Safeco Field in Seattle, SBC Arena in San Antonio, and many more).

Experience Economy

As we saw in the previous chapter, personal experience is a leading feature of the postmodern worldview, but it is also a leading feature of contemporary popular culture. Business writers Joseph Pine and James Gilmore say that the new economy is becoming an "experience economy."[8] Companies do not sell goods and services as much as they sell fun, adventure, and understanding. Entertainment industry insider Michael Wolff writes about the "fun-focused consumer": "Americans have time for entertainment and they're willing to pay for it."[9] Theme parks, restaurants, and retail stores are offering experiences to customers along with products and services. The REI store in Seattle is an example of experience retailing; not only does it offer the latest in sporting goods but customers can try out the rock-climbing experience on a fifty-foot climbing wall, or the experience of mountain biking on a four-hundred-yard bike trail.

Youth Culture

Contemporary popular culture is primarily geared to youth. The film and television industry has been youth-oriented since the early 1960s, with such popular shows as "Dobie Gillis," "77 Sunset Strip," and "The Monkees" featuring youthful stars and helping to spread the perception of a national youth culture. Baby Boomer teens grew up at the movies and in front of the television and made them a regular part of their lives—especially television. TV marks an important generational difference. The GI and Silent generations typically have a different attitude toward television from that of younger adults; they watch specific programs and usually keep the TV off when not watching it. Younger adults are more likely to watch whatever is on (aka "vegging") and leave the TV on even if they're not watching it.

Youth culture has its own music. This may seem obvious to us now, but it is useful to remember there was no such thing as youth music before World War II. Older men and women looked down upon the jazz and swing of the 1920s and 1930s, but those genres were hardly youth music. In the 1950s, Baby Boomer teens identified with rock and roll as their music, even though most of the early stars (Bill Haley, Elvis Presley, Chuck Berry, Jerry Lee Lewis) were from the Silent generation.

In the 1950s, American Baby Boomer teens were the first generational cohort to be identified as a target market, a group that companies could sell to directly. In Frank's *The Conquest of Cool*, we have seen, advertisers became hip in the early 1960s in order to attract younger consumers.[10] The result changed the face of advertising and made the youth culture a legitimate alternative to mainstream mass culture. Marketing and advertising executives now focus heavily on youth, hoping to build "brand loyalty" among new consumers. Not surprisingly, television advertising rates are highest for programs that have the largest audience of the coveted eighteen-to-twenty-five segment.

Not surprisingly, popular culture often overemphasizes the difference between today's youth and other generations. It may be profitable to treat youths and young adults as a distinct group of consumers, but artists and producers often exaggerate youth experience and perspectives. Attentive pastors and church leaders have noticed a similar effect in their youth groups, as young people have been separated artificially from the rest of the church. Meeting their special needs in a youth group has often escalated into a superior feeling that only youth really understand worship.

How Popular Culture Shapes the Worship Awakening

For years, missionaries and others working in cross-cultural settings have looked for ways to communicate the Christian message and lead Christian worship while being faithful to its message. What is essential to Christian worship, and what is cultural packaging? Views on this range from those who argue that nothing can be changed to those who allow that nearly everything is up for grabs. The Eastern Orthodox represent the former view; they believe the form of the liturgy and music must not be changed. Many evangelicals have adopted the latter view, allowing much change and adaptation in music and liturgical form to fit a local setting. Roman Catholics and mainline Protestant groups fall somewhere in between, accepting some change that does not alter the essence of worship, but holding on to a basic structure, or *ordo*, that reflects the tradition of the universal church.

Missionaries and liturgical scholars, we have seen, use terms such as *inculturation* or *contextualization* to describe the process of making communication and worship intelligible to people in a host culture.[11] The point is that to some degree Christian worship must have the sight, sound, and feel of the local culture if it is to be authentic in that culture. Nineteenth-century missionaries often treated their cultural forms as part of the Christian message they proclaimed. In the Caribbean, for example, Moravian churches have used traditional Moravian liturgy and hymns for generations, even after the missionaries left and congregations were able to support themselves. Since the 1960s, however, Caribbean islanders, including Moravians, have become more aware of their distinctive local cultural forms, including music. Not surprisingly, many younger members now prefer a worship service with Caribbean sounds and feel, including calypso and reggae musical styles.[12]

Most Protestants and Roman Catholics now agree that some inculturation or contextualization is necessary, and even good, when it comes to worship. But although a number of scholars concede or even encourage the process in the two-thirds world, they disagree whether a similar process applies when it comes to worship in North American culture. There are three basic ways a church responds to the influence of popular culture on worship: resist or avoid popular culture, adopt cultural forms wholesale, or critically adapt cultural forms.

Resisting and Avoiding

In the mid-twentieth century, few religious leaders had anything nice to say about the emerging electronic media popular culture. Religious conservatives condemned movies, television, and popular music as worldly and sinful, while liberals attacked them for promoting consumerism and materialism. With a few notable exceptions, such as the popular topical preaching of Harry Emerson Fosdick or Norman Vincent Peale, Protestants kept worship free from the sights and sounds of popular culture. Mainline musicians received classical Western musical training at Westminster Choir College, Yale's School of Sacred Music, denominational colleges, and church music programs at secular universities such as the University of Illinois and Indiana University.

Those who advocate resistance or avoidance of popular culture in worship usually have three concerns in mind. The first is a theological objection: popular culture is too worldly and not sacred enough for use in worship.[13] It is idolatrous, offering the false gods of materialism and self-satisfaction for the consumer to worship instead of the true God. The shallow, self-centered nature of popular entertainment is reason enough to keep it out of Christian worship, where the focus should be on God rather than the worshiper.

For another thing, many don't want to accommodate popular culture in worship because they prefer traditional liturgy and music. They avoid popular culture because they like hymns, stained glass, gothic or neocolonial architecture, and the rest. Others resist popular culture because they see an antitraditional bias in it that threatens to erode the church's appreciation of its heritage. Pop culture should be resisted or avoided because it does not value the traditions of the church.

Finally, many do not want to make use of pop culture on aesthetic grounds, because its forms of expression are not good enough for Christian worship. Contemporary worship music is kitsch, offering shallow, repetitive, "sub-Christian" lyrics set to simplistic, unsophisticated, poor-quality music. Multimedia communication, drama, and visual art water down the substance of Christian truth. Critics are troubled by music that sounds like the world and images that look like the world; they believe Christian worship should look and sound different. Instead of pandering to the impoverished tastes of popular culture, churches should elevate worshipers with forms that ennoble, educate, and remind us of the transcendent mystery of God.

Adopting Popular Culture

Beginning in the 1950s, another approach to popular culture began to emerge in Protestantism, beginning first in parachurch youth ministry and then spreading to the evangelical church (as we saw in Chapter Three). These groups attracted young people by tapping into youth culture for common ground upon which to communicate the gospel. Music was a key tool, and youth leaders in the fifties and sixties used it creatively to connect with teens. By the eighties, many churches had learned from their youth ministry how to engage popular culture creatively. A Presbyterian elder described his church's contemporary service as "a Young Life meeting for grown-ups."

The seeker church movement is a good example of the adoption approach because of its emphasis on effective communication. The purpose of adoption is dialogue with popular culture in which Christianity can be presented as a viable alternative to other religious and secular perspectives. Such seeker churches as Willow Creek and Ginghamsburg adopt pop culture forms when they use drama, movie and TV clips, and contemporary Christian music to reinforce their message. The seeker church pastor or worship leader is often a keen student of popular culture, having learned that an important first step in the process of using popular culture media for communication is understanding it. For communicators such as Pastor Randy Rowland at the Church at the Center in downtown Seattle, this means listening carefully to the popular culture of the city, especially the music scene, and creatively adopting its sounds and engaging the message in the service. In addition to accompanying worship music, the church band also plays one or two secular songs, one of which usually precedes the message. Songs are selected as an introduction or illustration of the message, and Rowland often comments at length on the lyrics.

The dialogue with popular culture goes beyond preaching to include all aspects of the service. Although most traditional elements of worship are abandoned in some churches as seeker-unfriendly, nearly all churches make some effort to translate important elements into a contemporary format. Many churches use such familiar things as the Lord's Prayer and the Apostles Creed, or familiar songs such as the Doxology and Christmas carols. At each service, the Church at the Center projects the Lord's Prayer and the Doxology onto the screen and frequently uses contemporary hymn arrangements.

The seeker church uses popular culture in the context of the service to create a sense of connection and identification with the world the seekers know and understand. It intentionally emphasizes the sight, sound, and feel of other familiar popular settings, beginning with the design of the building. It avoids building a structure that appears "churchy"; instead, the campus looks more like a community college than a church, and the sanctuary is more like a civic auditorium. Attenders sit in theater-style seats rather than pews. There are few, if any, Christian symbols or traditional pieces of furniture on the platform or walls, and the visual atmosphere is highlighted by theater-style lighting. From beginning to end, the whole service is a popular culture event, or spectacle, with secular music, TV and film clips, slice-of-life dramatic skits, and visual art.

The benefits of this approach are apparent, but the potential downside of this strategy is not so obvious. The common appeal to separating the nonnegotiables of worship from changeable cultural packaging misses the important way in which culture shapes our understanding of faith. Tex Sample, for one, uses another way of understanding adoption and dialogue, arguing for an incarnational approach to cultural engagement.[14] Sample and others like him acknowledge that worship and culture are not easily separated, but they point out that God took this risk of confusion by taking on flesh in Jesus Christ. God met humanity under specific historical and cultural conditions, namely, as a first-century, male, Palestinian Jew. In the incarnation, culture is neither ignored nor made absolute. An incarnational approach, it follows, engages culture without making too little or too much of it. To use the language of John's gospel, Christian worship should be "in the world, but not of the world." Being in the world means using modes of expression and communication common to the local culture, without contradicting the gospel.

Off the record, many seeker church leaders acknowledge the risk of confusion involved in this process of engaging popular culture. With the benefit of hindsight, nearly all admit to crossing the line more than once into confusing and misleading adoption of pop culture forms. The seeker church sees itself as experimental, and with experiment comes some inevitable failure. Accountability matters to most seeker church leaders; they point to a high commitment to the truth of the Christian message in Scripture and to regular and thorough feedback and evaluation of all aspects of their services.

Adapting Popular and Folk Culture Forms

Charismatics and the ethnic churches use an approach to popular culture that represents another avenue somewhere between resistance or avoidance and adoption.[15] Charismatics, African American, and Hispanic churches use the sights and sounds of their own culture for worship without intentionally using them for evangelistic purposes.

The most noticeable adaptation among such churches is music. Unlike the traditional church resisting contemporary musical styles and the seeker church using popular music for its communication value, an adaptive church uses music as a common language that allows the congregation to participate more fully. Music is drawn from culture in much the same way that language is used. In such a setting, the worship leader does not worry about the suitability of musical style; it is already suitable because it belongs to a common musical vocabulary. Nathan Corbitt, in *The Sound of the Harvest*, argues that the meaning of music is found in the persons who make music, rather than in the music itself.[16] Thus sounds that were once used in a non-Christian or nonreligious setting can be adapted by Christians for worship.

At Iglesia de la Comunidad, a Hispanic Presbyterian church in Glendale, California, the music for worship is a mix of familiar European hymn tunes with Spanish translation of the lyrics, as well as *coritos* (discussed in Chapter Five). The arrangements are all unmistakably Hispanic, using familiar Latin rhythms with plenty of percussion, as well as guitars and brass. According to Pastor Roberto Colón, musical styles from the culture are used to create an atmosphere of fiesta and *familia*, celebration and community. He notes that Hispanic churches continuing to use only European music for worship struggle to make worship meaningful for members and to engage newcomers.

Seeker service communication style is found in some charismatic and ethnic churches, but not yet to a high degree. Many churches, even smaller ones, use computer projection for song lyrics and with preaching, but few use video regularly. Secular songs are hardly ever used. At one charismatic church, video projection is used during prayer, displaying pictures of missionaries supported by the church, a map showing their location, and pertinent information. Many use projection for announcements before and after the service, cutting down the need for spoken announcements that take time away from worship.

The adaptive church is thus more thoroughly inculturated than the seeker church because the connection to popular and folk culture is organic and natural, rather than the product of a communication strategy. The adaptive church is less intentional about how music and other cultural forms are used, more eclectic and ad hoc. The seeker church uses many forms of popular culture for their communication value; the adaptive church tends to use just a few key forms as a means of creating an atmosphere of worship and community.

Interestingly, critics of the worship awakening who resist or avoid pop culture in worship take a sympathetic view of non-European folk culture forms. Popular music from the two-thirds world (Africa, Asia, South America) is acceptable for worship—even for North Americans—but North American popular music is not. The main reason for this distinction seems to be a negative attitude toward commercial production and distribution. North American pop music is ruled out for worship simply because the style comes from pop culture, while songs imported from the two-thirds world are thought to be a purer expression of the authentic, grassroots church. This assertion is difficult to maintain because the distinction between the grass roots and the marketplace is blurred.

Embracing and Engaging Popular Culture in Worship

In *Worship Evangelism*, Sally Morgenthaler understands the Great Commission (Matthew 28:18) to mean that the church is in the business of "making more and better worshipers."[17] The church worships in the world, and it must be intelligible and inviting to those who come. Even critics of the worship awakening acknowledge that a missionary church does not have the luxury of resisting or avoiding its host culture. But how do we do that?

How we engage popular culture should reflect our core theological beliefs and avoid the extreme of taking our cultural surroundings either too seriously or not seriously enough. As we have seen, the critic of the worship awakening generally views pop culture negatively. There is much to be negative about in pop culture, but by making it off-limits the critic unwittingly negates the incarnational mandate of the church to be in the world, though not of it. Labeling popular culture as idolatrous goes too far and runs the risk of failing to take it seriously.

On the other hand, some advocates of the worship awakening go too far in trying to connect with the host culture, unwittingly taking popular culture too seriously. Michael Slaughter likens electronic media to Gutenberg's invention of movable type printing. Electronic media and popular culture forms are God-given tools that are essential for the church in cross-cultural communication and ministry.[18] Those who fail to use them are doomed to eat dust on the information superhighway. In my estimation, this sentiment abandons any critical reflection on the negative aspects of popular culture, leaving us with a false love-it-or-lump-it alternative.

In many places, the worship wars have stalemated into a standoff between those who think using pop culture forms is absolutely essential for worship that honors God, and those who think using them is absolutely unacceptable for worship that honors God. The worship wars are likely to continue if the critic continues to demonize the opponent's approach. There is a way to think of the suitability of pop culture forms in worship other than the overly pessimistic "idolatry" view or the overly optimistic "essential tool" view.

Like any other cultural expression, pop culture forms are not inherently demonic or idolatrous, nor are they inherently good. They are fallen but not irredeemable and beyond the impact of God's grace. Reformed theology uses the category of "common grace" to describe how cultural forms can facilitate God's purpose. Richard Mouw, author of *Consulting the Faithful,* advocates a "hermeneutic of charity" when it comes to popular culture. "We cannot accept sinful culture as it is," he writes, "but neither can we simply reject it as altogether evil. Cultural formation is a part of the good creation. Contemporary culture, including contemporary popular culture, is a distorted version of something that God meant to be good. So we must 'un-distort' it."[19] A theologically responsible way of adapting popular culture forms in worship involves this process of undistorting them, or "retasking" them for use to the glory of God.

Pastor Rowland uses the analogy of the Israelites plundering the Egyptians' temples during their escape from Egypt to describe how the Church at the Center in Seattle adapts popular culture for worship. Just as the Israelites took the statues and furniture designed for the worship of Ra and converted it to use in worshiping Yahweh, so North American Christians can plunder popular culture for artifacts that can help us worship the Triune God.

Retasking Popular Culture

There are several principles to help us retask popular culture forms for worship. First, adapting or adopting pop forms should enhance the worship of God and allow the congregation to honor God more fully. Morgenthaler rightly asserts that worship is for God, not for the benefit of the worshipers.[20] Whatever we use in worship must pass this first test: Will it honor God? Because worship is the work of the whole people of God, what is used should then honor God as well. Because electronic media are capable of drawing attention to themselves, pastors and worship leaders must be discerning about how the congregation responds to them. Discernment is the ability to see beneath the appearance to the underlying reality at work in a congregation. Is a video clip effective because people enjoy video? Or is it effective because the narrative draws people to consider an issue in a way they normally wouldn't? Is a musical style working with the congregation because they can move and clap to it? Or is it working because they are able to express their worship to God more completely and authentically?

Second, adapting or adopting pop culture forms should acknowledge and use more and differing gifts, talents, and skills among the congregation. Increasingly among postmoderns, those gifts have to do with computer technology, video production, drama, visual art, and popular music. Something important happens when worshipers are able to contribute their gifts and skills to production of a worship service. The service becomes theirs in an active sense of participation, instead of just a passive sense of identification. There is a difference between worshiping in a service designed *by* us rather than *for* us.

Using these gifts effectively requires a new model of planning worship. For one thing, it means creating a service where the gifts can be used. As we have seen, a compelling argument for multiple styles of service is to accommodate a wider range of gifts and skills than a single style of worship can handle. It also means greater emphasis on teams to use people with specialized gifts and skills.

Third, adapting or adopting pop culture forms should strengthen the church's outreach and connection with the unchurched and nonbelievers. This is not the primary reason, but it is important for the missionary church in a postmodern and post-Christian setting. Retasking pop culture forms is not simply a way to entice newcomers. Rather, it is an expression of good hospitality. In *Welcoming the Stranger,* Patrick Kiefert uses the biblical concept of hospitality to explain how worship is evangelistic.[21] There is an important difference between using music, video, or computer technology as a hook or device to pull people in to a service and retasking them for worship in a way that expresses hospitality. They are user-friendly, but not necessarily user-focused. They create an opportunity for people to encounter God, rather than just an encounter with a song, a video, or a computer-generated presentation.

We have now briefly explored the social and cultural setting of the worship awakening. This survey does not explain everything about the worship awakening, though I hope we are able to see more clearly that it is both a product of its time and a response to the times. Also, this survey is not meant to excuse everything under the banner of the worship awakening. Worship innovators have made plenty of mistakes and offered plenty of wrong-headed explanations. As the movement matures, I hope that its advocates are able to hear better the criticism of others.

Finally, this survey is not a prediction of the future. The forces and trends we have examined here do not lead to any predetermined and inevitable outcome. God is the ruler; the future is in his hands. The Holy Spirit blows where it will, Jesus reminds us in John's gospel, and we would be foolish to think we can predict the future accurately on the basis of our limited insight. At the same time, we are responsible to act faithfully on the basis of what we know. In the Old Testament, the men of Issachar were commended because they were able to read the signs of the times and knew what to do. In the two chapters that follow, we explore some options for embracing the worship awakening and how pastors and church leaders can begin the process of worship renewal in their congregations.

Part III

Leading a Worship Awakening in Your Church

9

A Theology of the
Worship Awakening

When pastors and church leaders talk about worship, it seems the discussion often generates more heat than light. A quick glance at the articles and letters to the editor in church magazines or Web discussion groups reveals a high level of personal interest and passion. It also reveals quite a range of emotions—anger, anxiety, frustration, disappointment. Why does the worship debate generate such an intense response?

Clearly, there's a lot at stake for people on all sides of the worship discussion. For one thing, regardless of their liturgical and musical preference, most Christian leaders agree that worship is the top priority, or nearly so, for our individual lives and our congregations. Study after study shows worship continues to be a priority for leaders and people generally, even if they don't understand it or practice it very well. Again, leaders invest a lot of meaning and significance in their worship, in whatever form it takes. Although some complain that others just don't get it about worship, this doesn't seem to be the case. Because they are leaders, they are thinking of the welfare of others, and not just their own needs and preferences. They understand that decisions they make affect others. The scale of the debate can be read as an indicator of the importance of worship to many. Apart from, say, homosexuality, other issues just aren't as volatile as worship. Finally, we're intense about worship because we know worship services are the most visible activity of our congregation. James E.

White calls the Sunday service a congregation's "front door" to the wider community. In nearly all churches, more people come in through worship than any other activity.[1]

As important as it is to discuss worship, the current debate about worship innovation is cluttered with unhelpful definitions and assumptions, and poisoned with uncharitable attitudes. Some even call this the worship wars, as we saw in the preceding chapter. Sad to say, worship has been the excuse for church conflict—and even schism.

How does healthy discussion and debate about worship turn into destructive conflict over liturgical and musical style? There are several contributing factors, one of the most important being the assumptions we make about what is discussed and decided. In many cases, discussion escalates into debate and then erupts into conflict because people allow themselves to think of tradition and innovation as mutually exclusive. Either-or thinking is not the only factor behind the worship wars, but it is often the most difficult to address.

The either-or attitude manifests itself in how a pastor or church leader might view the worship wars: as a pitched battle between those who advocate innovation without regard for tradition and those who embrace tradition at the expense of innovation. In some cases, the reality fits the caricature. The terms *traditional* and *contemporary* contribute to the either-or dilemma. In the current debate, contemporary generally means worship shaped by contemporary popular music and multimedia communication, while traditional means worship shaped by liturgical practice and musical style of an earlier period (the 1950s, the Reformation, the fifth century).

But these common assumptions betray the original meanings of the words contemporary and traditional. The word *tradition* comes from the Latin *traduco*, which means to hand down or bring across. Far from meaning static and inflexible, tradition denotes a fluid and dynamic process of handing on from one generation to the next. My family's Thanksgiving Day tradition now looks entirely different from my childhood memories. Thanksgiving used to include football games on TV and a house full of relatives. Now we take walks on an Oregon beach and assemble jigsaw puzzles by a roaring fire. But there will always be turkey with oyster stuffing. The current practice does not need to be identical to the original to be traditional. When the word *tradition* is narrowed to mean only what is old, it is easy to get the impression that traditional practice and style has no value for the present. Yet even the most out-of-the-box alternative worship service contains elements that have been handed down from previous generations.

Similarly, the term *contemporary* means something different from what many take it to mean now. The Latin word literally means "with the times." Contemporary is simply what is happening now in our times. An Eric Clapton concert and Bach's B Minor Mass are both contemporary because both happened this spring in San Antonio. Contemporary describes when something is used, not when something is created. Many contemporary services use songs that are twenty-five years old, or older; among radio stations, such songs are known as golden oldies. When the word *contemporary* is narrowed to refer only to a liturgical or musical style shaped by current popular culture, it is easy to get the impression that this is some entirely new invention with no background. As we have seen in previous chapters, most of the innovations of the worship awakening are more traditional, in the original sense of the word, than many admit. Such a narrow view of contemporary blinds us to innovation that has taken place even in the most old-fashioned of churches.

As difficult as these misperceptions have made things for the pastor or church leader, the root of the conflict over worship goes deeper than vocabulary and definition. The issues are seldom what the partisans say they are. Instead, it often is the differing views of God that create the underlying tension in church and erupt into conflict. Theologically, we can put it this way: the nature and character of the God we worship shapes what we think is the best way to worship him.

Clear definitions help, but only to a point. What is needed is a theological framework through which we can view the worship awakening and the process of worship innovation. Such a framework focuses on renewal and newness as characteristics of God's interaction with his creation and his people.

The Cycle of Renewal

Worship is for God, and to please God it must be offered to him sincerely and authentically. Worship must be focused on God yet be accessible for people. Over the years, churches have struggled to keep a balance between these two insights. At times, the weight has come down more on the theological imperative to focus on the nature and character of God in worship. The need for theological renewal becomes apparent when familiar and comfortable rituals and practices obscure the content of Christian worship. Rejection of many aspects of the mass and other practices of late medieval Roman Catholicism was founded on the Reformers' conviction that they had obscured the gospel by focusing attention on the priesthood and the church rather than on scripture and Jesus Christ. At other times, the stress fell on the need to connect worship with people. Following the Reformation, groups such as the Methodists emphasized greater participation in worship through new liturgical practices and hymns, small-group fellowship, and large-scale camp meetings.

The history of Protestant worship reveals a cycle of decay and renewal among nearly every group. In most periods, decay includes a shift in musical style, a new approach to communication, and a change in culture that affects ritual. Liturgical scholar Frank Senn observes that "rituals can decay, no longer conveying the force or meaning in personal or social life they once had."[2] What one generation finds meaningful and significant can become stale and sterile to a later generation. Eventually, new liturgical and musical forms emerge to challenge and replace the older ones. Initially, there is almost always resistance to renewal. Theologians question the theological integrity of the movement, liturgical experts point out its deficiencies, musicians defend established musical forms. The arguments of the worship wars are nothing new. The objections to the worship awakening of the past thirty years have been heard before.

The diversity of the worship awakening makes the current movement different from its predecessors. Earlier worship renewal generally offered one alternative to the existing liturgical order. The revival worship of the early nineteenth century among the Methodists, Baptists, and others was a clear alternative to established Presbyterian and Congregationalist worship. Today there are several options: seeker service, the praise and worship movement, ethnic approaches, and the Liturgical Renewal movement. There are hybrid approaches that combine a number of these options.

Because it is so diverse, the worship awakening challenges some of our assumptions about the cycle of worship decay and renewal. For one thing, it challenges the common view of traditional versus renewal. Of course, history was never so simple, but it certainly is not simple now. The worship wars pitting traditional versus contemporary styles usually miss the point about the process of decay and renewal. Some innovations with the most profound impact on a congregation are quite traditional, such as the Taizé style of sung prayer. Meanwhile, countless contemporary innovations have been abandoned because they lacked theological integrity or failed to connect with people, or both.

Again, the diversity of the worship awakening challenges our understanding of authority in worship. The movement coincides with the collapse of denominational authority in general and the rapid decline of the mainline denominations in particular. Previous generations generally looked to the denomination for guidance and approval for worship innovation. Connectional churches, such as the Presbyterians and Methodists, supplied the local church with worship aids (hymnals, prayerbooks, devotional resources) through an in-house publishing company. Church musicians networked through an association sponsored by the denomination, such as the Presbyterian Association of Musicians. Denominational tradition worked just as strongly among congregational groups such as the

Baptists, and informally and unofficially through colleges, seminaries, and publishing companies. Liturgical and musical style and denominational identity often went hand-in-hand, mutually reinforcing each other.

The close association of worship style and denominational affiliation disappeared by the end of the twentieth century. Nazarene and Pentecostal churches adapted Episcopalian rites; Lutherans and Methodists experimented with seeker service; Baptists discovered charismatic-influenced praise and worship service. Immigration changed the landscape for many a denomination, adding new music, new liturgy, and new ritual to worship. All groups were hit hard by the exodus of the young Baby Boomers in the 1960s and 1970s, and many were affected by the return of some with their children in the late eighties and early nineties.

Finally, and perhaps most important, the diversity of the worship awakening challenges our assumptions about how to maintain the balance between a focus on God and relevance for people in worship. Many now see that this way of posing the problem creates problems of its own, in particular the danger of making worship primarily a human activity. In his important book *Worship, Community and the Triune Grace of God*, Scottish theologian James Torrance points out that worship begins not with us but with God, in particular with the mediation and priesthood of Jesus Christ: "The good news is that God comes to us in Jesus to stand in for us and bring fulfillment of his purposes of worship and communion. Jesus comes to be the priest of creation to do for us, men and women, what we failed to do, to offer the Father the worship and the praise we failed to offer, to glorify God by a life of perfect love and obedience, to be the one true servant of the Lord."[3] Through Christ's union with humanity in the incarnation, sealed by the Holy Spirit, we are connected to Christ in his worship of the Father: "[Jesus] calls us that we might be identified with him by the Spirit, not only in his communion with the Father, but also in his great priestly work and ministry of intercession, that our prayers on earth might be the echo of his prayers in heaven."[4]

At the heart of this understanding of the source of worship is the ancient insight that in the incarnation, God took our humanity upon himself. But Christ did not shed this humanity in the resurrection; instead, it is purified and made new in him. Torrance says: "Christ takes what is ours (our broken lives and unworthy prayers), sanctifies them, offers them without spot or blemish to the Father, and gives them back to us. . . . He takes our prayers and makes them his prayers, and we know our prayers are heard 'for Jesus' sake. Christian worship is, therefore, our participation through the Spirit in the Son's communion with the Father, in his vicarious life of worship and intercession."[5]

Because worship begins within the Trinity, within the being of God at the core, namely, the adoration of the Father by the Son, the polarizing either-or issues of the worship wars can be seen differently. Torrance observes that "anything we say about worship— the forms of worship, its practice and procedure—must be said in the light of him to whom it is a response. We must ask ourselves whether our forms of worship convey the gospel. To answer these questions, we have to look at the meaning, the content of worship, before we can decide whether our traditions and procedures are adequate."[6] If we worry about where the focus of our worship is, then we are asking the wrong question because it implies worship is merely a human affair. As Torrance reminds us, worship is not about what we do, but about what Triune God has done and is doing. The proper question is, How then do we express the reality of our participation in the ongoing worship of Jesus, our high priest?

Seen from this vantage point, the worship awakening is more than a shift from traditional church music to rock and roll, from traditional preaching to multimedia communication, from solo ministry to team-based ministry, from performance to participation, from intellectual to experiential, from monocultural to multicultural. It is a movement of God among his people to draw them closer to himself, and give more vital and vibrant expression to our earth-bound worship. Torrance rightly reminds us that all we can offer to God in worship and prayer is broken and incomplete. We are all beginners and learners; even the experts (myself included) are "thinking our confusion out loud," as CWM pioneer Chuck Fromm likes to say.

A Trinitarian understanding of worship offers two important insights that we consider in the remainder of this chapter. First, the diversity of sources and expressions found in the worship awakening bear witness to the creativity of the Triune God. God stands behind the diversity of his creation, and behind the variety of personal and cultural expressions that find their voice in new styles of music, communication, and the arts. Second, the newness of the worship awakening is a response to the command to sing a new song to the Lord that reflects and responds to the worship of heaven and, in the words of the Wesley hymn, "tunes our hearts" to sing praise to the Triune God.

A Theology of Variety

It is often said that variety is the spice of life. Variety is a sign of health in nearly every aspect of life—even in the health of the economy. Peter Klenow of the Federal Reserve Bank in Minneapolis thinks that an increasing variety of products and services is perhaps the most reliable indicator of economic vitality. Along with Mark Bils, Klenow is developing instruments that measure the economy's health by tracking the choices available to consumers. Virginia Postrel comments that "increasing variety raises Americans' standard of living, by giving us more of what we actually want rather than forcing us to make one-size-fits-all choices."[7] Not enough variety in the marketplace is a key reason the old-style centrally planned communist economies failed.

God's Creation Is Diverse

Variety is more than spice to Christian worship; it is essential. Variety and diversity are expressions of the creative activity of God. God is the Creator, and God is creative. It has been said that God could have created one kind of flower, but he chose to create thousands. God could have created one kind of person and then cloned him or her to make the rest of us, but as pastor and author Bruce Larson likes to say, each person is "a unique and unrepeatable miracle of God." Although each person is fallen and sinful, nevertheless we bear the divine in our individuality as well as in the diversity of our common humanity.

God's creation is good, and he takes delight in what he has made: "God saw all that he had made, and it was very good" (Genesis 1:31). Though defaced by the fall and continuing human sinfulness, creation has not ceased to be God's good creation. As William Dyrness explains: "God's pronouncement has the character of a promise, or, better, a guarantee. This now becomes a given of creation. The fall . . . introduces a tragic dimension of disorder and rebellion; but there is no hint in Scripture that creation's essential goodness is lost."[8] Creation is good because it reflects the glory and creativity of God. The psalmist sings, "The heavens declare the glory of God; the skies proclaim the work of his hands" (Psalm 19:1). Psalm 148 tells us that nature does more than passively reflect God's glory. Everything in all creation actively praises God as well: "Let them praise the name of the Lord, for he commanded and they were created" (Psalm 148:5).

Humanity Is Diverse

Humanity has a unique role in God's creation. Adam and Eve were created different from the rest of the creatures; God breathes his breath (*ruach*, breath or Spirit) into them alone. God gives them the role of caretaker of the garden, stewards of his creation. They are creatures, and yet their relationship with the Creator is different from that of the rest of creation. Eminent theologian T. F. Torrance notes that humanity was created to be the priest of creation, "whose office it is to interpret the books of nature written by the finger of God, to unravel the universe in its marvelous patterns and symmetries, and to bring it all into orderly articulation in such a way that it fulfills its proper end as the vast theatre of glory in which the Creator is worshipped and hymned and praised by his creatures. Without man, nature is dumb, but it is man's part to give it word: to be its mouth through which the whole universe gives voice to the glory and majesty of the living God."[9] When we worship God, we fulfill the destiny of creation as well as the destinies of our lives.

Worshiping God as his creatures and as priests of his creation pleases God; our worship as members of the "tribes and nations of the earth" pleases God. Some argue that cultural differences are not originally part of God's creation; rather, they are the result of the fall. But there is nothing in the Bible to suggest that God looks negatively on the diversity of the tribes and nations of the earth. For one thing, the election of Israel to be God's chosen people does not imply a rejection of all other nations. God explains that nothing other than his grace and covenant faithfulness prompted him to choose Israel: "The LORD did not set his affection on you and choose you because you were more numerous than other peoples, for you were the fewest of all peoples. But it was because the LORD loved you and kept the oath he swore to your forefathers that he brought you out with a mighty hand and redeemed you from the land of slavery, from the power of Pharaoh king of Egypt" (Deuteronomy 7:7–8). The prophets look forward to the day of the Lord, in which all the nations of the earth will worship God at Zion: "And I, because of their actions and their imaginations, am about to come and gather all nations and tongues, and they will come and see my glory" (Isaiah 66:18).

John's vision also includes the diversity of human cultures. The angels and the saints sing a new song to the exalted Christ: "You are worthy because you were slain and with your blood you purchased men for God from every tribe and language and people and nation. You have made them to be a kingdom and priests to serve our God" (Revelation 5:9–10). As Craig Keener comments, "The particular praise reflects the redemption of Israel from Egypt by the blood of the Passover lamb, except that the people of God now explicitly include representatives from every people, celebrating redemption in their multiethnic, diverse styles of worship."[10] Now the worship of every tribe and nation is acceptable and pleasing to God through the blood of Christ; God takes delight in the variety of his people.

The diversity of human creativity reflects the image of a creative Creator. Because humans are individually and culturally different, our creative expressions are bound to differ as well. As we have seen, our expression is shaped by our cultural surroundings (ethnic background, regional setting), but also by our generation and by commercial popular culture. A theology of variety embraces these differences as part of the good—though fallen—creation of God. This good-though-fallen perspective allows us to see creative expression through music, the arts, drama, multimedia, and so on as important without rejecting them on the one hand, or making them absolute and normative on the other. All expression is distorted in some way by sin, but all expression can be refocused or retasked as a vehicle for praise to God.

Guidelines for Adapting Cultural Expressions

Are there any limits on adapting personal and cultural expression for worship? The best guidance for Christians in this matter comes from Acts 15, which records the conclusions of the Church's first council, held in Jerusalem. The issue at hand was the circumcision of Gentile converts. Did Gentiles have to become Jews first before they became Christians? The council agreed with Paul and said no. Writing to Gentile believers, the apostles offered direction to the Church about how Gentile believers could be incorporated into the people of God along with Jewish believers[11]: "It seemed good to the Holy Spirit and to us not to burden you with anything beyond the following requirements: You are to abstain from food sacrificed to idols, from blood, from the meat of strangled animals, and from sexual immorality. You will do well to avoid these things" (Acts 15:28–29).

These principles may seem quaintly ancient to us now, but they contain some important principles that can guide us in the process of worship renewal today. First, the command to avoid food sacrificed to idols translates into a command not to adapt music or art that has already been intentionally used to worship something or someone else. In the same way all other food was fit for Jewish and Gentile Christians to eat, all other music and art forms are suitable for worship. Caution is needed when checking the sources of music. In Africa and Central America, for example, some popular tunes cause confusion for Christians because they have been used previously in worship in other religions. There is a difference between using a folk tune and using a tune associated with worship in other religions.

Second, the command to avoid blood and meat from strangled animals was intended to avert the kind of offense that can occur in a cross-cultural setting. For the apostles, who were Jewish Christians, a Christian's freedom from the ceremonial law should never be used as an excuse to embarrass or humiliate other believers. Gentiles were not bound to keep kosher, though they should be sensitive to those still adjusting to that freedom.

When it comes to music and art, this means respect and sensitivity to others. In North America, some musical styles are so thoroughly associated with beliefs and lifestyles that are antithetical to Christian values that they should be avoided in most cases. Gangsta rap and heavy metal, for example, are not irredeemable, but it is difficult to use them for worship beyond certain groups because of their association with violence, racism, drug use, and suicide. As I see it, this recommendation places a burden of sensitivity on those who advocate innovation. Innovators need to be respectful of those who continue to cling to older styles of liturgy music. The worship awakening has lost goodwill in many sections of the church because of how its advocates talk about other forms of worship. At the same time, it is important to note that this command follows, not precedes, the command that allows all expression except what is explicitly offered to a false god. The primary burden is for the traditionalist to accept innovation; in return, the innovator should be sensitive to the traditionalists and not rub their faces in the freedom to innovate.

Finally, the command to avoid immorality, especially sexual impurity, is self-explanatory. It refers here to personal conduct; it would not be stretching things too far to make it refer to music or art that has been associated with sexual themes. Clearly, it is inappropriate to use a song in worship whose original lyrics were about sex. But the common complaint that rock and roll as a genre is all about sex is only association and groundless. There is nothing inherently sexual about any style of music. According to rock critic Simon Frith, "It is . . . in what we bring to music rather than in what we find in it, that sexual suggestions lie."[12]

God revels in infinite variety and diversity, and blessed creation and the Church with it. We cheapen God's good creation and hold the Creator in contempt when we insist one culture's expression is the only means to offer acceptable and authentic worship to God.

New Song and Our Songs

Worship renewal is a twofold process of handing on tradition and discovering fresh contemporary use. God invites us into that process with a call to sing a new song.

New Song in the Bible

Authentic worship is a fresh response to God's nature and character, and his saving activity. Throughout the Bible, worship is accompanied by music, especially singing. Beholding God leads inevitably to worship and singing. But songs can become stale and lose their freshness over time. At several key passages, God's people are commanded to sing a "new song" to the Lord (Psalm 33:3; 40:3; 96:1; 98:1; 144:9; 149:1; Isaiah 42:10; 66:18; Revelation 5:9; 14:3). In the Old Testament, the command to sing a new song is part of the renewal of the covenant between God and Israel through the appointed festivals and rituals. As the Israelites experienced renewal and new grace from God, they responded with new praise to him.[13] In the book of Revelation, the angels and the saints sing a new song of praise for God's new covenant in Jesus Christ. George Ladd comments that "the new song is for a new redeemed order. New song stands in contrast to the songs sung in worship and adoration of the Creator. The new song is sung to the Lamb as redeemer."[14] The glory of God revealed in the new covenant and new creation evoke new forms of praise from God's people.

By all accounts, the early church was a singing church that enjoyed a variety of musical styles. The Jewish Christians inherited the psalter, and new Gentile believers brought hymns and spiritual songs to Christian worship. Paul highlights this diversity of musical styles in two passages, in Ephesians 5:19–20 ("Speak to one another with psalms, hymns and spiritual songs. Sing and make music in your hearts to the Lord, always giving thanks to God the Father for everything, in the name of the Lord Jesus Christ") and in Colossians 3:19 ("Let the word of Christ dwell in you richly as you teach and admonish one another with all wisdom, and as you sing psalms, hymns and spiritual songs with gratitude in your hearts to God").

The early church sang the old psalms in a new way. As the hymnbook of ancient Judaism, it is not surprising that the psalter became the first hymnbook of the early church. In particular, the first Christians cherished the "messianic psalms," which referred to the coming Christ. Hughes Old observes that "the New Testament writers evidently believed that certain psalms were to be understood as hymns of praise for God's saving work in Christ."[15] Because Psalms 113 to 118 featured prominently in Jewish Passover observance, they soon appeared in Christian Easter celebration. A few centuries later, the royal psalms (Psalms 2, 18, 45, 72, 89, 98, 99, 110, and 132) appeared in the service during the Christmas season because of their emphasis on God's faithfulness to the house of David. Old notes that "even today some of our favorite Christmas carols are based on a Christian interpretation of these 'royal psalms.' 'Hail to the Lord's Anointed' is a paraphrase of Psalm 72 and 'Joy to the World' is a paraphrase of Psalm 98."[16] The psalms helped the first Christians understand Christ; they gave the church ready-made means to praise him.

The early church used the old psalms in a new way, singing them to praise God revealed in Jesus Christ. They also created new psalms. One of these Christian psalms is Romans 11:33–39 ("Oh, the depth of the riches of the wisdom and knowledge of God! How unsearchable his judgments, and his paths beyond tracing out! Who has known the mind of the Lord? Or who has been his counselor? Who has ever given to God, that God should repay him? For from him and through him and to him are all things. To him be the glory forever! Amen"). The "Odes of Solomon" are a collection of Christian psalms that date from the late first or early second century. Larry Hurtado writes that "one feature of this collection is that in several odes it appears that Christ speaks in the first-person form, celebrating his redemptive victory and giving us the unique image of the singing Christ."[17]

Hymns are another genre of music for worship, coming from a different cultural background than the psalms did. Psalms were generally sung to Yahweh, the God of Israel; hymns were generally composed later and are more frequently songs about Yahweh. There are Jewish hymns dating from around the time of Jesus that suggest some segments of Judaism had adopted the genre. Hymns from pagan cultures were generally songs about the gods. Christian hymns differ from their pagan counterparts in content and use. There are fragments of early Christian hymns scattered throughout the New Testament; many of them are found in Paul's letters. Like any good preacher, Paul quotes familiar lyrics to drive home a point, and he may have written some of them himself.

Scholars do not agree on what Paul meant by the term "spiritual songs" (*ode pneumatikon*) in Ephesians 5:19 and Colossians 3:16. Some think Paul meant informal "ditties," or songs of worship based on folk tunes popular at the time, rather like today's praise choruses. Others think the term refers to songs sung while under the direct influence of the Holy Spirit (also known as "singing in the Spirit"). Either way, Paul clearly has in mind a kind of song for worship that is different from both psalms and hymns; all three belong in the church's worship.

Paul's witness to the musical diversity of the early church reveals an emphasis on both scripture and freedom, on tradition and innovation. From the earliest times, Christians have made the scripture, in particular the psalms, the bedrock of worship in song. Not surprisingly, times of worship renewal are marked by renewed appreciation of singing the scriptures as a means of expressing worship to God. The recent outpouring of worship songs that set scripture or scriptural allusions to contemporary folk or popular musical styles is a current example of something the church has done from the very beginning. Equally, Christians have been free to create new songs that continue in the same trajectory of scripture. The early Christian psalms and the psalmlike "Odes of Solomon" are examples of the freedom to move beyond the psalter. Hymns and spiritual songs came from pagan culture, but Christians used them freely to worship Christ. We see this process in the worship awakening as well, as Christians use new genres developed in commercial Western popular culture and in indigenous cultures elsewhere in the world.

New Song Today

These observations about the new song in scripture lead to some conclusions about new song today. First, biblical new song is more concerned with the content of songs than the musical style. Songs in the Bible come to us without music; we know they were set to music, but we don't know how they sounded. This is for the best, given our tendency to absolutize musical styles and relativize theological content. The focus of biblical songs is on God; *who* we praise matters much more than *how* we praise him. The new song reminds us that we sing to glorify God, not to engage in an educational or aesthetic exercise.

Second, biblical new song demonstrates that musical diversity is written into the genetic code of Christian worship. Although certain musical styles have become associated with certain groups over time, there is nothing necessary or inevitable about this association. The organ is not the sole instrument of Christian worship, as some have claimed. The organ did dominate Christian worship in the West for several hundred years, but its role is not thereby established for all time.

Down through the ages, revival and renewal movements have given birth to new songs. In a privately published research paper, Fromm wrote that "throughout history, music has been a primary means of expression for people whose lives have been touched and changed at the deepest levels. Its role in revival is indispensable and in any true spiritual awakening . . . new song will be found."[18] The worship awakening that began in the late 1960s should be seen in the same light. Historian Richard Lovelace views the Jesus movement of the late sixties and early seventies as a significant spiritual awakening in American Christianity.[19] The worship innovations of that movement, and its various spin-offs, deserve to be seen as new song for our time. Fromm feels that "although its form was often modeled on the surrounding pop culture, New Song of the seventies was, by and large, born of a work of the Holy Spirit and nurtured by a young and growing church. The ranks of Christian workers in the creative arts—utilizing the full spectrum of modern communications—evidenced a continued and genuine desire for reformation and renewal."[20] The worship awakening in all its forms is a fresh response to the God whose mercies are new and fresh every day; "because of the LORD's great love we are not consumed, for his compassions never fail. They are new every morning; great is your faithfulness" (Lamentations 3:23).

The newness of songs of praise to the Triune God has as much to do with the renewal of the people who sing them as it does with the date of composition. We are accustomed to thinking of new songs as ones that have never been *heard* before. This may be part of it, but it is also true that songs that no one has ever *sung* before are also new, regardless of when they were written.

In 1996, at a contemporary worship service in southern California, worship leader and songwriter Tommy Walker introduced his arrangement of the hymn "A Mighty Fortress Is Our God" to his young, unchurched congregation.[21] Many had never heard the song before. Walker took a few moments to teach a brief chorus he had written to go with it, and to explain the lyrics. Poking fun at himself, he said, "You can tell I didn't write this; I'd never use the word 'bulwark' in a song." The congregation embraced it enthusiastically.

The venerable hymn was a new song for the twentysomethings in the congregation who had not grown up in church. But it was also a new song musically and visually for me and others familiar with the traditional version. First, Walker's up-tempo arrangement made a warhorse fresh again. Singing a familiar hymn with a new arrangement is, as Fromm says, "like meeting an old friend in new clothes." Second, projecting the lyrics onto a screen made it for me a new song by helping me see the hymn's poetry, something I'd never noticed before when reading it out of a hymnal. Hymnologist Erik Routley once lamented the dismantling of poems in hymnals by observing that "our God is not a God of hyphens." The worship awakening is helping the Church recover an appreciation for the poetry of the all the songs we sing, old and new.

During the 1980s and early 1990s, some wondered if new worship music would completely replace hymnody. This fear has proved unfounded. For one thing, classical hymnody continues to thrive. Such lyricists and composers as Brian Wren, Thomas Troeger, Fred Pratt Green, Ruth Duck, Hal Hopson, and others continue to write new lyrics for existing hymn tunes as well as new hymn tunes in the classical style that are being included in newer hymnals. Worship scholar Michael Hawn observes that these new songs "have a language that connects better with contemporary culture and current human needs."[22] The evangelical church, for the most part, has not embraced these new hymns because of the nontraditional language for God and the strong emphasis on social justice. The general popularity of new hymns such as Daniel Schutte's "Here I Am, Lord" and Graham Kendrick's "Shine, Jesus, Shine" suggests the possibility of fruitful dialogue between contemporary classical hymnwriters and CWM songwriters.

Another reason for optimism about the future of hymns has been the interest in them shown by songwriters and arrangers such as Tommy Walker and Fernando Ortega, who have set texts and tunes and to a variety of popular musical styles. Ritual music—the Lord's Prayer, the Gloria in Excelsis, the Te Deum, and the Apostles Creed—are also being set to contemporary popular and folk styles. Biblical new song reminds us that the dynamic, fluid process of handing on tradition and discovering new expression continues, even in heaven. Katherine Hankey's gospel song "I Love to Tell the Story" puts it this way: "And when in scenes of glory / I sing the new, new song, / 'Twill be the old, old story / that I have loved so long."

10

Sources and Strategies for Worship Innovation

In addition to ignoring important theological issues, another crucial mistake among pastors and church leaders is thinking renewal in worship is simply a practical matter of using different music and multimedia. Contrary to what many of them think, renewal and innovation in worship are not the result of money and talent. The latest gear and talented artists help, but by themselves they do not make the difference. Innovative worship has succeeded with few resources, while churches with money and talent to burn have failed. Where a worship awakening takes root, there is theological consensus about God and worship, and an appropriate plan to implement change. Where experiments fail, there is usually no meaningful consensus and preparation is haphazard.

Embracing Variety

The worship awakening is about variety. A strategy for worship renewal in your church should embrace variety in a way that suits you. The first step is to discover your congregation's worship voices.

In Touch with the Grass Roots

The worship awakening is a grassroots movement, not a top-down program; it is a local church phenomenon, rather than the result of denominational direction or corporate marketing. Individual con-

gregations are being powerfully transformed by worship in a seemingly random fashion, like a Texas thunderstorm that misses my yard
but soaks my neighbor's across the street.

The worship awakening is not the result of slick marketing by
the contemporary worship music industry. For one thing, the free
market is truly free; no one is forced to buy anything producers offer
for sale. For another, the producers generally reflect worship trends
in the church, rather than create them. CWM executives and producers continuously search for new songs that are already being used
in churches. Their workshops and resources demonstrate how worship ministry is done elsewhere; customers come because they are
at least curious or have already made a decision to move in that
liturgical and musical direction.

The worship awakening is not a faucet that can be turned on
and off; nor is it a secret recipe to be discovered and applied. Books,
tapes, and conferences have done their share to give pastors and lay
leaders the impression that worship renewal is just a matter of technique and equipment. Pastors and lay leaders have proved to be a
gullible market for the impression. But technique and equipment
alone do not produce renewal ("Unless the LORD builds the house,
its builders labor in vain"; Psalm 127:1). Without the movement of
God's Spirit, changing the worship service or adding a new service
is simply rearranging the liturgical and musical furniture.

Denominational officials, pastors, and lay leaders cannot make
a worship awakening happen, but they can facilitate or prevent
awakening in their churches. God's Spirit doesn't work in these
matters without invitation and permission. Although churches that
weren't expecting it have experienced a worship awakening, no
church has experienced a worship awakening that didn't want it.
Lay leaders and longtime members are legendary for their resistance
to change, and some of that reputation is deserved. In too many
churches, a petty squabble between individuals and factions over
control has grieved the Spirit of God and thwarted a worship awakening before it could even begin. A suburban West Coast church

with a history of bickering and infighting among its elders went through several pastors and music directors over a period of just a few years. Yet the leadership continues to wonder why members are discouraged, why some are leaving, and why few visitors are joining.

Lay leaders can also stifle worship renewal by constantly criticizing or micromanaging innovation. A church in southern California launched a new-style service in the fall of 1994. Six months later, they stopped it because it hadn't grown. Along the way, they debated extensively about where to place the pulpit and piano, which songs to sing, where the singers should stand, what the bulletin should look like, and whether or not to have drums. As the old saying goes, it's hard for plants to survive if you keep pulling them up to see how the roots are doing.

In other cases, the pastor is the obstacle. Many of them have a top-down view of leadership and can only endorse in their church what they are able to control. One church in the South managed to begin a contemporary-style service over the senior pastor's objections. It didn't last long. This pastor used his control over the budget and staff time to sabotage the service, and it ended within six months.

Until lay leaders and pastors realize that God's Spirit controls renewal in worship, they are likely to resist anything that is out of their control. But when pastors and lay leaders work together with an attitude that welcomes and facilitates the renewing work of God's Spirit, it creates an atmosphere in which a worship awakening can happen.

Cathedrals and Bazaars

Looking back over the recent history of worship innovation, I conclude there have been two suitable environments for developing a new way to think about worship and how to do it. One is a church or organization with the resources to develop innovation—today's cathedrals. The other source of innovation is an informal network in which pastors and church leaders share information and help each other. They are today's bazaars.[1]

The idea of a cathedral for worship innovation is simple: gather and shape talented leaders and hand on the traditions. A cathedral is a center of liturgical and musical excellence. It is a learning environment; a cathedral often sponsors a school where young artists can learn their craft under the watchful eye of experts and the bishop. It is a laboratory where the talented and gifted can try out new things with an appreciative congregation that has a taste for excellence and innovation. But a cathedral is also a controlled environment. Although cautiously encouraged, innovation is carefully monitored; anything new must be scrutinized to ensure fidelity to tradition.

The cathedral model continues to this day in North American Protestantism, in various formats: a large downtown church, a college or music school, a denominational agency. These organizations still share the same vision as the medieval cathedral: to gather and shape talent by handing on certain traditions, as well as by encouraging certain kinds of liturgical innovation that conform to the values of the cathedral. The evangelical megachurches—Willow Creek, Saddleback, Ginghamsburg, and Community Church of Joy, among others—function like a cathedral too. They gather and hire gifted artists and leaders, who then train and lead others. Through conferences, books, and tapes, they are able to extend their philosophy of worship and their techniques to other churches.

The strength of the cathedral is found in its ability to conserve tradition, shape worship leaders with a vision of excellence, and equip them to achieve the vision. Some, like the evangelical megachurches, are occasionally at the forefront of worship innovation; but on the whole the cathedral does not do well at changing and adapting to a changing culture because it prizes tradition so highly. As we have seen, Willow Creek is struggling to come to terms with a changing society and culture and the implications thereof for seeker services. A cathedral may also become elitist by focusing on art for its own sake, losing touch with other churches that value art for its function in worship.

The other source for worship innovation is the bazaar. Throughout the world, people gather at markets and bazaars to buy and sell
things. The bazaar may be a flea market where people exchange
junk or a financial market where people exchange junk bonds. As
a forum for worship innovation, the bazaar is simply a meeting place
where people freely exchange ideas and practices. There is no controlling vision at a bazaar; no one gathers people together, as at a
cathedral. People come on their own, bringing what they have and
hoping someone there might be interested in it too.

The Christian Reformed Church (CRC) embraces a bazaar approach to encouraging worship renewal among its congregations.
Rather than invest resources in a top-down, directive strategy, the
CRC has attempted to network its local churches to help the ones
experiencing renewal rub something off on those that need it. The
two main tools for this task are the journal *Reformed Worship*, edited
by Emily Brink; and the Calvin Institute of Christian Worship
(CICW), directed by John Witvliet and housed at Calvin College
and Seminary, the denomination's flagship educational institutions.
Reformed Worship and CICW embrace the diversity of the worship
awakening. Their articles and events educate and expose pastors,
musicians, lay leaders, and members to the seeker church movement,
the praise and worship style, the Liturgical Renewal movement, global worship music and liturgy, and cultural and social trends. They lift
up the core theological insights of the Reformed tradition, such as
the centrality of the Word of God and the sacraments, the participation of the whole people, and the connection between corporate
and personal worship and everyday life, among others. Yet they
avoid endorsing a particular liturgical and musical style as defini-
tively Reformed. The result has been acceleration of the worship
awakening among CRC congregations.

The bazaar approach is likely to serve churches best in the future because change in culture and society—and thus in worship—
is happening more rapidly than ever before. Until the latter half of
the twentieth century, worship innovation spread slowly, usually as
people moved from one part of the country to another. Denomina-

tions and other publishers produced new hymnals and worship aids only every twenty to thirty years. By the end of the twentieth century, new songs and liturgical ideas traveled more quickly, by person-to-person contact at a conference or workshop, through books and articles, and through instantaneous transfer of information on the Internet. Worship innovation in the bazaar is quicker to adapt available technology than is worship in the cathedral.

Strategies for Embracing Change in Worship

There are two basic ways a church can embrace worship innovation. The first strategy is to add new elements to the existing service (blending). The second is to add a service with a new musical and liturgical style.

Blended Worship

A common approach to the worship awakening among Protestant churches is to create a blended service combining older and newer liturgical elements and musical styles. All Christian worship is blended to one degree or another because it uses some old and some new elements. The real issue is how old and new elements are mixed. For the moment, blended worship refers to an approach to incorporating newer worship music, drama, and multimedia technology within the framework of an established service. But blended worship can also mean working old elements into a new framework.

A blended worship strategy has strengths and weaknesses. On the upside, blended worship can be a creative mix of old and new that vividly demonstrates how traditional Protestant worship can be adapted to its cultural setting, or how contemporary music and liturgy can be done faithfully to a denomination's worship tradition. Jesus commends this approach: "Therefore every teacher of the law who has been instructed about the kingdom of heaven is like the owner of a house who brings out of his storeroom new treasures as well as old" (Matthew 13:52). Further, a service that brings older and newer elements together can be a spiritually enriching experience for the worshiper. People who worship in an effectively blended service report a healthy appreciation for the older elements of worship, particularly hymnody and the sacraments, while also affirming the importance of allowing worship to be accessible to new Christians and seekers.

On the downside, blended worship can be little more than a compromise strategy. In such a case, people attending a service designed with something for everybody usually feel the service has something to *offend* everybody. Not surprisingly, many churches that take this approach to blending still find themselves in conflict over worship, mostly because the core issues of conflict discussed in the previous chapter haven't been adequately addressed. Blended worship does not always bring unity; indeed, it may contribute to deep division in the long run.

The keys to effective blended worship are leadership, preparation, and execution—not the strategy itself. There are three important stages in planning and developing effective blended worship. First, a church that blends worship well adopts the strategy only after a lengthy process of congregational consultation and education. Good blended worship is intentional, not accidental. This point is crucial in my experience of churches considering a change in worship.

Not surprisingly, blended worship works better in a church where there is a high level of spiritual maturity, particularly among lay leaders. By spiritual maturity, I mean a capacity to set aside personal preferences and taste in favor of biblical priorities and the interest of the congregation as a whole. The spiritually immature leader, on the other hand, argues about which style is better, or why tradition should or should not be abandoned. These leaders threaten to withhold money or leave the church if their preferences do not prevail. In other words, worship issues are about them, not about God or the rest of the congregation.

It is easy to see how a blended worship strategy would be doomed to failure in such an environment. If lay leaders cannot discuss worship except in terms of personal preference and taste, it is usually best to consider a new service or postpone any decision about worship innovation until the leaders mature or are replaced.

Change in an existing service almost always evokes criticism from the congregation, and pastors and lay leaders should expect to hear negative comments from many about change as well as see some marginal members leave. Some will offer constructive criticism that can help improve things in the service; the wise leader is publicly thankful for anything that makes the service better. Others grouse about things they don't like or things that are now gone. The wise leader treats such comments graciously and avoids dismissing them as cranky.

The wise leader also understands the grieving process involved in such change. Because people perceive change as loss, members are apt to go through some or all of the well-known stages of grief. With worship, the grief can be deep because many members think of the worship service as a primary source of spiritual identity and faith formation. The longer a person has experienced worship in a certain liturgical and musical style, the more she or he invests the style with an exclusive spiritual meaning and significance. In many cases, pastors and lay leaders find out how strongly people feel about worship only after things have changed. Like a still pool, the real depth of attachment to existing musical and liturgical styles is discovered only when it is disturbed.

This leads to another observation about effective blending: the more established the service, the harder it is to blend. This is not necessarily an age issue. A two-hundred-year-old church might be more flexible when it comes to worship than many churches just twenty years old; but in general, the longer it has been since the church introduced significant change in the service, the harder it is to do it again.

For most established churches, significant change in worship means things like purchasing a new hymnal, an extensive remodeling of the sanctuary, new liturgical elements that involve congregational participation, introducing a new musical style for choral and congregational singing, or the arrival of a new pastor. At one church in the West founded in the 1940s, the order of worship in 1999 is virtually identical to that of services in 1949. Not surprisingly, the lay leaders—most of whom were charter members—were reluctant to consider even the most modest of changes. On the other hand, a new church is not necessarily more flexible and open to change. One church planter told me that lay leaders in his church started to say "we've never done it that way before" after only nine months. Blending may not be a good strategy if a church does not have a positive history of accepting changes in the established service.

The second main principle about effective blending is that the church's worship ministry must lead well in diverse musical and liturgical styles. To make a blended approach work, the pastor must communicate the value of diversity in style. Like many in the congregation, the pastor has strong opinions about liturgy and music. It is difficult to convince a congregation to embrace liturgical and musical variety if the pastor prefers one style in particular. Pastors and church leaders need to consider carefully what they can endorse sincerely and convincingly.

The pastor also has to be comfortable leading in a number of styles. It is one thing to believe in liturgical and musical variety; it's another to be a good leader in several styles. At one large church in the South, the senior pastor avoids preaching in his church's contemporary service because he thinks it is irreverent to appear in any service without a coat and tie. When he does lead the service, he is clearly uncomfortable wearing an open shirt and slacks.

In a blended service, the musicians have to be able to play and sing a number of styles comfortably to lead the congregation well. The pastor or church leader should find out if the musicians are willing and able to facilitate the change in store. Not every church musician leaps at the opportunity to try something new musically, especially a popular style. Many classically trained musicians are defensive about expanding their repertoire to include contemporary musical style, for philosophical and musical reasons; they have strong opinions about popular music that should be respected. Some go further, feeling that popular music is unworthy of the church and beneath them as an artist. They have an over-my-dead-body attitude about playing contemporary worship music and helping to introduce it into the church. Many a church has experienced intense conflict between high-art musicians and the pastor or lay leader who wants to introduce change. In some cases, the musicians go along and feel as though they've compromised themselves. Others quit in frustration or are fired.

On the other hand, it is only fair to point out that pastors and lay leaders often overlook the limits of musical ability when they naïvely assume a trained musician is willing and able to play anything. Most classically trained church musicians have a strong background in theory and performance but not much experience with playing in a band or in pop improvisation. Because their estimation of their own capability is often high, they are reluctant to play something in front of others that they don't understand well and can't play well.

Contemporary worship music is different from traditional church music. Grounded in popular music, CWM features strong rhythm and unaccustomed harmonization. Good pop musicians play by ear as well as following sheet music, and pop bands arrange songs while in rehearsal ("woodshedding"). Musicians who depend on a complete musical score often don't know what to play when handed a piece of music that includes only a melody line and the names of chords. This is not to say they can't or won't learn; many musicians are working hard to play contemporary styles, listening to new music, taking lessons in pop improvisation, and spending time in rehearsal with a band. The pastor or lay leader must recognize and encourage the efforts these musicians are making to serve the church in a way for which their music degree did not prepare them.

Time is another limiting factor. Church musicians are often volunteers or part-time staff who already give all the time they can to the music program. Asking them to learn and teach new musical styles may require more time than they have. Many churches overlook this in hiring and compensating musicians; as a result, the director feels as if he or she is working longer and harder without proper recognition.

On the other side of the stylistic spectrum, many worship leaders with pop music experience do not have much exposure to traditional worship music, especially classic choral and instrumental literature. In a seeker or charismatic church, formal musical skills are generally secondary to the ability to lead congregational singing and a band. The worship leader may not read music and have little, if any, formal musical training.

Where can a church find the kind of talent to lead blended worship? Unfortunately, it doesn't grow on trees. Few musicians are equally comfortable in contemporary and traditional church music styles. The church looking for musicians to lead blended worship is often disappointed to find that the pool of experienced musicians with such breadth is shallow. This may improve in the future as younger musicians are trained in a wider variety of musical styles. Until recently, traditional church music programs—in steady decline since the 1970s—did not expose students to contemporary worship music. Now several Christian colleges offer a more diverse curriculum.[2] As a result, a church looking for crossover musicians may want to take a chance on a young musician straight out of college and allow him or her to grow into greater responsibility.

What's the difference between good and poor approaches to blending liturgical and stylistic elements in a service? Sally Morgenthaler suggests it is simply the difference between placing two things together and fusing them. In the first approach, "worship juxtaposition," styles and elements are placed next to each other without any connection. Symbolically, we can say that juxtaposition is A + B = AB. In the second approach, which Morgenthaler calls "worship fusion," the elements are brought together in such a way that both are mutually transformed and the product of that fusion is a new, third thing. Symbolically, it is A + B = C.

As we saw in previous chapters, African American and Hispanic churches have practiced worship fusion for generations. Ancient folk practices and rituals have been transformed by their understanding of the gospel and biblical worship; at the same time, their culture has transformed elements of the liturgy, such as corporate prayer and the Lord's Supper. They have also transformed classic hymns by altering the harmony and rhythm, and by translating into Spanish.

Lutheran worship leader Handt Hanson has a similar approach in mind when he advocates planning worship from the "radical middle." "I stand squarely in the middle," he says, "not Milquetoast in the middle, but radically in the middle . . . where we can learn to speak each other's language and enter into ongoing dialogue."[3] Hanson's notion of a radical and dynamic middle is a helpful way of thinking about blending worship service because it suggests that planning and leading worship is a process, not a product. To many pastors and church leaders, blended worship is a product to be sought ("If we can achieve the right blend, everyone will be happy"). Unfortunately, many churches find out too late that there is no magic formula or secret recipe that works every time. Planning and leading worship is an ongoing process of experimentation, trial and error, success and failure, learning and adjusting. For Hanson, the question is not whether to sing traditional hymns or contemporary songs. Rather, it is how they are being sung: "The question is less of, 'Which song shall we sing?' and more of, 'Is it a good song?' The criteria for planning a worship service should have less to do with style and more to do with whether or not the worship experience engages people."[4]

Morgenthaler helpfully points out that there are at least four ways to think of how to combine old and new elements in a service.[5] The first two approaches, limited repackaging and extensive repackaging, blend forward and amount to incorporating new elements in an existing service structure.[6] Limited repackaging often entails just one or two new elements and a little contemporary worship music or other contemporary element. For example, a church

replaces the opening hymn with two or three contemporary worship songs accompanied by a piano, and a brief drama might be
added before the sermon, which is delivered from the pulpit. But
the rest of the service remains intact.

Extensive repackaging takes the process further. A church adopting this approach uses a band to accompany all the congregational
singing, which is a mix of hymns and contemporary worship music.
Song lyrics as well as other liturgical texts are projected on a screen
(large-print bulletins are available for the visually impaired), and
video clips and PowerPoint graphics are used throughout the message, which is delivered away from the pulpit. An extreme form of
repackaging is the "rave mass," in which the traditional Anglican
Eucharistic liturgy is retained but multimedia is used and dance
music plays continuously throughout the service.[7] Both forms of
repackaging, however, maintain the traditional structure of the service in a way that is easy to recognize.

The second approach, to blend backward, reverses the process
of blending. Rather than work from the established order of service,
a backward blend develops a new order of service and then adds
older elements and music to it. A modest backward blend is a seeker
service or charismatic praise and worship service using little traditional liturgical language or music and few such symbols. There are
signs that a more extensive backward blend is catching on among
some of those churches.[8] Many now feature at least one hymn per
service and are experimenting with ancient prayers, litanies, an-
tiphonal and unison scripture readings, and creeds. At a seeker-
oriented church in western Michigan, for example, the band plays a
hymn each Sunday. In that heavily Dutch Reformed area, hymns
are familiar to many unchurched people. Churches with a praise
and worship focus in the service are also intentionally incorporating traditional elements into it. In *Blended Worship: Achieving Substance and Relevance in Worship*, Robert Webber offers some interesting
examples of what he calls convergence among charismatic and conservative evangelical churches that are adapting historic, traditional
worship elements and music in their services.[9]

Morgenthaler's categories of blending are a useful reminder that there is no one right way of blending. There is no secret recipe or magic formula that produces authentic worship in every church. One-size-fits-all thinking is perhaps the greatest barrier a church must overcome in experiencing a worship awakening because it views a blended service as a product instead of a process.

Starting a New Service

Although some churches experiment with new liturgical and musical styles in an existing service, others add a new-style service to their schedule. This strategy avoids the problems that emerge when the church replaces a service with something new, but it also has challenges of its own. For most churches, a new-style service nearly always features popular music styles and multimedia communication, though a few churches have added new services that are more liturgical—such as a Taizé-style service—with some success.

Multiple services have been a part of the church landscape for a long time. Presbyterian churches, for example, historically offered different Sunday morning and evening services, though the practice declined after World War II. Offering two or more identical services on Sunday morning seems to be a development of the early twentieth century. Many urban Roman Catholic parishes offered several masses, including one on Saturday evening, to handle their growing congregations. Large downtown Protestant churches that featured "pulpit princes" also found it necessary to offer more than one service to accommodate the crowds. After World War II, rapidly growing suburban churches also adopted the multiple service strategy. Until the mid-1980s, however, these additional services were usually identical to the so-called main service at eleven o'clock. They were, in effect, overflow services, intended to allow a church to serve a membership that exceeded the sanctuary's seating capacity.

Whatever liturgical and musical styles are under consideration, there are three main reasons for adding a new service.

Honoring God in New Ways

The first reason for adding a new service is to honor God. Our primary motivation for a service should be worshiping God, before anything else. We have seen already how some seeker service advocates create confusion by allowing another priority for a service besides the worship of God. A hard but useful question for church leaders to ask of their existing services is this: how do our services prevent people from focusing on God? Are we too focused on our liturgy, or our music, or our preaching styles? Does our commitment to our worship traditions deflect us from honoring God? It may well be that in many cases, a church needs a new service to allow people to worship without the baggage of inherited traditions and customs. While with Maranatha! Music, I accompanied the Praise Band to a large church in the midwest where we had been asked to lead worship for their first ever Saturday evening contemporary service. I was nervous, because the church was an established congregation widely known for its traditional Sunday morning service and excellent choral music program. My nervousness grew as the sanctuary filled with many older people. As the team members prepared to begin the service, I told them to hope for the best, but to prepare for the worst; this might be a tough crowd to win over to a new way of worship. I was completely wrong. The congregation embraced the new style of worship enthusiastically. After the service, several older women came to me to thank us for coming to their church. "We've been praying for this for years," one told me. I didn't realize that there was a widespread desire in that church for a worship awakening that had finally been allowed to surface. A new service may be the way a church is able to renew its focus on God.

Using New Gifts

Another reason for starting a new-style service is to create a context for the gifts and talents God has given to the congregation that are not being used, or are underused, in existing services.

The first group of underused gifts are musical ones. Americans are amateur musicians. The decline in music education in public schools has not limited music making. Instrument sales remain steady, and sales of pop music instruments (acoustic and electric guitars, drums, and electronic keyboards) continue to grow. Yet musicians without formal musical education are often unable to sing and play in traditional church music programs that require the ability to read music and a knowledge of music theory. Despite the popularity of music making, church leaders frequently wonder if there will be people to play and sing in their new services. Most churches have far more musical and artistic talent than they realize. Musicians and artists are waiting to see a need they can fill.

Drama is another area of underused gifts. Although drama was developed in churches in the middle ages, new attempts to include drama in worship have received mixed reviews in traditional services; in some places it is well received, in others there is a negative response. Drama thrives, however, in seeker churches and in many praise-and-worship-oriented churches that appreciate those with gifts and skills in writing, directing, acting, and technical areas.

Visual artists constitute another group that goes underused in many churches. Interestingly, our culture is experiencing a renaissance of interest in the visual arts. In many cities, tickets to traveling exhibitions of masters such as van Gogh sell out immediately. The Liturgical Renewal movement has helped some churches make use of some arts, such as banners and other crafts. Contemporary churches such as Coast Hills Community Church in Aliso Viejo, California, and the Warehouse Fellowship in Sacramento encourage visual artists to participate in the worship ministry. At Coast Hills, worship pastor Monty Kelso supervises two staff members who direct teams of amateur and professional painters, sculptors, and scenic and graphic designers who contribute artwork that decorates the church building and is also used in worship services as illustration and illumination of the pastors' messages.[10]

Finally, new-style services use the gifts of those with expertise in multimedia technology. As digital video technology becomes less expensive and easier to use, creative members are looking for a way to use it for the benefit of the worshiping community. A new style service gives a church a fresh setting in which to employ these gifts in worship creatively. Not surprisingly, people with such gifts gravitate to a church that values them.

In my estimation, established Protestant worship services are usually not flexible enough to accommodate all the gifts God gives a congregation, particularly in our era of artistic and stylistic diversity. This is true even in a smaller church. Pastors and worship leaders who try too much innovation in existing services are likely to frustrate those who prefer the familiar and are uncomfortable with anything new. The process is also likely to frustrate those who try to fit their gifts into an unreceptive and unappreciative environment.

The crisis that faces most churches now is not a lack of resources but rather the failure of imagination to use the resources God has already given. As important as financial and human resources are, money and talent are not as vital for the success of a new-style service as some might think. More often than not, in my experience, it is poor leadership that leads to failure, not a lack of cash and star power. A church with plenty of money and talent may watch a new service fail, while a smaller church without deep pockets or a pool of talent succeeds. The real key to success is leadership, not talent and resources. What makes the difference is not what a church has, but what it does with what it has. To be sure, the long-term prospects for effectiveness and growth are better in a service that has both leadership and adequate resources, but resources alone seldom spell the difference between a successful new service and a failing one.

Reaching New People

Blending new elements in an existing service can only accomplish so much, and generally appeals more to those who already attend than it does to newcomers. Methodist pastor and worship leader Andy Langford notes that "the single most effective way for established congregations to reach new audiences and especially the newer generations is to begin a distinctly second or third worship service. Starting a new service will serve significantly more people than simply reforming or adding new elements to an already established Sunday service."[11] Studies indicate that a church adding a service is more likely to grow than one just changing the order of service. In fact, according to research conducted by Charles Arn, among churches that add a new service, 80 percent experience growth *in both services*.[12] Arn goes on to present a compelling case for adding a new worship service, listing six reasons most churches should consider doing so.[13]

First, adding a new service is the most effective way to reach unchurched people. Confirming Langford's assertion, Arn notes that "a new service will focus your church's attention on the unchurched."[14] A new service is like a new church, where the outward focus and enthusiasm is greater than in an established church. Additionally, a new service allows a church to repackage the message: "Starting a new service allows you to shed cultural or sociological forms that may be keeping you from effectively reaching a new group of people."[15] Finally, new service give a member an opportunity to invite a friend. Research indicates that the overwhelming majority of visitors come to churches because someone invited them. Yet most mainline church members do not invite friends and neighbors. A recent survey conducted by the PCUSA reveals that the average Presbyterian invites someone to church once every 11.5 years.

Second, a new offering serves more people. Kennon Callahan observes that "the more options you offer, the more people you will help."[16] Even with identical services, worshipers have a choice of which service to attend. Not surprisingly, as leisure time has become more important to many families and retired people, alternative times for service are attractive to many, particularly in the recreation-oriented Western states. As Arn puts it, "when the decision is no longer 'take it or leave it,' but 'when,' 'what,' 'how,' or 'where,' you greatly increase people's choices. And the more choices you provide for a worship service, the more people will say yes to one of them."[17]

Third, a new service reaches new kinds of people. Most services have a core homogeneous group, whether church leaders know it or not. An existing service made up of one group is not likely to be effective with other groups, despite attempts to improve it. Arn writes: "A mistake some churches make in an effort to broaden the generational or spiritual range of people attracted to their existing service(s) is to diversify the music or liturgical style. In so doing, however, most churches actually diminish their effectiveness of their present service(s) among every people group, including their predominant one."[18]

Fourth, a new service breaks the normal life cycle of a church. Like any organization, a church goes through a life cycle of growth, plateau, and decline, which runs for about forty to fifty years without intervention. Arn's research suggests that adding a new service counts as an intervention and can continue a growth phase or bring a church off a plateau.[19]

Fifth, a new service allows change while retaining the familiar. Arn believes it is better to grow through addition than replacement: "Through adding a new service without deleting your existing one, you double your outreach and ministry potential while allowing those members who prefer the present service to continue receiving their spiritual nourishment."[20]

Finally, a new service brings back inactive members. This is perhaps the most interesting result of Arn's research. In churches that add a new service, member attendance increases from just over 40 percent to 60 percent or more. Arn thinks that "once a formerly active member stops attending church for longer than six months, it generally becomes too uncomfortable and too embarrassing for that person to return. A new service, however, provides a perfect excuse for many inactive members to give that church a second chance. When sensitively invited, 15 to 20 percent of resident inactive members can be expected to try your new service."[21]

Arn and others agree that a new service increases the range of options people have. Yet this is unlikely to help people unless the choices are conveniently scheduled. Until recently, churches that added a new service on Sunday morning faced tricky scheduling problems as they attempted to accommodate nursery and Sunday school along with the new service. But something new and considerably different happened when, beginning in the mid-1980s, mainline and evangelical Protestant churches started following the example of Willow Creek, Saddleback, and other innovative churches in offering Saturday night services. Roman Catholic parishes have offered a Saturday evening mass for decades, but this is a new venture for Protestants. Sunday evening is also a good time for a new service. University Presbyterian Church in Seattle offers two contemporary services on Sunday evening. Still other churches are experimenting with midweek services. The Next Level Church in Denver, for example, offers worship service on Tuesday evening and has nothing scheduled on Sunday morning. According to Worship Pastor John Miller, some of the members participate in small groups or attend other churches.

The location of a service is another choice that a church may be willing to give the attendees. Some churches now hold new-style services in another setting at the same time as a traditional service. Holding service for youths and young adults in a gym or youth room is common. Services may be held offsite in a coffeehouse, social hall, or public school facility. Perimeter Church in Atlanta holds service in numerous satellite locations throughout the area. A local worship team leads music and prayers, and a TV feed connects each site to the main church for the sermon by the pastor. A church with limited capacity or with unhelpful architecture may find that a new location presents new options for worship.

A new service in another language is often the best way to reach and include an ethnic group, particularly in an area where there is a large first-generation immigrant community. In southern California, one of the most ethnically diverse areas on the planet, it is common for a church to host several smaller ethnic congregations. In some of these churches, the service is part of the outreach of the church, while in others an independent congregation simply rents space from the host congregation. Churches that have worked to develop partnership among the groups meeting in the same building find the process difficult, yet rewarding.

Problems with Multiple-Style Strategy

There are several potential dangers for a church developing a multiple-style strategy. The first danger area is dividing the congregation. Marva Dawn, among others, urges pastors not to consider multiple styles because of the danger of disunity: "It seems unwise to me to create two different Sunday worship services utilizing two different styles of music because almost always that splits the congregation into two camps. Moreover, the split between 'traditional' and 'contemporary' usually divides the parish along age lines, and consequently younger and newer believers lose the opportunity to gain from the faith experience and maturity of older members. Such a split allows a congregation to escape talking about worship and types of music and precludes genuine communal conversation about the weaknesses and strengths of various styles."[22]

Although the danger of division is real in a church that has different styles of service, the split Dawn fears is not unavoidable. At Forest Hills Presbyterian Church, where I serve, our two contrasting-style services are coordinated to have a common theme reinforced by the scripture readings and sermon, a common prayer focus, and common music. There are usually at least two songs in common, a contemporary worship song and a hymn. As the worship leader, Darrin Newhardt, puts it, "We contemporarize a hymn in the contemporary service, and we traditionalize a chorus in the traditional service." In addition, the elders of the church are careful to communicate that one service is neither better nor more valuable than the other. They view both as necessary to achieving the full voice in worship God wants the church to have, and other new services may be added in the future.

Another danger area for multiple-style strategy is imbalance in commitment and inconsistency. Callahan observes that "some congregations think they offer two services of worship. In fact they offer one strong, excellent service of worship, usually at eleven o' clock on Sunday morning. They also offer what they call an early service; in reality it's more like a warm-up practice for the 'real' service at eleven o' clock."[23] In many churches, the early service began in the 1950s as an overflow or convenience service. But deterioration set in over time. In some churches, only part of the choir participates, or a less able organist accompanies, or an associate pastor presides in place of the senior pastor. In such a case, a conspiracy of neglected details converges to proclaim the church's real attitude: "This service isn't the real deal." Callahan comments that "this parochial perspective results in an early worship service that is less than a full service."[24] Pastors, musicians, and lay leaders should give full attention and faithful direction to all services, not just the favored time slots.

A similar problem is found in a church with different services; in many cases, commitment to a new-style service is not on a par with commitment to the existing service. The quality of liturgical leadership and musical presentation is much lower. The reason for this is not hard to detect. Many churches begin new-style service assuming that it requires less commitment than existing ones. Some churches have started a contemporary service believing it would not cost them anything! Not surprisingly, the service struggles to achieve even a respectable level of quality and stops after a few months. To match the quality level of an existing traditional service, a contemporary service generally requires more commitment in finances, people, planning, and preparation. Pastors and lay leadership need to count the cost before building their new service, as well as establish equity among services.

Leadership is included in the need for balance and consistency among services. In some established churches, senior pastors have been reluctant to become involved in a new-style service, either because they don't care for it or they don't want to offend tradition-minded members. This has led to an unhealthy situation in which an associate pastor preaches mostly at the contemporary service, while the senior pastor is rarely seen outside the traditional service. This leadership strategy sends a clear message to the congregation that the new service is a second-rate worship offering unworthy of the senior pastor's time. In one large midwestern church, the contemporary service split from the church to form a new congregation, led by the associate pastor who preached at it weekly. By the same token, a church offering different services in which the preacher of the day is present at all services is likely to report few problems with congregational unity. The church should reconsider a new-style service if the senior pastor is reluctant or unwilling to preach for it.

Now that we've come to the end of the journey, what do we know? We know the territory of the worship awakening is better mapped than ever before; it is no longer terra incognita. We know that the worship awakening is marked by variety rather than uniformity. There is no one direction for all churches; pastors and worship leaders must chart the course for their own congregation.

Finally, we know that leading a church to embrace a worship awakening is not easy or risk-free. There's no magic formula to determine which liturgical and musical styles work best in your church. There are no guarantees that blending your existing service or starting a new service will work as expected; failure is always a possibility, even in the best of circumstances. Fear of failure has led some churches to put off worship innovation; they have counted the cost and decided to wait for things to change before altering their worship (new pastor, more new members). There are no recipes for success, but now we know what makes the process smoother. If you've already embarked, I hope you've learned what you need to know to stay the course. If you're planning to set sail soon, I hope you've learned what you need to launch well and get under way. May the refreshing breeze of God's Spirit be at your back as you discover new ways to worship him.

The Author

Robb Redman is currently pastor of Forest Hills Presbyterian Church in Helotes, Texas, a suburb of San Antonio. He holds advanced degrees from New College, University of Edinburgh, Scotland, and the University of Erlangen, Germany. From 1991 to 1997, he taught at Fuller Theological Seminary and directed the Doctor of Ministry program.

Redman has taught worship and ministry at several seminaries, speaks regularly at conferences and workshops, and works as a consultant for congregations and church groups. He is a frequent contributor to *Worship Leader* magazine and other journals and Websites. He and his wife, Pam, a middle school choir director and children's worship leader, live in San Antonio, Texas.

Notes

Introduction

1. Trueheart, C. "The Next Church." *Atlantic Monthly*, Aug. 1996, 278(2), pp. 37ff.

2. Miller, C. *Postmoderns: The Beliefs, Hopes and Fears of Young Americans*. Nashville: Discipleship Resources, 1996, p. 19.

3. For an overview of some of these streams, see Basden, P. *The Worship Maze: Finding a Style to Fit Your Church*. Downers Grove, Ill.: IVP, 1999; Towns, E. *Putting an End to Worship Wars*. Nashville: Broadman and Holman, 1997. From the perspective of different traditions of spirituality, see Foster, R. *Streams of Living Water: Celebrating the Great Traditions of Christian Faith*. San Francisco: Harper San Francisco, 1998.

Chapter One

1. For a description and analysis of the seeker church movement, see Sargeant, K. *Seeker Churches: Promoting Traditional Religion in a Nontraditional Way*. New Brunswick, N.J.: Rutgers University Press, 2000; Pritchard, G. *Willow Creek Seeker Services: Evaluating a New Way of Doing Church*. Grand Rapids, Mich.: Baker, 1996, pp. 54–76.

2. White, J. F. *Protestant Worship: Traditions in Transition*. Louisville: W/JKP, 1989. White's term *frontier worship* can be misleading. Revival worship began in frontier camp meetings, but the style was quickly adopted by urban (and later suburban) churches nearly everywhere.

3. Schmidt, L. E. *Holy Fairs: Scottish Communions and American Revivals in the Early Modern Period.* Princeton, N.J.: Princeton University Press, 1989.

4. Ruth, L. *A Little Heaven Below: Worship at Early Methodist Quarterly Meetings.* Nashville: Kingswood, 2000, p. 22.

5. Ruth (2000).

6. Ruth (2000).

7. White (1989), p. 176.

8. Quoted in White (1989), p. 177.

9. Some argue that this perspective is present in each of the major Protestant traditions to some degree. David Luecke, for example, argues that the Lutheran understanding of the "adiaphora" (things indifferent) and key passages in Lutheran confessional documents suggest its liturgical tradition is more flexible than many Lutherans in Finney's day were willing to admit. Luecke, D. *The Other Story of Lutherans at Worship.* Phoenix: Fellowship Ministries, 1995.

10. Hatch, N. *The Democratization of American Religion.* New Haven: Yale University Press, 1989, p. 197.

11. See Blumhofer, E. *Aimee Semple McPherson: Everybody's Sister.* Grand Rapids, Mich.: Eerdmans, 1993; Epstein, D. *Sister Aimee: The Life of Aimee Semple McPherson.* Orlando: Harcourt Brace, 1993.

12. Miller, K. "How Schuller Shaped Your Ministry." *Leadership,* 1997, 18(2), 114–118.

13. McGavran, D. *Understanding Church Growth.* (3rd ed.) Grand Rapids, Mich.: Eerdmans, 1990, p. 163. See also McGavran, D. *Bridges of God.* New York: Friendship Press, 1955.

14. Callahan, K. *Dynamic Worship: Mission, Grace, Praise, and Power.* San Francisco: HarperCollins, 1994, p. 3. See also Keifert, P. *Welcoming the Stranger: A Public Theology of Hospitality.* Minneapolis: Fortress, 1992; White, J. E. *Opening the Front Door: Worship and Church Growth.* Nashville: Convention Press, 1992.

15. Pritchard (1996), p. 189.

16. Wenz, R. *Room for God? A Worship Challenge for a Church-Growth and Marketing Era.* Grand Rapids, Mich.: Baker, 1994, p. 21.

17. Pritchard (1996), p. 193.

18. Pritchard (1996), p. 200.

19. Pritchard (1996), p. 242.

20. Dawn, M. *Reaching Out Without Dumbing Down: A Theology of Worship for the Turn-of-the-Century Culture*. Grand Rapids, Mich.: Eerdmans, 1995, p. 192. Although she does not mention it, the practice of changing services to accommodate the preferences of attendees did not begin with the seeker service movement. Episcopalian churches have long offered the Service of Morning Prayer as an option to the usual "full" eucharistic service. Other Episcopal and Lutheran churches offer an abbreviated eucharistic service (humorously known as "liturgy lite") with little or no singing, fewer prayers, and a shorter homily.

21. Pritchard (1996), p. 247.

22. Morgenthaler, S. *Worship Evangelism*. Grand Rapids, Mich.: Zondervan, 1995, p. 44.

23. Morgenthaler (1995), p. 45.

24. See, for example, Dobson, E. *How to Start a Seeker Service*. Grand Rapids, Mich.: Zondervan, 1993.

25. See Morgenthaler (1995); Dawn (1995); and Kiefert (1992). See also Olson, M. *How Does Worship Evangelize?* Minneapolis: Augsburg Fortress, 1995; Schattauer, T. (ed.). *Inside Out: Worship in an Age of Mission*. Minneapolis: Fortress, 1999. Two books from the mid-1980s have also had an impact: Webber, R. *Celebrating Our Faith: Evangelism Through Worship*. San Francisco: Harper, 1986; and Armstrong, R. *The Pastor-Evangelist in Worship*. Philadelphia: Westminster Press, 1986.

26. E-mail to author from Curt Coffield, Feb. 12, 2001.

Chapter Two

1. White (1989).

2. White (1989), p. 158.

3. White (1989), p. 160.

4. For more information on the roots of Pentecostalism in early

Methodism, see Dayton, D. W. *The Theological Roots of Pentecostal-ism.* Grand Rapids, Mich.: Zondervan, 1987.

5. Estep, B. "A Holiness Model of Worship." In R. Webber (ed.), *The Complete Library of Christian Worship.* Vol. 2: *Twenty Centuries of Christian Worship.* Nashville: Abbott-Martyn, 1994.

6. On the holiness understanding of baptism of the Holy Spirit, see Lederle, H. *Treasures Old and New: Interpretations of "Spirit-Baptism" in the Charismatic Renewal Movement.* Peabody, Mass.: Hendrickson, 1988.

7. Dayton (1987), p. 170.

8. Costen, M. "An African-American Model of Worship." In Webber (1994), p. 249.

9. Costen, M. "African-American Worship." In Webber (1994).

10. White, J. F. (1989), p. 196.

11. Cox, H. *Fire from Heaven: The Rise of Pentecostal Spirituality and the Reshaping of Religion in the Twenty-First Century.* Reading, Mass.: Addison-Wesley, 1995.

12. Blumhofer, E. "The Holiness-Pentecostal Movement." In Webber (1994), p. 106. See also Synan, V. *The Holiness-Pentecostal Tradition: Charismatic Movements in the 20th Century.* Grand Rapids. Mich.: Eerdmans, 1991.

13. Fromm, C. E. "New Song: The Sound of Spiritual Awakening." Privately published, 1983, p. 13.

14. Blumhofer (1994), p. 107.

15. Hamon, B. *The Eternal Church.* Point Washington, Fla.: Christian International, 1981, p. 257.

16. Alford, D. L. "Worship." In S. M. Burgess and G. M. McGee (eds.), *The Dictionary of Pentecostal and Charismatic Movements.* Grand Rapids, Mich.: Eerdmans, 1988, p. 693.

17. Cox (1995), p. 278.

18. For more on the charismatic understanding of Spirit-baptism, see Lederle (1988); and Bruner, F. D. *A Theology of the Holy Spirit: The*

Pentecostal Experience and the New Testament Witness. Grand Rapids, Mich.: Eerdmans, 1970.

19. Wagner, C. P. *The Third Wave of the Holy Spirit.* Ann Arbor: Servant, 1988; Wagner, C. P. *The New Apostolic Churches.* Ventura, Calif.: Regal/Gospel Light, 1998.

20. Miller, D. *Reinventing American Protestantism.* Berkeley: University of California Press, 1997.

21. Liesch, B. *The New Worship: Straight Talk on Music and the Church.* Grand Rapids, Mich.: Baker, 1996.

22. This approach is taught regularly at Vineyard worship conferences and is summarized here by Liesch (1996).

23. Liesch (1996).

24. See Cornwall, J. *Let Us Worship.* South Plainfield, N.J.: Bridge, 1983; and Sorge, B. *Exploring Worship.* (2nd ed.) St. Louis: Oasis House, 2001. A useful summary can be found in Liesch (1996).

25. Liesch (1996), p. 66.

26. Sorge (2001).

27. Sorge (2001), p. 68.

28. Sorge (2001), p. 68.

29. Sorge (2001), p. 69.

30. Sorge (2001), pp. 69–70.

31. Sorge (2001), p. 71.

32. Sorge (2001), p. 71.

33. See Anderson, R. S. *Ministry on the Fireline.* Downers Grove, Ill.: IVP, 1993.

34. See Hoge, D., and Roozen, D. (eds.). *Understanding Church Growth and Decline, 1950–1978.* New York: Pilgrim Press, 1979; Kelley, D. M. *Why Conservative Churches Are Growing.* (2nd ed.) New York: HarperCollins, 1977; Gibbs, E. *In Name Only: Tackling the Problem of Nominal Christianity.* Ann Arbor: Servant, 1994.

35. See Howard, T. *Evangelical Is Not Enough.* New York: Ignatius,

1988. Such popular evangelical writers as Richard Foster, Dallas Willard, and Henry Blackaby, among others, also point to a need to balance an intellectual understanding of faith with affective (emotion) and volitional (will) dimensions. See Foster, R. *Streams of Living Water*. San Francisco: Harper, 1999; Willard, D. *The Spirit of the Disciplines*. San Francisco: Harper, 1988; Blackaby, H., and King, C. V. *Experiencing God: How to Live the Full Adventure of Knowing and Doing the Will of God*. Nashville: LifeWay, 1990.

36. Sorge, S. "The Surging Spirit and Reformed Worship: Liturgical Implications for Pentecostal-Presbyterian Dialogue." Paper presented to the Office of Theology and Worship Pastor/Theologian Consultation, San Antonio, Feb. 28–Mar. 1, 2000, p. 6.

37. Sorge (2000), p. 6.

38. McLean, T. B. *New Harmonies: Choosing Contemporary Music for Worship*. Washington, D.C.: Alban Institute, 1999, p. 13.

39. McLean (1999).

40. Cladis, G. *Leading the Team-Based Church*. San Francisco: Jossey-Bass, 1999, p. ix.

Chapter Three

1. See Best, H. *Music Through the Eyes of Faith*. San Francisco: Harper, 1991; and Corbitt, N. *The Sound of the Harvest: Music's Mission in the Church and the World*. Grand Rapids, Mich.: Baker, 1998.

2. Simmons, M. "Hymnody: Its Place in Twentieth Century Presbyterianism." In M. Coalter, J. Mulder, and L. Weeks (eds.), *The Confessional Mosaic: Presbyterians and Twentieth Century Theology*. Louisville: Westminster/John Knox Press, 1990.

3. *Renew!* Carol Stream, Ill.: Hope, 1999. Other recent hymnals with some CWM are *The Baptist Hymnal*. Philadelphia: Judson Press, 1991; *Sing to the Lord*. Kansas City, Mo.: Lillenas, 1993; *Songs of Faith*. West Monroe, La.: Howard, 1997; and *Worship and Rejoice*. Carol Stream, Ill.: Hope, 2001.

4. Moore, R. L. *Selling God: American Religion in the Marketplace of Culture*. New York: Oxford University Press, 1994, p. 185.

5. Hustad, D. *Jubilate II: Church Music in Worship and Renewal*. Carol Stream, Ill.: Hope, 1993, p. 253.

6. Hustad (1993), p. 252.

7. Fromm (1983).

8. Yohan Anderson's nearly ubiquitous collection, entitled simply *Songs*, has gone through several editions and is still popular with youth and lay spiritual renewal groups. It is an eclectic mix of Sunday School songs, choruses, Roman Catholic folk mass tunes, sacred and secular folk songs, camp songs, and some better known CWM. Anderson, Y. *Songs*. San Anselmo, Calif.: Songs and Creations, Inc., 1997. In a similar vein, see Salsbury, S. *The Freeze Dried Song Book*. (3rd ed.) Privately published, 2001.

9. See Stedman, R. *Body Life*. Ventura, Calif.: Regal, 1972. For the history of the Calvary Chapel movement, see Ellwood, R. *The Sixties Spiritual Awakening*. Rutgers University Press, 1992; D. Miller (1997); and McIntosh, M., and Ries, R. "The History and Philosophy of the Calvary Chapel Movement." D.Min. dissertation, Fuller Theological Seminary, 1992.

10. Rock and folk were indistinguishably intertwined in the early years of CWM. Many sixties rockers, including a number of early Christian rock artists, started off in folk circles.

11. Myers, K. *All God's Children and Blue Suede Shoes*. Westchester, Mass.: Crossway, 1989, p. 155.

12. D. Miller (1997), p. 184.

13. Frame, J. *Contemporary Worship Music: A Biblical Defense*. Phillipsburg, N.J.: Presbyterian and Reformed, 1997.

14. Fromm (1983), p. 20.

15. Smemby, M. "The Praise and Worship Music Industry." *Worship Leader*, Sept.–Oct. 1999, p. 20.

16. Redman, R. "The Sound of Enthusiasm: How Generation X is Reshaping Contemporary Worship." *Worship Leader*, Oct. 2001, pp. 27–29. See also DiSabatino, D. "Making a Joyful Noise Around the World." *Worship Leader*, Nov. 2002, pp. 21–22; and Redman, M.

The Unquenchable Worshipper: Coming Back to the Heart of Worship.
Ventura, Calif.: Regal, 2002.

17. Riddle, M. "O for a Thousand Tongues." CCM magazine, Mar. 1998.

18. Peacock, C. *At the Crossroads.* Nashville: Broadman and Holman, 1999, p. 5.

19. Pine, J., and Gilmore, J. *The Experience Economy.* Cambridge, Mass.: Harvard Business Press, 1999, p. 11.

20. *Global Praise 1* (1996), *Global Praise 2* (2000), *Russian Praise* (1999), and *Caribbean Praise* (2000), as well as the *African Praise Songbook* (New York: General Board of Missions, 1998).

21. Langford, A. (ed.). *The Abingdon/Cokesbury Chorus Book I.* Nashville: Abingdon, 1996; *The Faith We Sing.* Nashville: Abingdon, 2000.

22. White, L. (ed.). *Lift Up Your Hearts: Songs for Creative Worship.* Louisville, Ky.: Geneva Press, 1999.

23. *With One Voice.* Minneapolis: Augsburg Fortress, 1995; *Worship and Praise Songbook.* Minneapolis: Augsburg Fortress, 1999.

24. *Sing! A New Creation.* Grand Rapids, Mich.: CRC Publications, 2001. See Redman, R. "Songs from Praise and Worship Sources" in E. Brink (ed.), *Sing! A New Creation: Leader's Edition.* Grand Rapids, Mich.: CRC Publications, 2002.

25. Collins, D. E., and Weidler, S. C. *Sound Decisions: Evaluating Contemporary Music for Lutheran Worship.* Minneapolis: Evangelical Lutheran Church in America and Augsburg Fortress, 1997; McLean, T. B. *New Harmonies: Choosing Contemporary Music for Worship.* Washington, D.C.: Alban Institute, 1999.

26. Johansson, C. *Music and Ministry: A Biblical Counterpoint.* Peabody, Mass.: Hendrickson, 1984, p. 48.

27. Rowland, R. "Stuck in a Musical Ghetto." *Worship Leader,* Sept.–Oct. 1999, p. 12.

28. Anderson, R. *Minding God's Business.* Grand Rapids, Mich.: Eerdmans, 1986.

Chapter Four

1. Fenwick, J., and Spinks, B. *Worship in Transition: The Liturgical Movement in the Twentieth Century.* New York: Continuum, 1995.

2. Fenwick and Spinks (1995), p. 25. On the relationship between personal and corporate prayer, see Bradshaw, P. *Two Ways of Praying.* Nashville: Abingdon, 1995.

3. Fenwick and Spinks (1995), p. 64.

4. Martinez, G. "The Impact of The Constitution on the Sacred Liturgy." In Webber (1994). See also Fenwick and Spinks (1995), pp. 61–70.

5. Fenwick and Spinks (1995), pp. 66–68. In 1975, the Congregation became the Congregation for Divine Worship and the Discipline of the Sacraments, as it is known today.

6. Martinez (1994). Roman Catholic theologian Anscar Chupungco is a leading advocate of this concept. See Witvliet, J. "Theological and Conceptual Models for Liturgy and Culture." *Liturgy Digest,* 1996, 3(2), 5–46.

7. Martinez (1994), p. 108.

8. Martinez (1994), p. 110.

9. Fenwick and Spinks (1995), pp. 115–116.

10. *Baptism, Eucharist, and Ministry.* Geneva: WCC Press, 1982.

11. Newman, D. R. "The Protestant Liturgical Renewal." In Webber (1994), p. 117.

12. Fenwick and Spinks (1995). This is less the case for Anglicans and Lutherans, who already used a "purified" pre-Reformation form of the Mass.

13. Byars, R. "Challenging the Ethos: A History of Presbyterian Worship Resources in the Twentieth Century." In M. Coalter, J. Mulder, and L. Weeks (eds.), *The Confessional Mosaic: Presbyterians and Twentieth-Century Theology.* Louisville: Westminster/John Knox, 1990, pp. 134–161.

14. Webber, R. "The Convergence Movement." In Christian Century,

1982, 99(3), quoted in Webber (1994), pp. 134–140. See also Webber, R. *Blended Worship: Achieving Substance and Relevance in Worship*. Peabody, Mass.: Hendrickson, 1996; and his video series *Ancient-Future Worship: A Model for the 21st Century*. Wheaton, Ill.: Institute for Worship Studies, 1999.

15. Webber (1994), p. 137.

16. Webber (1994), p. 138.

17. Webber (1994), p. 139.

18. Webber (1994), p. 139.

19. White, J. F. "A Protestant Worship Manifesto." *Christian Century*, 1982, 99(3), quoted in Webber (1994), pp. 332–337.

20. White (1982), p. 333.

21. White (1982), p. 333.

22. The International Day of Prayer for the Persecuted Church is observed on the fourth Sunday in November; it began in 1996 under the direction of the World Evangelical Fellowship (WEF).

23. See, for example, *The Book of Common Worship* (Louisville: Presbyterian Publishing House, 1993); and the *United Methodist Book of Worship* (Nashville: Abingdon, 1992).

24. The typical Protestant practice was to celebrate the Lord's Supper quarterly, with an additional celebration on Maundy Thursday or Good Friday.

25. White (1982), p. 335.

26. See Foley, E. *Ritual Music*. Washington, D.C.: Pastoral Press, 1995.

27. A number of CWM writers, among them John Michael Talbot, Walt Harrah, Graham Kendrick, Rick Founds, and Jamie Harvill, have set these traditional liturgical texts to contemporary music. Integrity Music's Renewal Music series offers both contemporary settings of these texts as well as contemporary arrangements of traditional Roman Catholic liturgical pieces. GIA and Oregon Catholic Press (OCP), among others, offer more contemporary versions of traditional liturgical pieces.

28. Hawn, C. M. (ed.). *Halle, Halle: We Sing the World Round*. Garland, Tex.: Choristers Guild, 1999.

29. White, S. J. *Christian Worship and Technological Change*. Nashville: Abingdon, 1994.

30. White (1994), p. 51.

31. White (1994), p. 53.

32. White (1994), p. 54.

33. Old, H. *The Shaping of the Reformed Baptismal Rites in the Sixteenth Century*. Grand Rapids, Mich.: Eerdmans, 1992.

34. White (1994), p. 56.

35. White (1994), p. 57.

36. Fenwick and Spinks (1995), p. 112.

Chapter Five

1. Drucker, P. *Post-Capitalist Society*. San Francisco: HarperCollins, 1993, p. 1.

2. Regele, M. *The Death of the Church*. Grand Rapids, Mich.: Zondervan, 1996.

3. Regele (1996).

4. Regele (1996), pp. 106, 108.

5. Maynard-Reid, P. *Diverse Worship: African-American, Caribbean, and Hispanic Perspectives*. Downers Grove, Ill.: InterVarsity Press, 2000, p. 60.

6. Maynard-Reid (2000), p. 61.

7. Maynard-Reid (2000), p. 62.

8. Costen, M. W. *African American Christian Worship*. Nashville: Abingdon, 1993, pp. 37–38.

9. Costen (1993).

10. Costen (1993), pp. 48–49.

11. Costen (1993), p. 50.

12. Lincoln, C. E., and Mamiya, L. H. *The Black Church in the African American Experience*. Durham, N.C.: Duke University Press, 1990, quoted in Maynard-Reid (2000), p. 69.

13. On African American worship music, see Maynard-Reid (2000), pp. 93–104 and Costen (1993), pp. 93–104.

14. Quoted in Maynard-Reid (2000), p. 90.

15. Maynard-Reid (2000), p. 168.

16. Gonzalez, J. *Alabadle! Hispanic Christian Worship*. Nashville: Abingdon, 1996, p. 20.

17. Maynard-Reid (2000), p. 179.

18. C. Michael Hawn, personal communication to the author, July 26, 2001.

19. Maynard-Reid (2000), p. 183.

20. Maynard-Reid (2000), p. 181.

21. Gonzalez (1996), p. 21.

22. Maynard-Reid (2000), p. 188.

23. Costen (1993), pp. 127–134. See also Aghowa, B. E. *Praising in Black and White*. Philadelphia: Pilgrim Press, 1993.

24. J. F. White (1989), p. 213.

25. Maynard-Reid (2000), p. 66.

26. Quoted in Maynard-Reid (2000), p. 73.

27. McGavran, D. *Understanding Church Growth*. (3rd ed.) Grand Rapids, Mich.: Zondervan, 1990. McGavran first raised the point in *Bridges of God* (New York: Friendship Press, 1955).

28. Van Engen, C. *God's Missionary People*. Grand Rapids, Mich.: Baker, 1991.

29. Wagner, C. P. *Your Church Can Be Healthy*. Nashville: Abingdon, 1979.

Chapter Six

1. Hoge, D., Johnson, B., and Luidens, D. *Vanishing Boundaries: The Religion of Protestant Baby Boomers*. Louisville: Westminster/John Knox Press, 1994.

2. Murren, D. *The Baby Boomerang*. Ventura, Calif.: Regal, 1992; Roof, W. C. *A Generation of Seekers*. San Francisco: Harper, 1994.

3. Miller (1997).

4. Strauss, W., and Howe, N. *Generations: The History of America's Future*. New York: Morrow, 1991. See also Wuthnow, R. *The Restructuring of American Religion*. Princeton, N.J.: Princeton University Press, 1988.

5. Strauss and Howe (1991), p. 60.

6. Strauss and Howe (1991), p. 63.

7. On the cycle of generational types, see Strauss and Howe (1991).

8. Strauss and Howe (1991), p. 35: "Most historians look upon this rhythm as, at most, a curious coincidence. We look upon it as key evidence that a generational cycle is at work, ensuring a rather tight correspondence between constellations and events."

9. Strauss and Howe (1991), pp. 33–34.

10. Strauss and Howe (1991), p. 31.

11. Strauss and Howe (1991), p. 350.

12. Howe and Strauss carefully address the strengths and weaknesses of generational theory. See Strauss, W., and Howe, N. (1991), pp. 433–453.

13. Regele, M. *The Death of the Church*. Grand Rapids, Mich.: Zondervan, 1995.

14. Hoge, Johnson, and Luidens (1994), p. 7.

15. Regele (1995), p. 106.

16. Hoge, Johnson, and Luidens (1994), p. 198.

17. George, C., and Logan, B. *Leading and Managing Your Church*. Tarrytown, N.Y.: Revell, 1987.

18. Vaughn, J. Megachurches and America's Future. Grand Rapids, Mich.: Baker, 1993.

19. Steele, D. "The Pilgrimage to Mega." *Presbyterian Outlook*, 2000, *182*(12), 11–13.

20. George, C. *Prepare Your Church for the Future*. Grand Rapids, Mich.: Revell/Baker, 1992, pp. 26–41.

21. D. Miller (1997), 173–174.

22. Redman, R. "New Paradigms for Worship and Ministry with Single Adults." *Worship Leader*, 1999, 8(3), 30–32.

23. Celek, T., and Zander, D. *Inside the Soul of a New Generation*. Grand Rapids, Mich.: Zondervan, 1995.

24. Byars, R. "Are the Historic Churches Obsolete?" *Reformed Liturgy and Music*, 2000, 34(1), 12.

25. Webber, R. "Finding Hope in the Coming Generation," *Worship Leader*, 2000, 9(5), 12; "Youth Discovering Ancient Worship," *Worship Leader*, 2000, 9(6), 12.

Chapter Seven

1. Grenz, S. *A Primer on Postmodernism*. Grand Rapids, Mich.: Eerdmans, 1996, 11–12.

2. Grenz (1996), p. 56.

3. Barna, G. "Worship in the Third Millennium." In M. Warden (ed.), *Experience God in Worship*. Loveland, Colo.: Group Publishing, 2000.

4. Pritchard, G. *Willow Creek Seeker Services: Evaluating a New Way of Doing Church*. Grand Rapids, Mich.: Baker, 1996, p. 223.

5. Pritchard (1996), p. 265.

6. Sargeant (2000), p. 85.

7. Sargeant (2000), pp. 83–86.

8. Sargeant (2000), pp. 178–184.

9. See Anderson, R. S. *Ministry on the Fireline*. Downers Grove, Ill.: InterVarsity Press, 1995.

10. Webber, R. *Worship Old and New*. Grand Rapids, Mich.: Zondervan, 1982; *Ancient-Future Faith: Rethinking Evangelicalism for a Postmodern World*. Grand Rapids, Mich.: Baker, 1999.

11. Corbitt (1998).

12. Grenz (1996), p. 14.

13. Anderson, W. *The Future of the Self*. New York: Putnam, 1997, pp. 35–45.

14. Gilligan, C. *In a Different Voice: Psychological Theory and Women's Development*. Cambridge, Mass.: Harvard University Press, 1982.

15. Grenz (1996), p. 14.

16. Grenz (1996), p. 170.

17. Ong, W. *Orality and Literacy: The Technologizing of the Word*. New York: Routledge, 1982.

18. Stephens, M. *The Rise of the Image, the Fall of the Word*. New York: Oxford University Press, 1998, pp. 20–21.

19. Stephens (1998), p. 208.

20. Sargeant (2000), p. 72.

21. Pritchard (1996), p. 216.

22. Pederson, S. *Drama Ministry*. Grand Rapids, Mich.: Zondervan, 1999, p. 16.

23. Miller, K. (ed.). *The Handbook for Multisensory Worship*. Nashville: Abingdon, 1999; and Wilson, L. *Making Media Ministry*. Nashville: Abingdon, 1999.

24. Slaughter, M. *Out on the Edge*. Nashville: Abingdon, 1998.

25. Gaddy, W., and Nixon, D. (eds.). *Worship: A Symphony for the Senses*. Nashville: Smith and Helwys, 1998, p. 16.

26. Webber (1982), p. 17.

27. Webber (1999), p. 94.

28. Webber, "Youth Discovering Ancient Worship" (2000), p. 12.

29. Cox, H. *Fire from Heaven*. Boston: Addison-Wesley, 1995, p. 81.

30. D. Miller (1997), pp. 80–107.

31. DiSabatino, D. "The Unforgettable Fire: Pentecostals and the Role of Experience in Worship." *Worship Leader*, 2000, 9(6), 21.

Chapter Eight

1. Levine, L. *Highbrow/Lowbrow: The Emergence of Cultural Hierarchy in America.* Cambridge, Mass.: Harvard University Press, 1988.

2. On the simultaneous convergence and collapse of mass media in the 1970s and its ongoing effect on American society and culture, see Frum, D. *How We Got Here: The 70s, the Decade That Brought You Modern Life—For Better or Worse.* New York: Basic Books, 2000.

3. Wolff, M. *The Entertainment Economy.* New York: Random House, 1999.

4. Stephens (1998).

5. Romanowski, W. *Pop Culture Wars.* Downers Grove, Ill.: InterVarsity Press, 1996, p. 313.

6. Frank, T. *The Conquest of Cool.* Chicago: University of Chicago Press, 1997.

7. Frank (1997), p. 31.

8. Pine, J., and Gilmore, J. *The Experience Economy.* Cambridge: Harvard Business School Press, 1999.

9. Wolff (1999), p. 32.

10. Frank (1997), pp. 133–167.

11. See Kraft, C. *Christianity in Culture: A Study in Dynamic Biblical Theologizing in Cross Cultural Perspective.* Maryknoll, N.Y.: Orbis, 1979; and Witvliet (1996).

12. I am indebted to my student Dion Christopher for his report on worship among the Caribbean Moravians.

13. See Dawn (1995), and Frankforter, F. D. *Stones for Bread: A Critique of Contemporary Worship.* Louisville: Westminster/John Knox Press, 2001.

14. Sample, T. *The Spectacle of Worship in a Wired World.* Nashville: Abingdon, 1998.

15. See Boschman, L. *Future Worship.* Ventura, Calif.: Gospel Light, 1999.

16. Corbitt (1998).

17. Morgenthaler (1995).

18. Slaughter (1998).

19. Mouw, R. J. *Consulting the Faithful: What Christian Intellectuals Can Learn from Popular Religion*. Downers Grove, Ill.: InterVarsity Press, 1994, p. 16.

20. Morgenthaler (1995), pp. 96–123.

21. Kiefert, P. *Welcoming the Stranger: A Public Theology of Worship*. Minneapolis: Augsburg, 1992.

Chapter Nine

1. White (1992).

2. Senn, F. *Christian Liturgy: Catholic and Evangelical*. Philadelphia: Fortress, 1997, p. 8.

3. Torrance, J. B. *Worship, Community and the Triune Grace of God*. Downers Grove, Ill.: InterVarsity Press, 1996, p. 14.

4. Torrance (1996), p. 14.

5. Torrance (1996), p. 15.

6. Torrance (1996), p. 16.

7. Postrel, V. "Variety is a Good Gauge of Progress. But How Well Can Economists Measure It?" *New York Times*, Apr. 19, 2001, p. C2.

8. Dyrness, W. *Let the Earth Rejoice: A Biblical Theology of Wholistic Mission*. Westchester, Ill.: Crossway Books, 1983, p. 22.

9. Torrance, T. F. *The Ground and Grammar of Theology*. Belfast: Christian Journals, 1980, pp. 5–6.

10. Keener, C. S. *The IVP Bible Background Commentary: New Testament*. Downers Grove, Ill.: InterVarsity Press, 1993, p. 779.

11. Stein, R. H. "Jerusalem." (Entry.) In G. Hawthorne, R. Martin, and D. Reid (eds.), *Dictionary of Paul and His Letters*. Downers Grove, Ill.: InterVarsity Press, 1993, 471. The text, in part: "The issue at stake, according to Luke, is not justification but rather social intercourse between Jews and Gentiles. The decree does not add a requirement for Gentiles who are seeking salvation. Rather they are

directions given by the Spirit (Acts 15:28) which seek to promote sensitivity on the part of Gentile Christians with respect to issues that were especially offensive to Jews."

12. Frith, S. *Performing Rites: On the Value of Popular Music*. Cambridge, Mass.: Harvard University Press, 1996, p. 143.

13. Kraus, H.-J. *Psalms 1–59*. Philadelphia: Augsburg, 1988.

14. Ladd, G. *Revelation*. Grand Rapids, Mich.: Eerdmans, 1972, pp. 90–91.

15. Old, H. *Praying with the Bible*. Philadelphia: Geneva Press, 1980, p. 57.

16. Old (1980), p. 58.

17. Hurtado, L. "Christology." (Entry.) In R. Martin and P. Davids (eds.), *The Dictionary of the Later New Testament and Its Developments*. Downers Grove, Ill.: InterVarsity Press, 1997, p. 181.

18. Fromm (1983), p. 1.

19. Lovelace, R. *Dynamics of Spiritual Life*. Downers Grove, Ill.: Inter-Varsity Press, 1979.

20. Fromm (1983), p. 20.

21. The arrangement can be heard on "The Making of a Godly Man" (Maranatha! Music, 1996).

22. C. M. Hawn, personal communication to the author, July 26, 2001.

Chapter Ten

1. Raymond, E. "The Cathedral and the Bazaar." (www.tuxedo.org/~esr/writings/cathedral-bazaar/cathedral-bazaar.html)

2. Redman, R. "Expanding Your Worship Worldview: Education and Training for Worship Leaders." *Worship Leader*, 2000, 9(3), 18–22; "Going to School with the Next Generation of Worship Leaders." *Worship Leader*, 1999, 8(2), 26–28.

3. Hanson, H. *Worship Inside Out*. Burnsville, Minn.: Changing Church Resources, 1995, 1; emphasis in original.

4. Hanson (1995), p. 1.

5. Morgenthaler, S. "Planning Worship." In *Celebration Hymnal Worship Leaders Handbook*. Waco, Tex.: Word, 1996.

6. See Webber, R. *Planning Blended Worship*. Nashville: Abingdon, 1998.

7. Ward, P. *Worship and Youth Culture*. London: Marshall Pickering, 1993.

8. See Liesch (1996).

9. Webber (1996).

10. Seay, D. "Eye Has Not Seen: Flourishing Ministries Nurture a Christian Arts Renaissance." *Worship Leader*, 1999, 8(1), 25.

11. Langford, A. *Transitions in Worship*. Nashville: Abingdon, 1998, p. 105.

12. Arn, C. *How to Start a New Service*. Grand Rapids, Mich.: Baker, 1997.

13. See also Callahan, K. *Dynamic Worship*. Nashville: Abingdon, 1994; Hunter, G. G. *Church for the Unchurched*. Nashville: Abingdon, 1996; Schaller, L. *44 Steps Off the Plateau*. Nashville: Abingdon, 1995; and White (1992).

14. Arn (1997), p. 25.

15. Arn (1997), p. 26.

16. Callahan (1994), p. 102.

17. Arn (1997), p. 27.

18. Arn (1997), p. 31.

19. Arn (1997).

20. Arn (1997), p. 38.

21. Arn (1997), p. 38.

22. Dawn (1995), p. 177.

23. Callahan (1994), p. 102.

24. Callahan, p. 103.

Index

Ethnic groups, inclusion and integration of, 106–108, 211–212. *See also specific ethnic groups*
Ethnic identity, 102
Ethnically targeted churches, 110–111, 177
Ethnocentrism, reverse, resorting to, 91
Ethnography, relying on, 12
Eucharist, 76–77, 79, 84, 85, 204, 219n20. *See also* Communion; Lord's Supper
Evangelical Lutheran Church of America, 66
Evangelical Quaker congregation, 34
Evangelicals: priority of, 8, 18; and revival worship, 5–9; and scheduling, 211; and seeker services, 14, 15, 17–19; view of, 91–92, 159. *See also* Conservative evangelical churches; Convergence movement
Event sponsorship, 157
Experience economy, 157
Experiencing God. *See* Baptism in the Holy Spirit
Experiential approach. *See* Holistic and experiential approach
Expository preaching, 7, 82
Extensive backward blend, 204
Extensive repackaging, 203, 204

F

Failure, fear of, 214
Faith articulation, 108
False god, worshiping a, 184, 185
Family, 5, 102, 104, 164
"Father, I Adore You" (Coehelo), 55
Fear of failure, 214
Feminists, 139
Fenwick, J., 74, 77, 92
Fiesta, 101–103, 104, 164
Finney, C. G., 7–9, 12
Fitts, B., 66
Folk (lowbrow) culture, 152, 165
Folk music, 51, 53, 184, 188, 223n10
Food sacrificed to idols, command to avoid, 183, 184

Forecasting, caution in, 121
Forest Hills Presbyterian Church, 212
Formalism, critique of, 91
Forward blend, 203–204
Fosdick, H. E., 160
Founds, R., 43, 226n27
Frame, J., 54
France, community in, 90
Frank, T., 156, 158
Free-flowing praise, 35–36, 46, 221n22
Frith, S., 185
Fromm, C., xi, 29, 51, 53, 62, 180, 189, 190
Frontier worship, 5–9, 23–24, 217n2. *See also* Revivalists
Frontline ministries, 126
Fulfillment theology, 17
Full gospel teaching, controversy over, 33
Fuller Theological Seminary, 12
Fusion, 148, 202, 203
Fusion music, 103, 106

G

Gaddy, W., 147
Gaither, B., 51
Gaither, G., 51
Gangsta rap lyrics, 155, 184
Garlington, J., 64
Gathering, the, 81
General Board of Discipleship, 66
General Board of Global Missions, 66
Generalization, caution in, 120–121
Generation, defined, 118
Generation X: defining, 118, 119; and the homogenous unit principle, 127–128; and liturgical renewal, 148; new churches for, 126, 127; and seeker services, 19–20; targeting, 111; view of, 129; worldview of, 131. *See also* Younger adults
Generational constellation, 120, 229n8
Generational cycles, 119, 120, 128, 176, 229n8

218n9; and fusion, 148; interest in, 129; and modernism, 147; preference for, 161; revitalizing, 8; setting aside, 3, 4; and worship music, 86, 226n27
Traditional, meaning of, 47, 48, 174
Traditional worship, conflict over. *See* Worship wars
Traditional worship music: and Baby Boom generation, 53, 116; interest in, 129; and Jesus music, 54; and Millennial generation, 50, 51; negative overtone associated with, 48; new arrangements for, 190–191; new settings for, 86, 222n27; preference for, 161; recovering, 86; setting aside, 3, 4; and worship leader skill, 202
Traduco, 174
Transformation, social and cultural, periods of, 95
Transitioning neighborhoods, options in, 112
Translation, 74, 75, 203; bilingual, 211
Trinitarian perspective, 138, 179, 180
Triune God, 179, 180, 189
Troeger, T., 190
"True Prayer of the Church, The" (Beauduin), 73–74
Trueheart, C., xiii
Truth, 132–134, 135–136, 137–138, 161, 163
Two-thirds world, 90, 160, 165

U

U2, 57
Unchurched and nonbelievers. *See* Seeker entries
Understanding Church Growth (McGavran), 110
United Kingdom, influence of music from, 57
United Methodist Church, 66, 90
Universal Studios, 142
University Baptist Church, 126
University of Illinois, 160
University Presbyterian Church, 211

Urban areas, 106, 111, 124, 205
Urban music, 112
U.S. Census Bureau, 96
USA Today, 144
Usability value, 58, 60, 66
User-friendly service, 13–15; versus user-focused, 168

V

van Engen, C., 110
Variety, 180–185, 192–197. *See also* Diversity
Vatican II reforms, 73, 74, 75, 76, 78
Video games, 142, 153
Video images, 4, 142, 143, 154. *See also* Television
Video projection, 165
Vineyard Association of Churches, 34, 70, 117
Vineyard Ministries International, 56, 69
Vineyard model, 35–36, 44, 221n22
Vineyard Music Group, 56, 57, 62, 69, 70
Virtual reality games, 142, 153
Visibility, 173–174
Visitor-friendly service, importance of, 13
Visitors, inviting, 209
Visual aids. *See* Multimedia communication
Visual artistic talent, congregational, utilizing, 207
Visual arts, 3, 4, 161, 207

W

Wagner, C. P., 12, 13
Wagner, P., 112
Walker, T., 43–44, 63–64, 65, 112, 190, 191
Walker, W. T., 101
Wallace, R., 157
Warehouse Fellowship, 207
Warhol, A., 154
Warren, R., 12, 135
Webber, R., 50, 78–80, 90, 129–130, 138, 148, 204
"Welcome Back," 53